Psychological Aspects of Society: Book 2

THE SOCIAL INDIVIDUAL

PSYCHOLOGICAL ASPECTS OF SOCIETY: BOOK 2

The Social Individual
John Rowan

DAVIS-POYNTER
LONDON

First published in 1973 by
Davis-Poynter Limited
20 Garrick Street, London WC2E 9BJ

Copyright © 1973 by John Rowan

ISBN 0 7067 0125 9

Printed in Great Britain
by Ebenezer Baylis & Son Ltd
The Trinity Press, Worcester, and London

This book is dedicated to
David Krech

CONTENTS

Contents

INTRODUCTION

This is the second of four books which comprise a complete guide to social psychology. Book 2: *The Social Individual* stands by itself but makes use of a number of fundamental concepts which are explained more fully in the first volume.

The book falls into two parts. In the first the individual, as seen by social psychology, is followed through the stages of life, from birth to death; much use is made of evidence from experimental research, and although some of the conclusions may appear to be radical, the studies quoted are highly orthodox.

The second part of the book examines the whole question of research. I take the view that anyone who wants to study social psychology seriously must be prepared to look at research in a critical way. It is not enough to swallow whole the assertions of the textbook or research paper. Here I am giving the reader the tools or weapons required to attack a research study in a constructive way, and also to carry out original research.

But this part of the book also goes on to examine the whole question of what the researcher is doing in society. What role is he or she playing in the process of social change which is now going on so fast? Is the psychologist an upholder of the established order, or an agent of radical change? On what ground is the social psychologist standing when carrying out 'objective research'?

The next volume in the series will deal with groups and organizations, and the fourth book will be concerned with social problems.

A*

THE SOCIAL INDIVIDUAL

CHAPTER ONE

The Early Experience

Social psychology is very much interested in the individual person, and it is one of the mistakes of many textbooks to define the individual out of social psychology, saying that it is the study of groups exclusively. The view we shall be sharing in this book is that social psychology is the central discipline in psychology, in relation to which all other kinds of psychology are specialisms.

So we start at the beginning of life. Any beginning to life must be a matter of decision, rather than being self-evident. However far back we go, someone else can always point to some previous stage even further back. Freud went back to the infant at the breast. Rank went back to the trauma of birth. Many writers recently have referred to the important events going on within the womb. Scientology goes back into the previous lives of the person – and even back to pre-human stages in evolution.

Where we start is where we choose to start. And social psychology chooses to start with the first social interaction, between infant and parent. Every theory of psychology attaches some importance to this interaction, because a great deal of learning takes place over a very short period, as Gesell[1] has well described in detail.

Maternal Deprivation

But a great wave swept across this whole field in the 1950's because of the publication in 1951 of John Bowlby's report for the World Health Organization[2] in which he stated that maternal deprivation at a certain critical period in an infant's life caused that person to grow up into an affectionless and psychopathic character. In the original report, this was backed up by an analysis in Freudian terms, supported by some general considerations drawn from embryology - for example, that 'the starvation of rats on the 24th day of life left traces on behaviour clearly discernible in adult life, while a similar experience at 36 days had no such effect'. But by the time he came to check over the revised version of the report which came

out in book form in 1953[3] he had come across the work of ethologists like Lorenz[4] who had shown in their studies of imprint-
ing that there were critical periods in the maturation of birds,
such that attachment to a mother figure either happened over a
very short period, or did not happen at all. This again seemed to
support the general case that this kind of thing could happen with
human babies too.

It just so happened that Lorenz' very well written and exciting
book came out at just about the same time as Bowlby's, and the
connection was easily made: what Bowlby had discovered was a
human critical period – a point in development when a relatively
small amount of maternal deprivation could bring about irrever-
sible changes, making a person totally unable to have or show
affection for the rest of his days. This seemed a new and important
scientific discovery, having direct relevance to the way in which
infants and young children were treated – and the conclusion which
was most often drawn was that babies should never be put into institutions, but always given to foster parents, if the mother died or
went away.

Unfortunately the message which at first seemed so loud and
clear was much less so when looked at closely. For example, when
was this critical period? There are at least 17 different answers in
the book:

1. Three to six months of age. (p. 28)
2. First 6 months and proper mothering delayed until after two and a
   half years. (p. 56)
3. Six to twelve months. (p. 27)
4. Beginning in the period 6–12 months and lasting for five months
   or longer. (p. 225)
5. The first year of life. (p. 212)
6. Prolonged and severe deprivation, beginning in the first year of life
   and continuing for as long as three years. (p. 224)
7. Between one and three years of age. (p. 33)
8. Between one and a half and two and a half. (p. 29)
9. Before about two and a half. (p. 33)
10. In the first three years. (p. 39)
11. In the second and third years. (p. 28)
12. Deprivation for at least three months and probably more than six,
    during the first three or four years. (p. 54)
13. Between two and four years. (p. 214)
14. During the first five years of life. (p. 41)

15. In their early years. (p. 46)
16. Between the ages of five and seven or eight a fair proportion are
    unable to adjust satisfactorily to separations. (p. 33)
17. Before a child's tenth birthday. (p. 229)

All these periods are quoted by Bowlby or by Ainsworth as evidence
in favour of his case. But this at once looks much less like the discovery of a critical period and much more like a general problem of
social relationships, not really tied very closely to any one period
in a child's life. The research carried out in the years that followed
seems to bear out this general position. Ainsworth, a collaborator of
Bowlby's, finally concluded that:

> It seems unlikely that either separation or deprivation alone is the
> effective antecedent of delinquency, even in the 'affectionless' character,
> but rather that the antecedent is likely to be some special form of dis-
> tortion in early parent-child relations, perhaps alone, but more probably
> in conjunction with separation or deprivation experiences or both.[5]

So this amounts to virtual withdrawal of the original dramatic
statement. And even the conclusion about foster homes always
being better than institutions has not survived intact. Foster homes
also produce emotional problems, as O'Connor[6] reminds us.

Inadequate as the original Bowlby theory may have been, it did
have the effect of stimulating a great deal of research into the social
reactions of young children. It is now a very flourishing field, and
much of interest has been discovered. One of the most interesting
areas is the question of what is the best age to adopt children, in
order to do the least harm to them. Yarrow[7] seems to have shown
rather convincingly that the earlier that adoption or transfer to
foster parents can take place, the less harm will be done; but if the
transfer is left as late as seven months, severe emotional ill-effects
will be experienced by the infant. Many people have now seen the
film showing the sad reactions of a two-year-old to being put in a
home while his mother was away in hospital. Bowlby[8] has now
developed a new theory about this, in which he says that these reactions resemble those found in mourning adults. But the key question is – however severe these emotional experiences are at the time,
do they have permanent effects?

It seems that they do not necessarily have long-lasting effects at
all. In a study carried out by Dennis & Najarian[9] in Beirut, children
in a hospital crêche were subjected to a bare environment because of

staffing shortages which cut the staffing ratio to one in ten. The situation led to test score differences at three to ten months when crêche children were compared with children at home. However, at the later ages of four and a half to six years, differences had largely disappeared. The same kind of result was found by Rathbun *et al.*[10] and by Rabin & Mohr [11] – the first with 38 immigrant children adopted in the USA, and the second in kibbutz children compared with village children in Israel.

This research was followed up by Dennis & Sayegh[12] in a further experiment which tested the effect of supplementary experiences on the test results of deprived children in their Beirut clinic. Results showed that simple supplementary experiences significantly increased test scores. This fits in with the work of Skeels and his co-workers[13] in Iowa.

Research has also gone backwards, in an attempt to study the infant experiences of those who in adulthood are either backward intellectually or who show flattened effect. Howells[14] took a neurotic and a control group, and examined their childhood experience. There were no significant differences. Some of Howells' later work[15] even shows that under certain conditions parent-child separation can be beneficial.

One of the most important studies is that by Hilda Lewis[16] dealing with a reception centre in Kent during World War 2. After a detailed examination of the figures available for 500 children, and a two-year follow-up, she concluded that her data:

> fail to confirm the belief that a characteristic form of delinquent personality, recognizable on psychiatric examination, commonly ensues upon a child's separation from his mother in his early years.

So it looks as though we must conclude that, however severe and unpleasant the short-term emotional experiences may be, over quite a variety of ages, they are not regularly translated into long-term damage.

This was already the conclusion of Orlansky[17] some years ago, after an extensive review of sociological and anthropological studies:

> We conclude that the rigidity of character structuring during the first year or two years of life has been exaggerated by many authorities, and that the events of childhood and later years are of great importance in reinforcing or changing the character structure tentatively formed during infancy.

What it seems we are now saying, therefore, is that the weight of evidence seems to fall in the direction of saying that maternal deprivation has important short-term effects, but does not cause lasting damage. But before we can be entirely happy about such a conclusion, we need to be clearer about two key words in the statement – 'deprivation' and 'damage'.

There are at least three important things which deprivation can mean in practice. First, it can mean deprivation of a familiar and loved person; second, it can mean deprivation of a familiar and loved place; and third, it can mean sensory deprivation. It is unfortunately true that in most studies, all three have been present at the same time, and therefore quite impossible to tease apart.

Nevertheless, there is now a good deal of evidence that when Bowlby thought he was talking about the first kind of deprivation, he was quite often talking about the second or third instead. Yet the practical implications are quite different. And there is even a fourth kind of deprivation which has less often been considered – deprivation of other children of a similar age – again with different implications.

In each of these cases there is some relevant animal evidence which is worth consideration. First, there is the work of the Harlows[18] on mother love in the rhesus monkey, which shows that separation from the mother has to be very prolonged (total isolation for six months or more) before it has any lasting effects. Their later work with chimpanzees showed even greater powers of recovery for the chimpanzee, which is of course much closer to man. If we can extrapolate from this at all, it shows that human beings would have to suffer much more severe isolation than any which is normally encountered in institutions before any important permanent damage resulted.

The same research also shows that mixing with other young monkeys can be just as good as having a mother. Monkeys who were reared alone with only a mechanical mother for company were considerably disturbed, particularly in their sex and play behaviour; but if they were allowed to mix with others of the same age, their behaviour was quite normal. This cannot be extrapolated to human beings, of course, but it is quite suggestive and certainly the human evidence does not contradict it.

Sensory deprivation has been the subject of a great deal of research, and this is not the place to review it all, but it seems clear that both animals and men need a certain level of sensory stimulation to remain healthy—Hebb[19] has a good summary and discussion of this whole area. If in a children's home the nurses hang up sheets round the cots to keep the children quiet and manageable, this is of course a severe form of sensory deprivation.

On the question of removal from a loved place, Douglas & Blomfield[20] found that children suffer apparently more from change of place than from change of parent. This fits in with a great deal of animal work quoted by Scott[21] who says:

> The process of forming an emotional attachment to a particular set of physical surroundings may be called primary localization, indicating that it is quite similar to the process of primary socialization, or forming an attachment to the particular individuals in the social environment.

We can now see that in addition to all the forms of deprivation outlined by Bowlby – insufficiency of interaction, distorted relations and discontinuity of relations – in respect of a mother or mother-substitute, there are also three other forms of deprivation to be considered – peer deprivation, sensory deprivation and place deprivation – each of which may contribute different effects.*

Now let us turn to the other key word – 'damage'. Bowlby states that there are four kinds of damage which can be caused by maternal deprivation: backwardness in verbalization; growth retardation; failure in emotional response; and intellectual backwardness, including not only lowered IQ but also lack of ability in abstract thinking. But there has never been any clear statement as to which of these ought to be more visible in any given set of circumstances, and therefore which are the most relevant things to test for. Consequently there have been a majority of pieces of research which have tested one but not the others, and have either found or not found some effect; this has led to a good deal of controversy as to which are the relevant findings and which are to be ignored.

Backwardness in verbalization is not very easy to measure, because of the wide variation between children in any case, and the heavy situational dependence of verbalization, but the work of

---

* Looked at from the point of view of the young child, this could mean that children can love places as well as people. And following this train of thought, perhaps it is also true that children can love things. Perhaps taking away a favourite toy or pet can be just as traumatic, and have just as lasting effects, as any other of the forms of deprivation we have considered.

Skeels, already mentioned, seems to show that this can be rectified fairly readily by suitable treatment.

Growth retardation is not very often measured, and it seems rather unconnected with any theoretical expectations – more or less any kind of shock could produce some impairment of growth, and there seems nothing specific to deprivation about it, in any form.

Failure in emotional response is highly central, but is hard to measure in any convincing way. For example, O'Connor[22] criticizes the Goldfarb work relied on so heavily by Bowlby in the following way:

> Although the institution children in this particular study were more disturbed than foster home children, the evidence consisted of check-listing behaviour items such as for example 'disobedient', 'apparent craving for affection', 'inability to concentrate' and 'complains easily' which, however meaningful clinically, are notoriously subjective and unreliable unless rigorously checked and counterchecked by observers who do not know of the hypothesis.

More recent work has been more defensible from a methodological point of view, but the problem is still a difficult one, and some writers, such as Zigler,[23] have gone over to such alternatives as measuring 'motivation for social reinforcement' (measured by how long the child will persist on a boring task in order to gain the attention and support of an adult). This seems like the classic evasion of the psychologist, in measuring things which are easy to measure, rather than what is relevant to the issue.

Intellectual backwardness is also difficult to measure, unless one restricts oneself to measuring IQs. And guess what – most investigations have merely measured IQ! But again, it seems very possible to raise IQ levels by suitable stimulation at a later date: Clarke & Clarke[24] show that children coming into a mental institution from homes where they had been neglected and beaten actually gained ten IQ points over the ensuing two-year period.

It seems, then, that those forms of damage which can be specified at all exactly can be remedied at a later date; and it seems likely that those other forms which at present are not clearly specified can also be remedied as soon as we know what they are.

But so far, everything we have said is negative. We have seen that children can be adversely affected by certain experiences in their early years, and that these adverse effects can in most cases be over-come by later experience of a remedial kind. But what about the positive aspect? Are there any positive experiences we can give to children which will have the effect of making them *more* adequate in later life?

Positive Provision

Let us again look at some animal studies to see if we can get any clues. There is some interesting work by Denenberg[25] with young rats; if one simply picks them out of the nest one at a time, puts them in a separate cage, and then returns them to the mother's cage a few times, they grow faster, live longer and stand physical stress better than animals which have been left undisturbed. They are also less emotionally disturbed by anxiety-provoking situations. This kind of handling is most effective in the first week of life.

Now what is it about this handling that brings about the effect? Levine[26] found that not only gentle handling from cage to cage, but also electric shock and mechanical shaking would work, and Schaefer[27] found that cold had the same effect. These results again confirm the principle that stimulation is necessary for the development of basic behavioral capacities.

But do these findings have any bearing on human beings? Lan-dauer & Whiting[28] surveyed a large sample of primitive societies where measurements of adult size are known, and found that mem-bers of those societies where some drastic treatment of new-born infants is practised, such as plunging them into cold water, or cir-cumcision, or scarification, or head moulding, etc., are on the average taller than members of societies which do not practise such drastic treatment. They suggest that in our own society, the practice of inoculation may have a similar effect.

But how relevant is being taller to anything we want for our children? Terman[29] found, in a large-scale investigation, that taller children are on average more intelligent and have more socially acceptable personalities than shorter ones, so there may be some relevance.

These suggestions fit in very well with the theory put forward by Schaffer & Emerson,[30] that there are three stages in a baby's rela-tionships to people. The first stage is non-social; the infant seeks optimal arousal from all aspects of his environment. The second stage is indiscriminately social; the infant views human beings as particularly satisfying objects and makes special efforts to be near them. The third stage is more discriminating; the infant now forms attachments to specific people, not necessarily always the mother. If this theory is correct, it is at the first stage that extra stimulation of a non-specific kind would be most effective.

The interesting thing is that the infant can himself determine this to some extent. Bowlby[31] has pointed out that the baby is born with six response patterns which increase nearness to another person. Crying initially, smiling later and calling later still, all bring attention and stimulation; clinging and sucking initially, and following later, all maintain attachment. And Karelitz et al.[32] found that the frequency of crying outbursts in infants under ten days of age was correlated positively with intelligence at three years of age; this suggests that such behaviour gets attention, handling and general stimulation at a point where it can do the most good.

The unfortunate thing is that often this highly adaptive and efficient form of communication by the very young infant is ignored by the people looking after him. This seems to be because of a systematic distortion of perception remarked on in the Newson[33] research study in Nottingham:

> Baby cries; mother, sooner or later, picks him up; baby stops crying. To this, the restrictive mother typically reacts: he stopped crying as soon as I picked him up – so there was nothing wrong with him at all, he was just having me on. The result is that the baby is put back again to cry it out, sometimes with a smack to drive home the lesson. . . . (The basic attitude is) suspicion of the baby as a small enemy in a continual battle of wits.

It seems clear, then, that there are three stages of stimulation: first, giving more stimulation than is asked for; second, giving accurate responses to the infant's attempts to communicate his needs; and third, giving less stimulation than is asked for. And it appears that, on the whole, the effects are beneficial in direct relation to this scale.

Obviously the main reason why infants are not treated in the optimum way – given more stimulation than they ask for – is because it would be a lot more trouble for the parents. But what would happen if they overcame their reluctance to do more than the minimum necessary (or even less) and did try to give much more attention to the infant?

Marcelle Geber[34] worked for a period with the Ganda tribe in Uganda, and found remarkably fast development, bringing back almost unbelievable films of newborn infants, who could hold their heads upright when pulled up into a sitting position, at the age of nine hours old. In this tribe there are intense preparations of the mother during pregnancy, and a complete focus on the oncoming birth and its care subsequent to birth. The mother never lets the child cry, and knows exactly when it is going to urinate or defecate, and holds it accordingly. The maturation of the child is amazingly fast under this treatment. Unfortunately it is only continued up to the time of weaning, when the child is abruptly sent away to a grandmother; if it were continued we would expect the adults to be remarkably advanced.*

Some evidence for the validity of this general account is also given in the book by Deakin[35] which gives details of the outstanding development of four children whose parents – particularly the mother – gave them more attention than the average. They became unusually well-developed physically and mentally, appearing to be three or four years ahead of their contemporaries at the age of 12 or so. The mother did all her work when the children were asleep – often not getting to bed until 3 am or 4 am – and spent almost every waking minute with them.

It appears to be a sad fact that the medical profession has not caught up with this thinking. The Newsons say in their book already quoted:

> It will be noticed, in the quotations that follow, that the assertion that 'crying does a child no harm' seems to have been presented with an authoritarian certainty which is hardly a good advertisement for the scientific humility of the medical profession . . .
>
> 'We were worried it might rupture him, he cried so hard, and for two hours sometimes, just screaming; but the doctor said, "Rubbish, it can't do him any harm, just let him cry it out"; so I'm going by what he says.'
>
> 'When she was born, she cried on and off for a whole day. I was worried, but the midwife said, "Put her in the bathroom and shut the door so you can't hear her, it won't hurt her." But I didn't.'

These babies were having their needs for stimulation, which they

---

* For some interesting comments on this work, see Neil Warren, 'African infant precocity', *Psychol. Bull.* 78, 1972.

were able to express with great efficiency, systematically denied. This certainly is harmful, just as the denial of any other basic need is harmful. We shall be seeing throughout this book that we are doing more harm to each other than we think; this is one instance where the evidence certainly points in that direction. But we are now more interested in how we can actively help the development of the infant in the optimum way, rather than in merely avoiding harm.

One way is to give more stimulation, for example by letting children explore a varied environment and get into difficulties with it, rather than by confining it to a cot or playpen. There is evidence from Pasamanick[36] and Williams & Scott[37] that children in disadvantaged households often have improved motor development, simply because they have more freedom of movement there. All through this chapter, we are mainly talking about children under a year old.

In other words, we can do a great deal just by leaving children alone in a relatively complicated environment which is not too easy to master. Hebb[38] put this to the test with rats as long ago as 1947 – he took some of his laboratory rats home and allowed them to be brought up as pets. When they were taken back and put into a test maze, they did much better than rats reared in the usual cages. Later, Forgays & Read[39] did a better controlled test using a large cage containing a number of objects and playthings; again superior performance on a number of tests was obtained. The best scores were due to rats exposed to the free environment immediately after weaning, at 21 days of age. Rats exposed before or after that period still did better than the ordinary rats, but not so strikingly well. Thus there is an optimum period which is especially sensitive to this treatment, as the same amount of time spent in the free environment produces a less favourable result in both older and younger animals.

This again leads us back to the earlier thought in another form – is there any age at which stimulation of human infants would have maximal beneficial effect? It seems that here the best indication we have is the behaviour of the infant itself. McGraw[40] suggests as a result of her research on twins that the critical period in each case is the time following the age when the child is first capable of performing the act effectively. Since in some cases the development of the capacity is dependent on practice itself, such an optimum period is difficult to establish and may differ from individual to individual. In the absence of concrete practical information, it is a matter, very largely, of providing maximum opportunity.

At the earliest stage, this will mean frequent approaches to the infant, and not only response but also anticipation of its needs - even providing more stimulation than may immediately be comfortable on occasion. This in a purely physical way.

At the next stage, it will be a question of providing a great deal of human stimulation - the more people the better, so that the infant can get a great variety of human impacts.

And at the third stage, it will be necessary to provide some few more intense relationships, starting perhaps with just one. Schaffer & Emerson, in the study already quoted, found that at about 7 months old (but as early as 22 weeks and as late as 13 months) the infant showed specific attachment to just one person, which became more intense in the next three or four months. Once they had shown one such specific attachment, there was a rapid increase in the number of persons the babies became attached to. The formation of additional attachments progressed so rapidly that in some infants the forming of multiple attachments seemed to appear simultaneously with the first attachment. If we want to avoid the worst results of separation from one person, it seems that one way of doing this would be to deliberately set up a situation in which it would be easy for the infant to become attached to a number of familiar adults straight away.

It seems clear that the nuclear family familiar to us in Western culture is not very well adapted to the needs of infants. There is not enough room in our small houses for a great deal of freedom of movement; we have too many precious possessions to allow infants a free run even in the space which we have; and there are too few adults about in the child's environment. There are other restrictions, too, which we shall be meeting in the next chapter.

Whether this be so or not, it is certainly important to remember that even the new-born baby is actively engaging with his or her social and physical environment—not just passively being acted upon by it. To some extent the baby actually has a hand in creating its own environment, and is starting to interpret it right from the word 'Go!'. And each one is individual; Thomas[41] has shown that differences appear in early infancy relating to autonomic response patterns, social responsiveness, sleeping and feeding patterns, sensory thresholds, motility and perceptual responses.* And adults respond to these differences; Moss[42] found, in his study of mother-child interaction at the ages of three weeks and three months, that it is not only the child who adapts to the mother's treatment, but also the mother who adapts to changes in the child. The important thing is to recognize this explicitly and act upon it, rather than trying to pretend it is not true.

Rigid and inflexible treatment does not work with babies any better than it does with people; perhaps this is because babies are people. Unfortunately there are even more parents who think they ought to be rigid and inflexible, but cannot manage to be so; consequently they are responsive in a half-hearted and guilty way which gives little pleasure either to them or to their children. It seems that if one really responded to the needs of infants in the very first weeks of life and later too, the results might be truly astonishing. But it could be that this would require important changes in adult attitudes and even, perhaps, in the structure of the family. Can parents who have themselves been raised in a restricted way and been made defensive by their other life experiences bring themselves to change sufficiently to treat their babies in an open and responsive or anticipatory way? Or are they trapped in the way in which Freud[43] has urged:

> The superego of the child is not really built up on the model of the parents, but on that of the parents' superego, it takes over the same content, it becomes the vehicle of tradition and of all the age-long values which have been handed down in this way from generation to generation.

Or are they trapped in another way; by social pressures coming from the whole way in which society is run – the separation and domination of workers by bosses, of women by men, of blacks by whites, of pupils by teachers and of children by parents? Is the pattern too strong to break?

We shall see later on that there is hope, largely centred on the power of small groups and large media to produce psychological and social changes. Given the right circumstances, which can be

* See also the article by A. Thomas, S. Chess and H. G. Birch on 'The origin of personality' in the **Scientific American** for August 1970, which deals with three types of babies – easy children (40%), difficult children (10%) and slow-to-warm-up children (15%).

consciously set up, people's attitudes and outlook can change in the directions which they desire.

In a very full discussion of personality changes throughout life, Maddi[44] concludes that: 'There seems ample evidence for radical changes in personality following the childhood years.' If children can develop, parents can, too.

REFERENCES

1. A Gesell & F. L. Ilg. Infant and child in the culture of today, Harper 1943
2. J. Bowlby. Maternal care and mental health, Schocken 1966 (1951)
3. J. Bowlby. Child care and the growth of love, Penguin 1953
4. K. Lorenz. King Solomon's ring, Thomas Y. Crowell 1952
5. M. D. S. Ainsworth. The effects of maternal deprivation: A review of findings and controversy in the context of research strategy, in Deprivation of maternal care, Schocken 1966 (1962)
6. N. O'Connor. The evidence for the permanently disturbing effects of mother-child separation, Acta Psychol. (Amst.) 12, 1956
7. L. J. Yarrow. Separation from parents during early childhood, in M. L. Hoffman & L. W. Hoffman (eds), Review of child development research, Russell Sage Foundation 1964
8. J. Bowlby. Childhood mourning and psychiatric illness, in P. Lomas (ed). The predicament of the family, Hogarth 1967
9. W. Dennis & P. Najarian. Infant development under environmental handicap, Psychol. Monog. 71, 1957
10. C. Rathbun et al. The restitutive process in children following radical separation from family and culture, Amer. J. Orthopsychiat. 28, 1958
11. A. J. Rabin & G. J. Mohr. Behaviour research in collective settlements in Israel. VI. Infants and children under conditions of 'intermittent' mothering in the Kibbutz, Amer. J. Orthopsychiat. 28, 1958
12. W. Dennis & Y. Sayegh. The effect of supplementary experiences upon the behavioral development of infants in institutions, Child Develop. 36, 1965
13. H. M. Skeels et al. A Study of environmental stimulation: An orphanage pre-school project, Iowa Studies in Child Welfare 15, No. 4, 1938. See also his Adult status of children with contrasting early life experiences, Monogr. Soc. Res. Child Dev. 31, 1966.
14. J. G. Howells. Day foster care and the nursery, Lancet 1956
15. J. G. Howells, Child-parent separation as a therapeutic procedure, Amer. J. Psychiat. 119 (10) 1963
16. H. Lewis. Deprived children, Nuffield and Oxford University Press 1954
17. H. Orlansky. Infant care and personality, Psychol. Rev. 46, 1949
18. H. F. Harlow & M. K. Harlow. Social deprivation in monkeys, Scientific American 207, No. 5, 1962
19. D. O. Hebb. The mammal and his environment, in I. D. Steiner & M. Fishbein (eds), Current studies in social psychology, Holt, Rinehart & Winston 1965 (1955)
20. J. W. B. Douglas & J. M. Blomfield. Children under five, Allen & Unwin 1958
21. J. P. Scott. Early experience and the organization of behaviour, Brooks/Cole 1968

22. N. O'Connor. Children in restricted environments, in G. Newton & S. Levine (eds). Early experience and behaviour, Thomas 1968. See also M. Rutter, Maternal Deprivation Reassessed, Penguin 1972
23. E. Zigler. Social reinforcement, environment and the child, Amer. J. Orthopsychiat. 33, 1963
24. A. D. B. Clarke & A. M. Clarke. Recovery from the effects of deprivation, Acta Psychol. (Amst.) 16, 1959
25. V. H. Denenberg. Stimulation in infancy, emotional reactivity, and exploratory behaviour, in D. H. Glass (ed), Biology and behaviour, Russell Sage Foundation 1967
26. S. Levine. The effects of infantile experience on adult behaviour, in A. J. Bachrach (ed), Experimental foundations of clinical psychology, Basic Books 1962
27. T. Schaefer. The search for a critical factor in early handling, some methodological implications, in same ref as 22
28. T. K. Landauer & J. W. Whiting. Infantile stimulation and adult stature of human males, American Anthropologist 66, 1964
29. L. M. Terman. Mental and physical traits of a thousand gifted children, in R. G. Barker *et al.* (eds). Child behaviour and development, McGraw-Hill 1943
30. H. R. Schaffer & P. E. Emerson. The development of social attachments in infancy, Monograph. Soc. Res. Child. Devel. 29, 1964
31. J. Bowlby. Attachment and loss, Vol. 1, Hogarth 1969
32. S. Karelitz *et al.* Relation of crying activity in early infancy to speech and intellectual development at age three years, Child Developmt. 35, 1964
33. J. Newson & E. Newson. Patterns of infant care in an urban community, Penguin 1965 (1963)
34. M. Geber. The psychomotor development of African children in the first year, and the influence of maternal behaviour, J. soc. Psychol. 47, 1958
35. M. Deakin, The children on the hill, André Deutsch 1972
36. B. Pasamanick. Comparative study of the behavioral development of negro infants, J. Genet. Psychol. 69, 1946
37. J. R. Williams & R. B. Scott. Growth and development of negro infants: Motor development and its relationship to child-rearing practices in two groups of negro infants, Child Developmt. 24, 1935
38. D. O. Hebb. The effects of early experience on problem-solving at maturity, Amer. Psychologist, 2, 1947
39. D. G. Forgays & J. M. Read. Crucial periods for free-environmental experience in the rat, J. Comp. physiol. Psychol. 55, 1962
40. M. B. McGraw. Later development of children specially trained during infancy, Child Developmt. 10, 1939
41. A. Thomas. Behavioral individuality in early childhood, New York University Press 1963
42. H. A. Moss. Sex, age and state as determinants of mother-infant interaction, Merrill-Palmer Q .13, 1967
43. S. Freud. New introductory lectures, Hogarth 1949 (1933)
44. S. R. Maddi. Personality theories: A comparative analysis, Dorsey Press 1968

CHAPTER TWO

Socialization

Babies become children in a social system. It may be that the whole notion of a child is a social invention, but in any case the processes of maturation and socialization go on side by side and in an interacting way. Secord & Backman[1] say:

> Socialization is an interactional process whereby a person's behaviour is modified to conform to expectations held by members of the group to which he belongs.

This definition makes it clear that it is not only children who are socialized – we all become exposed to socialization pressures when we enter a new group. But adult socialization is often called secondary socialization, to distinguish it from the primary socialization which happens to children. We shall be looking at it in the next volume.

Historically, interest in socialization arose out of concern with the way in which children became moral, developed a conscience, or were tamed. In theory, there are two main problems which can appear: undersocialization, where the child grows up too aggressive and with insufficient attention to others; and oversocialization, where the child grows up dependent and helpless. But in practice the major emphasis has always been on the problems of undersocialization.

One of the most influential concepts was that of the superego, put forward by Freud. Hall & Lindzey[2] put it succinctly:

> The superego is modelled upon the earliest parental images, when the parents were thought to be perfect and omnipotent . . . Superego takes over the role of external authority figures and exacts conformity to society. The person is then said to be socialized.

This is not the place for a full discussion of the Freudian view, since we have already looked at the whole theory, and seen that it is very doubtful whether the concept of a superego makes any sense at all. (Vol. 1, Chapter 2.)

The other main source of ideas about the conscience has been behaviorist psychology. Eysenck[3] put this position more honestly than most:

> How does conscience originate? Our contention will be that conscience is simply a conditioned reflex, and that it originates in the same way as do phobic and neurotic responses . . . In this process of conditioning, much help would, of course, be forthcoming from the law of generalization which we have encountered previously.

It will again be clear from our earlier discussion of the whole behaviorist position that this cannot be accepted as an adequate account. Conditioning accounts for very little of the learning which human beings do, even on the most generous interpretation of the terms involved.

Most research in the field of socialization has been oriented round the efficacy of various kinds of discipline in taming the young child. This has sometimes been a one-off piece of research, sometimes a cross-cultural comparison; very rarely has it been longitudinal. Let us look at one of each, to see the approaches and some of the findings.

Survey Research

The very influential Sears *et al.*[4] research was a survey of mothers carried out in 1956. It was based entirely on the verbal reports of these mothers, about their practice in relation to their five-year-old children, all of whom were in Boston (USA) kindergartens. Many of these questions went back a number of years, covering things like age of weaning and toilet training, etc. But one of the most interesting and often-quoted findings was about the relation of permissiveness and punishment to the control of aggression. By permissiveness is meant that the mother believed it to be all right for the child to express angry emotions, and would not attempt to stop this happening. Punishment means in this context any behaviour of the mother which is seen by the child as punishing – *after* the aggression has taken place. This was rated as more or less severe. The results are shown in the table on page 30.

TABLE I

Association between mothers' reported behaviour and aggressiveness reported in their children.

PER CENT HIGHLY AGGRESSIVE

MOTHERS' BEHAVIOUR	Boys (n = 195)	Girls (n = 162)
Low permissiveness, low punishment	4	13
Low permissiveness, high punishment	20	19
High permissiveness, low punishment	25	21
High permissiveness, high punishment	42	38

Note—Both columns total only 91 per cent because in a few cases the mother's behaviour could not be assessed from the data available.

What is so interesting here is the difference between the two extremes, both of which deal with behaviour which is, on the face of it, rather inconsistent. The first group on the table were mothers who did not permit aggression from their children, but stopped it by other means than punishment. Looked at in this light, their behaviour can be seen to be more consistent, not less; punishment is itself a form of aggression, and they were disapproving of it not only by precept but also by their own practice, thus offering a role model to imitate. The last group on the table were mothers who felt they should allow their children to express aggression, but could restrain their own impulses to suppress the child's aggression only so long, and then they would blow up. When the punishment came, it was likely to be severe. So these mothers were providing a living model of aggression at the very moment when they were trying to teach the child not to be aggressive; and what happened was that the children learnt more from the example of successful aggression than they did from the pain of punishment.

This is certainly very interesting, and a very nice example of simple multivariate analysis, being much more revealing than looking at permissiveness by itself, or punishment by itself; but is this good evidence that we can rely on? How good are these reports of permissiveness, these reports of punishment, these reports of aggression? Well, not very good. Yarrow and his colleagues[5] tried to replicate the findings more recently, and found that all the data collected in this way – from mothers' reports – tended to be un-reliable and shaky. Sears and his co-workers[6] also looked at the data more critically in a later piece of research and found very low corre-lations as soon as they tried to compare data on the same child from different sources. And Danziger[7] draws the moral:

> Parental punitiveness is shown to be positively associated with reported aggression on the part of the child only when the mother is the source of information both about her own behaviour and the behaviour of her child. Such correlations are of course spurious. They merely show that the mother sees her relationship with the child in relatively consistent terms of hostility and counter-hostility. They tell us nothing about the child's actual behaviour or about its causes.

So we have arrived at a pretty shattering conclusion. The nice pattern that seemed so plausible turns out to be an artefact of the research method used. Instead of the neat interaction of well-defined variables, we have the whole messy atmosphere of homes in which relationships are generally good, or generally bad, or some-where in the middle.

Cross-Cultural Research

Can we do any better with the cross-cultural research? The most influential study here has been the one by Whiting and Child[8] which examined 75 societies to find what relationship existed be-tween child-rearing practices (weaning, toilet training, sex training, independence training, aggression training) and customary re-sponses to illness; illness was taken as a typical focus of guilt feel-ings – people with a guilty conscience think that if they are ill it is their own fault in some way. The authors wanted to test the idea that the earlier the socialization, the stronger the guilt feelings. The results are shown in the table on page 32.

These figures show that indeed it is true that the earlier the socialization, the stronger the guilt feelings, particularly for sexual training. This seems very plausible, and seems to add to our under-standing of how socialization works.

But is this so in fact? How good is this data, based as it must be on the work of a multitude of different investigators, working under diverse and always difficult conditions? How much of the informa-tion comes from actual observation, and how much from reports

TABLE 2

Relation between patient self-blame for illness and estimated age of onset for certain aspects of socialization.

ASPECT OF SOCIALIZATION

Age at onset	Weaning	Toilet training	Modesty training	Training in hetero-sexual inhibition	Independence training
Below 1·0	11·0 (2)	4·0 (2)			
1·0 to 1·9	11·6 (5)	11·9 (8)			
2·0 to 2·4	11·0 (10)	11·7 (7)			15·8 (4)
2·5 to 2·9	9·1 (9)	9·0 (1)			9·9 (8)
3·0 to 3·9	9·5 (4)	14·0 (1)	13·6 (4)		9·0 (9)
4·0 to 5·9	4·0 (2)	8·0 (1)	10·5 (3)		3·2 (11)
6·0 to 7·9			9·2 (5)	12·1 (7)	6·0 (1)
8·0 to 9·9				9·0 (3)	
10·0 and above			9·0 (1)	5·5 (4)	
Correlation	−0·42**	+0·21	−0·50*	−0·74**	−0·34*

Note – The figures given show the mean index of self-blame. The figures in brackets show the number of societies on which this mean is based. The correlations with one star are significant at the 5% level, and those with two stars at the 1% level.

after – and perhaps long after – the event? And how close is the variable measured – reported self-blame – to the intended quality – strength of guilt feelings or conscience? And are the findings from primitive societies relevant in any case to our much more complex situation? Even more fundamentally, is the primitive society itself constant? Danziger refers to Margaret Mead[9] when he says:

> . . . The cross-cultural comparison of societies at a particular point in time has something very accidental about it. It is like the comparison of a number of stills, chosen at random from various films.

It seems, then, that the cross-cultural approach to the study of socialization is also problematical. It can be useful, but needs a very critical eye in evaluating the results. In the present case, even if we accepted the results completely at their face value, there would still remain the question of meaning; what are the implications for us? Do we identify a strong conscience with guilt feelings? Do we want guilt feelings to be so strong that they make us blame ourselves when we get ill? How much and what kind of guilt feeling is desirable, or undesirable? So many questions, and so few answers! Is longitudinal research any better?

We shall, in Chapter 12, be looking at the major socialization study in this field, that by Kagan & Moss[10] which followed up three-year-old children to fourteen and into the early twenties. Our conclusion will be that very little consistency appeared, and most of what did appear seemed to be due to sex-role typing rather than anything else. In other words, children change quite a lot over time. (See also the excellent treatment by Maddi[11] of this whole question.)

So has any research discovered anything in the field of socialization? There does appear to be one major area of agreement.

Types of Influence

All the research seems to show that 'love oriented discipline' or 'withdrawal of love techniques' are more effective in controlling children and developing a conscience in them than is direct physical punishment. Aronfreed[12] has suggested that these are vague terms, and wants instead to talk of 'induction discipline' (excluding the child, expressing disappointment in it, depriving it of privileges, reasoning with it, and in this way giving it self-initiated controls); and 'sensitization discipline' (physical chastisement, yelling, verbal threats and so on, which are much more external and lead the child to watch out for danger rather than looking inward in any way).

But this seems equally unsatisfactory – why should we divorce the attempt to influence children from the attempt to influence adults? If we cast our minds back to the work of Kelman[13] mentioned in the previous volume, it seems clear at once that sensitization discipline is just the same as the attempt to produce *compliance* by the use of superior power.

But induction discipline fails to make the distinction between *identification* (based on attraction to the influencing person) and *internalization* (based on seeing the point for oneself). It also omits the question of perceived legitimacy, which we saw that Kelman also left out. Perhaps this may be allowable for younger children, who may not make the necessary distinctions; but perhaps it is also a question of helping them to make such distinctions earlier than they normally do. As young as four years old, many children already have the notion of fairness in a fairly clear form.

It seems evident, then, that future research could be much more specific in separating out these different forms of influence. But what still remains is an unambiguous message that influence attempts which merely aim at compliance are the least likely of all to produce self-control in the sense of a knowledge and understanding of personal rules of conduct.

This is usually thought to mean that aiming at compliance is bad, and aiming at identification or internalization is good, but Lynn[14] raises a telling point on this which puts the whole matter in rather a different light. He points up the similarity between induction discipline and brainwashing:

> The essence of brainwashing, according to Sargant,[15] lies in the *alternating signals method*, i.e. the brainwasher first induces fear in his prey by threatening jail, Siberia, Hell, etc., and then offers an escape message to the effect 'only do or believe such and such and you will avoid these terrors'. If the victim does not break with the first alternation the process is repeated. The other components of brainwashing – solitary confinement, starvation, physical weakening and the like – should be understood as appendages to the basic alternating signals procedure. Now this analysis is stating that the brainwasher must play *two roles*, which he must alternate. The first role is as threatener and anxiety inducer. The second role is that of friend, protector and anxiety reducer. Both roles are essential if the victim is to be influenced in the most efficient manner.

Compare this with the account of induction discipline given by Secord & Backman in the book already quoted:

> . . . maximum strength of conscience results from an alternation of acceptance and rejection, paralleling the alternation of reward and punishment in the development of dependency . . . The children having mothers who were relatively warm toward them, but who made their love contingent on the child's good behaviour, appeared to have the most well-developed consciences.

The parallel is striking. It raises a number of disturbing questions about too easy acceptance of the desirability of instilling our rules into the minds of our children so that they become a firm and fixed internal conscience. Do we really want or need to brainwash our children?

Positive and Negative Views of Man

And this opens up the general point that both Freud and the behaviorists hold a negative view of man, which has entered into this whole question of control and conscience in a very powerful way. As we saw in the first volume, they both see man as essentially a mass of unacceptable selfish impulses which society must clamp down on. At the same time, the child is supposed to react to discipline in a fairly passive and mechanical way.

This whole view is criticized strongly in the latest edition of the Handbook:[16]

> This view leads to seeing socialization as a very difficult enterprise in which society seeks to mould a recalcitrant organism ... The tendency of socialization theorists to focus on such systems of behaviour as orality, toilet training, aggression and sexual behaviour has contributed to the predominance of the negative view of man ... A very different picture of socialization might have emerged had the early socialization theorists concentrated instead on the child's acquisition of language ... Looking at the two-year-old's command of bladder and bowel, we may find evidence that it was imposed through stern discipline; if we instead look at his command of language, we are more likely to feel that he has gladly seized upon a tool society offered him.

There are really two separate points here—one is that the child is to be trusted to mature in his own way and in his own time, because he is fundamentally a social being in any case; and the other is that he is active rather than passive in that process of self-development.

The former point is made most strongly by Carl Rogers, who has again and again urged that a child's impulses are basically socialized right from the start – in other words, if he has a wish to hurt another child, he also has a wish to be liked by that other child, and to be approved of by his parents, and to preserve and enhance his phenomenal self – as we saw in Chapter 3 of the first volume. If we allow free rein to *all* his impulses, and encourage them to be integrated, he will behave in a way which makes a lot of sense. In Rogers' own words:[17]

One of the most revolutionary concepts to grow out of our clinical experience is the growing recognition that the innermost core of man's nature, the deepest layers of his personality, the base of his 'animal nature', is positive in nature – is basically socialized, forward-moving, rational and realistic . . . We do not need to ask who will socialize him, for one of his own deepest needs is for affiliation and communication with others . . . He is realistically able to control himself, and he is incorrigibly socialized in his desires. There is no beast in man. There is only man in man . . .

What can happen, however, is that through various processes, the child's impulses become separated instead of integrated. Wishes of different kinds may then become compartmentalized and isolated in various ways, so that they do not get the benefit of internal 'collective criticism', so to speak. It may then need some form of therapy to bring the parts back together again – a good example of this process may be found in the excellent book by Axline[18] which gives a moving picture of the return to health of a five-year-old boy.

Unfortunately, there are certain regular ways in which this sort of thing happens in our culture. For example, we have already touched on the powerful force of sex-role typing; this does harm to both males and females by cutting them off from forms of experience which are natural to them but 'belong' to the other sex. And there is also a pattern, which seems specifically male and is still very dominant in our society, of actually valuing the separation and isolation of aspects of life. The culture seems to favour the separation of emotion from intellect, of the imaginative from the practical, of children from teachers, of blacks from whites and, of course, men from women. This kind of alienation of different aspects of ourselves one from the other may be something we have to combat at the social, cultural or even political level, rather than just in the family itself. (See Chapter 8.)

The other point, about the child being active rather than passive, is also an important one. We saw in the early chapters of the first volume how White urged that competence and mastery were motives just as important for the child as any of the 'drives' postulated by behaviorists or ethologists. And a lot of recent work tends in the same direction. For example, Peiper's work[19] has made it clear that the behaviour of the newborn is much more competent than has previously been supposed. Kessen[20] in his review of research on infancy, has brought out the same emphasis. Bell[21] has

argued that a passive model is not even appropriate to the socialization of animals, much less man. And in a later paper, Bell[22] has further shown that children are busy socializing parents, just as parents
are trying to socialize children. Once one thinks about it, it is obvious that two children of the same parents can elicit quite different
behaviour from those parents, depending on their own characteristics. This again cuts across both Freudian and behaviorist formula-
tions, both of which assume relatively fixed mechanisms operating
within the child.

So a large body of evidence has now built up to show that the
child must be considered as actively demanding certain kinds of
treatment from parents and other caretakers, at the same time as
they are demanding certain kinds of behaviour from him. But it
goes further than this. Not only does the child ask for certain things
to be given to him – he also processes what he gets in his own way.
This is the practical expression of the learning relationship which
we drew attention to in Chapter 5 of the first volume. In other
words, parents attempt to get across certain lessons – but the lesson
which is received may not be quite the same as that which the parent
thought he was sending out. This view of the child as an active
processor of the society's norms and standards is a far cry from the
approach which views socialization as a simple transmission of
norms from one generation to the next.

Main Variables Studied

The main variables which have been studied in the field of socialization are the following:

1. *Oral behaviour* Sucking, timing of feedings and age and nature of
   weaning;
2. *Excretory behaviour* Toilet training;
3. *Sexual behaviour* Various anxiety patterns;
4. *Aggression;*
5. *Dependence* Seeking the help of others as a method of attaining
   one's goals; attachment and deprivation relevant to social sensitivity:
6. *Achievement motivation;*
7. *Warmth* See the paper by Maccoby[23] for a discussion of this difficult
   variable;
8. *Family structure.*

But as we are now in a position to see, most of this research has been seriously flawed by the unwarranted assumptions it has made about the nature of the process involved. If we assume a one-way process, we can only get one-way results. And the whole thing seems to stem from the view which we have questioned, that the parents are basically right and have all the answers, and the child is basically likely to go wrong and continually needs to be pushed into the right path.

It is this set of assumptions which has resulted in the vast body of work which has centred round the last of the variables to be studied:

9. *Punishment.*

This is sufficiently important to be considered by itself.

Punishment

One of the most important continuing controversies in the field of socialization has been the efficacy of punishment. The standard position in psychology for many years was that rewards and punishment – the stick and the carrot – were highly effective, and in fact the only way in which organisms learned.

During the 1950's a great deal of new evidence came along which seemed to show that punishment was ineffective. It seemed that although punishment could temporarily suppress a particular form of conduct, it did not permanently weaken the motivation to perform such actions.

But reviews of the research literature since then, for example by Church[24] and by Solomon,[25] seem to show that punishment can be extremely effective, so long as (a) it is done at the right time – even a few seconds can make a significant difference – and (b) it is mild rather than severe. We have already looked at (b) in Chapter 7 of the first volume, so let us concentrate for a moment on (a). Solomon has something to say about this, but the main investigator has been Aronfreed.[26]

In one experiment with 9- and 10-year-old boys, each one had to choose between two toys on each of nine training trials. A different pair of toys was used on each trial, but each pair consisted of one toy that was highly attractive and another that was relatively unattractive. All of the toys were small replicas of common objects. The child was instructed to pick up the toy in each pair that he wished to talk about, and then to describe its functions at the request of the experimenter. He was also told that certain toys were *only supposed to be for older boys*, and that he was not supposed to choose these toys.

On each trial, the child could pick up the unattractive toy and describe its function. But when he chose an attractive toy, the experimenter said 'No! That's for the older boys.'

Now in one condition, he said it just as the child was reaching for an attractive toy and before he actually touched it.

In the second condition, he said it roughly two or three seconds after the toy had been lifted, and took the toy out of the boy's hand.

All the children at first chose the attractive toys. But they quickly shifted to the unattractive toys, and consistently chose them after the first two or three trials.

However, the group who were punished while reaching learned more quickly.

The more dramatic effect of the timing of punishment appeared during a common test for internalization that directly followed.

Two test objects were introduced as the first pair of toys in another choice task. Again, one toy was highly attractive and the other was unattractive. The experimenter then left the room on a pretext that would obviously take him far from the scene, and the child remained alone for five minutes within a protective nest of room-divider screens. The results were as follows:

TABLE 3

Results of temptation test

	PUNISHED BEFORE TOUCHING	PUNISHED AFTER TOUCHING
LEFT ATTRACTIVE TOY ALONE (Based on 34 children)	74%	29%

Remember that the first group had actually had fewer punishments, because they learned quicker. So the only reason must have been in the timing of the punishment.

This experiment was later replicated and extended to girls aged 8–10 years old, and to female experimenters. Similar experiments were done on reward.

Why does this happen? The explanation Aronfreed gives is that anxiety about choice is maximal just before the choice is made. By punishing at that point, you link the forbidden thing with this high degree of anxiety arousal. 'Anxiety becomes attached to the intrinsic cues of an incipient transgression.' This link is of the nature of fear-memory, and hence very powerful whenever it is re-aroused.

Punishment at this optimal point makes the child actually feel guilty when he touches the forbidden object; punishment at some other point makes him *know he is supposed to feel guilty*, which is a very different thing.

Aronfreed found that the internalization of the taboo was assisted if a 'reason why' was given. But it made no difference whether this reason was external – 'Those toys are difficult to tell about, so they are more suitable for older children' – or internal – 'It is wrong to want to have toys that are for the older children.'

It appears, then, from this whole line of experimentation, that it is possible to use punishment to socialize children, in a very direct and manipulative sense. But if this is so, then the moral question about brain-washing arises once more. Do we have the right to brainwash our children? Bennis & Slater[27] say:

> The democratic family is based on an expectation that tomorrow will be different from today, and that there is, hence, some ambiguity as to how to socialize the child. 'Socialization for what?' is its fundamental question.

This is indeed the whole point which we have now raised in this chapter. It becomes clear that many of the assumptions behind the whole field of socialization research are autocratic assumptions, and not democratic assumptions at all. This is probably because what goes on in the family is generally autocratic rather than democratic. Laing goes further:[28]

> Love and violence, properly speaking, are polar opposites. Love lets the other be, but with affection and concern. Violence attempts to constrain the other's freedom, to force him to act in the way we desire, but with ultimate lack of concern, with indifference to the other's own existence or destiny.

If this seems to go too far, and to be making too strong a case for the harmfulness of much that goes on within the family, we can at least respect the sense of what is being said, and realize that it is not so far from what is being said more temperately and more acceptably by highly-respected authorities like Gesell & Ilg[29] when they say:

The spirit of liberty has its deepmost roots in the biological impulse toward optimal growth. Babies as well as adults are endowed with this inalienable impulsion . . . If parents and teachers begin with the assumption that they can make over and mold a child into a preconceived pattern, they are bound to become autocratic. If, on the contrary, parents begin with the assumption that every baby comes into the world with a unique individuality, their task will be to interpret the child's individuality and to give it the best possible chance to grow and find itself.

Our attempt to approach socialization through the way of external sanctions seems, then, to have brought us to a point which is hardly satisfactory. Perhaps it would be better to approach it through the way of internal maturation in a social setting. Let us now go on to this different approach.

REFERENCES

1. P. F. Secord & C. W. Backman. Social psychology, McGraw-Hill 1964
2. C. S. Hall & G. Lindzey. Theories of personality, Wiley 1957
3. H. J. Eysenck. Fact and fiction in psychology, Penguin 1965
4. R. R. Sears *et al.* Patterns of child rearing, Harper & Row 1957
5. M. R. Yarrow *et al.* Child rearing: An inquiry into research and methods, Jossey-Bass 1968
6. R. R. Sears *et al.* Identification and child rearing, Stanford University Press 1965
7. K. Danziger. Socialization, Penguin 1971
8. J. W. M. Whiting & I. L. Child. Child training and personality, Yale 1953
9. M. Mead. New lives for old, Morrow 1956
10. J. Kagan & H. A. Moss. Birth to maturity, Wiley 1962
11. S. R. Maddi. Personality theories: A comparative analysis, Dorsey Press 1968
12. J. Aronfreed. Aversive control of socialization, in W. J. Arnold (ed). Nebraska Symposium on Motivation 1968
13. H. C. Kelman. Compliance, identification and internalization; Three processes of attitude change, J. Conflict Resolution 2, 1958
14. R. Lynn. Brainwashing techniques in leadership and child rearing, Brit. J. Soc. clin. Psychol. 5, 1966
15. W. Sargant. Battle for the mind, Heinemann 1957
16. E. Zigler & I. L. Child. Socialization, in G. Lindzey & E. Aronson, Handbook of social psychology (2nd ed), Vol. 3, 1969
17. C. R. Rogers. On becoming a person, Constable 1961
18. V. Axline. Dibs: In search of self, Houghton Mifflin 1964
19. A. Peiper. Cerebral function in infancy and childhood, Consultants Bureau 1963
20. W. Kessen. Research in the psychological development of infants: An overview, Merrill-Palmer Quart. 9, 1963
21. R. Q. Bell. Developmental psychology, Annu. Rev. Psychol. 1965
22. R. Q. Bell. A reinterpretation of the direction of effects in studies of socialization, Psychol. Rev. 75, 1968

23. E. E. Maccoby. The choice of variables in the study of socialization, Sociometry 24, 1961. Reprinted in I. D. Steiner & M. Fishbein, Current studies in social psychology, Holt, Rinehart & Winston 1965

24. R. M. Church. The varied effects of punishment on behaviour, Psychol. Rev. 70, 1963

25. R. L. Solomon, Punishment, Amer. Psychologist 19, 1964

26. J. Aronfreed. Conduct and conscience, Academic Press 1968

27. W. Bennis & P. E. Slater. The temporary society

28. R. D. Laing. The politics of experience, Penguin 1967

29. A. Gesell & F. L. Ilg. Infant and child in the culture of today, Hamish Hamilton 1965 (1943)

CHAPTER THREE

Moral Development

What happens when we try to look at things like right and wrong, transgression of norms, altruism and so on from the point of view of a natural development within the child?

If the general position which we have taken up is true, then it should be demonstrable that the child naturally grows into a moral being, mindful of the social situations in which he finds himself.

But it is not necessarily true that this is a gradual and unbroken process. What seems to be the case is that moral development is a matter of stages or levels which the child passes through. The order of the levels is invariable, but the exact age at which each stage is reached is not. Let us look at each of these stages in turn, and then discuss some of the difficulties raised by such a conception.

Stage One: Non-Moral

At the earliest periods in a child's life, it is not conscious of the idea of a rule. And it is the idea of a rule which is the beginning of morality. So children of this age – under 4 or sometimes a little older – cannot have much sense of morality at all. They may certainly have a sense that some things they do are punished – they are often surrounded with threats of punishment, as the Newsons[1] have shown – but if they avoid the action, it is rather from a wish to avoid punishment than from any real feeling that the action is wrong. In fact, some parents make a distinction between young children 'being naughty' and older children 'doing wrong'. The traditional Catholic teaching, of course, is that children know the difference between right and wrong at seven years old, and not before, so there is nothing very controversial about the existence of this particular stage.

Piaget[2] calls it an egocentric stage, but this is dangerous, because it suggests a kind of behaviour which we find in adults, and which

Piaget did not mean at all. What he meant was that the child at this stage sees and thinks about his world from his own point of view (as we saw in Chapter 4 of the first volume) and is unable to conceive that there are other perspectives. His thought is completely dominated by those features of the environment that he is perceiving or noticing at the time; in Piaget's term his thought is centred. Since he cannot free himself from this limited perception, he cannot compensate for the distortions which it must introduce. This is something like a physical limitation, which the child cannot overcome, any more than he can overcome the inability to reach a light switch which is too high, or the inability to turn a handle which is too stiff.

Kohlberg[3] found in his research that two separate stages could be distinguished within this general level. One stage had to do with punishment and its avoidance. 'There is no true moral obligation, no concept of the rights of others, and no true respect for authority; only conforming deference to those who have the power to punish.' It is possible to speak of obedience at this stage, but it is important to realize that it is not obedience to rules, but obedience to persons. This is a hard lesson for parents to learn, and many of them never do learn it. The other stage which Kohlberg found was a kind of primitive idea of exchange. The child knows what he wants, and is willing to admit that other people have wants too. So he is able to 'trade' by giving in to someone else's wants if that will enable him to get what he wants. It is a kind of 'giving in for reward' effect. So both of these stages are concerned with straight rewards and punishments for approved or disapproved persons, and they are both concerned with persons rather than with rules or principles.

Kay[4] has shown that a large number of investigators have all found this level to fit in with the analysis which has been outlined here. He calls it a 'prudential attitude'. But again it is necessary to remember that this is not like what we would call a prudential attitude in an adult, and which we might feel to be inadequate or harmful as a moral stance. It is a kind of 'prudence' which knows nothing else, and has no alternative which could be substituted. It is pre-moral.

Stage Two: Morality as a Set of Rules

We come here to morality proper, in one way, and yet fall short of it in another. All the emphasis is on what is done, and none on why it is done. The rules are sacred, in the sense of coming from 'on high' in a generalized sense – their origin cannot be questioned. Piaget calls this a heteronomous stage, meaning that the locus of control is always outside the child himself or herself. At this stage there is a genuine respect for authority, and even a certain legalism. Piaget says:

> The obligation to speak the truth, not to steal, etc., are all so many duties which the child feels deeply although they do not emanate from his own mind. They are commands coming from the adult and accepted by the child. Originally, therefore, the morality of duty is essentially heteronomous. Right is to obey the will of the adult. Wrong is to have a will of one's own.

This is the age from roughly four to eight years old, though as we must always stress, the point is not the age-range, but the sequence of stages.

There is a kind of obsessive quality about this kind of morality, which reminds one of the taboos of savage tribes. The knowledge of what is right and wrong is an absolute knowledge – there is no qualification. If someone does something wrong by accident, or out of the best of intentions, it is still just as wrong, and no allowances can be made.

It is a curious thing about this attitude to morality that it does not necessarily result in better behaviour. The child may know that something is absolutely wrong, and still do it, because the other factors in the situation are stronger. But he knows that he has done wrong, and may feel guilty, or may expect to be punished if found out.

This seems very close to Kohlberg's 'law and order' stage, which he found to consist in showing respect for authority and maintaining the given social order for its own sake. But Kohlberg also found another stage of morality which runs as it were between what we have called stage one and stage two; this he called 'personal concordance'. Personal concordance was defined as a 'good boy' morality of maintaining good relations with others; at this stage the child is oriented towards personal approval, and to pleasing and helping others. The right action is defined by the general consensus of others, and the motive behind right action is the desire to remain accepted by others.

I am not sure about personal concordance. I think it may hide two or three different things, and to be more complex than it looks.

For the moment, let us just register Kohlberg's disagreement with most of the other observers.

It seems generally best to regard stage two as a stage of almost religious observance of the rules for their own sake, because they are there. The phrase 'it's not allowed' is a final statement – it does not need any further elaboration or justification. And motives are irrelevant.

Stage Three: Morality as Social Agreement

This next stage is again a kind of maimed morality; it is still heteronomous, though in a different way. It consists in a search for norms and a wish to conform to those norms, but now with a clear recognition that the norms are not absolute, but come from a set of people and serve definite purposes.

In Piaget's terms, this is a reciprocal stage, because rules are often now accepted as the expression of reciprocity and give-and-take between social equals. It is something like an ethic of mutual respect. It is no longer sufficient simply to know the requirements of the rules and fulfil them.

An action is now seen to be good if it is socially fair. The possibility now emerges of having arguments about what is right, based on this notion of fairness. The possibility also emerges of weighing one set of values against another set, and arriving at some sort of order of importance—thus saving life may be seen as more important than saving property, and breaking rules may be worse in the one case than in the other.

So there is much more understanding of why the rules are there, and there may be a growing refusal to accept rules whose point cannot be seen. At this stage, which commences roughly at the age of nine or ten, there is relative freedom from the fixed boundaries of the two earlier stages, and much more ability to see the other person's point of view. Mead[5] has a good statement about this:

> In so far as the child does take the attitude of the other and allows that attitude of the other to determine the thing he is going to do with reference to a common end, he is becoming an organic member of society.

But it must be remembered that the child at this stage has very little sense of himself as a person. He is very much a satellite of his parents, and looks at the world from a largely unexamined centre.

So the norms which he accepts are accepted in a very automatic way – simply as emanating from a group with which he identifies – and can weigh just as heavily and arbitrarily as the earlier absolute rules which were obtained from the parents.

Motives are recognized, but in a rather external way, as simply applying to people, rather than as coming out of people 'from the inside'.

This is very much like Kohlberg's fifth stage, that of 'social contract', where the main consideration is general law-like principles involving the rights of others. It is a law-making stage, as distinguished from the law-obeying stage which it emerges from.

Stage Four: Morality as Conscience

This can only emerge in adolescence, and not necessarily early in adolescence, because it involves the conception of oneself as a person, distinct from one's family or other group.

We do not mean by conscience the Freudian superego, which is irrational and unexaminable, but simply the reference to one's own inner voice, rather than some external authority, whether rule, law or group norm. At this stage we get statements like – *I'm not the kind of person to do that*. Kohlberg calls this the stage of 'individual principles', and for him it is the sixth and highest form of morality.

This is the first stage where we find a genuine autonomy – in other words, the rules come from inside rather than from outside. In philosophy, it is only autonomous morality which is counted as morality at all. Everything else is merely prudence or expedient behaviour, performed in order to get by, and survive.

It is a key feature of this stage that it means emancipation from roles. And as such it involves finding oneself as a person. It means a lot of self-examination, and a heavy emphasis on motives, seen now as really internal.

At this stage we should say that no act should be called right unless it proceeds from motives which are right. It is acting from the right motives which actually constitutes rightness. Actions are done by people, and do not exist in abstraction from real people acting in real situations. It is the rectitude of the heart which produces actions which are right, and no set of rules is good enough to form a substitute for this. If the motives are right, the actions – even though they break ordinary rules or laws – will also be right.

This was originally a religious view, and it lays the stress upon the conscience or inner voice. At its self-confident height, the guarantee of the rectitude of the heart is the critical eye of God, which tears away all shams and self-deceit, and never permits the moral eye to delude itself. In our own day, when it is much harder to believe in God, the possibility of self-deception remains very much open.

Stage Five: Morality Proper

It is only when the previous four stages have been passed through that we can talk of morality proper. For important though the conscience is as a discovery, and as a release from external pressures, there is something unexaminable about it, and it therefore falls short of full rationality. But it is only with full rationality that we can conduct moral discourse that is worth the name.

And once we are talking morality in the full sense, all the problems of ethics come upon us. Utilitarianism, the ethics of duty, natural law, the ethic of progress, Marxism, existentialism, all have to be discussed, adopted, acted on.

However, the interesting thing is that nothing of this stage has been researched at all – though Kohlberg's sixth stage does include some mention of universal principles. So we do not have to deal with any of this here – but it is worth pointing out that books on moral development in children hardly contain anything about morality in the full sense at all.

What may be worth some attention here is some discussion of what happens in adult life. Obviously adults do not go on treating their parents as unquestioned authorities all through life, but neither do they adopt the highest stage of morality and stick to that!

What seems to happen is that adults revert to an adult version of one of the four stages which we have outlined for children – but because it is an adult version, it varies and re-forms in certain ways.

The adult version of stage four is someone who is a morally conscious person. One feels that all the time he or she is saying, 'is this right for me?', and trying to make his or her life a consistent whole. But often this is a much more relaxed person than the adolescent who has just discovered the conscience, and there is not the same self-condemnation for falling short, nor the same denunciation of others for their hypocrisy.

The adult version of stage three is the conformist, who wants to keep well in with everyone. He sinks himself in his roles, and if

48

action in one role is inconsistent with action in another role, that is not too worrying. He does not refer to principles very much, and is able to bend the rules when it seems to be justified. He does not have a high sense of his own worth, and may have a great need for other people's approval.

The key thing about this is the absence of any principle to refer to; sometimes, indeed, it results in a kind of 'moral' censure of people who do have principles as narrow or repressive. It has great survival value in any culture – the song about the Vicar of Bray demonstrates this. But it comes very low on any scale of morality, as we shall see.

The adult version of stage two is dominated by fixed principles, but whereas with the child this took a personal form, in the adult it takes a more abstract form. So instead of referring to infallible authority figures, the adult refers more often to permanent principles of law and order. And because this makes rational argument about morality possible – one principle may conflict with another, and so on – this is actually a more advanced moral stage than the adult version of stage three.

So although in the child stage two comes before stage three, in the adult the positions reverse, and stage two becomes a higher and more specifically moral stage than stage three. This is a twist which has not been remarked on by most of the authorities in this field, though it is obvious enough once it is pointed out.

There is a further twist, in that there is a more sophisticated version of the law-and-order stage, which instead of merely looking at the laws and duties which are already laid down, and acknowledging obedience to them, starts thinking in terms of making the laws and changing the laws. This is what Kohlberg calls the 'social contract' stage, and we saw earlier that it was implicit in the stage three outlook of the child – what Piaget called the reciprocal stage. But in the adult it flowers out of the law-and-order stage, and often argues in terms of the general welfare.

The adult version of stage one – the pre-moral stage – must obviously be very different in a number of ways, because in the child it is based on an incapacity to understand the nature of a rule; while practically all adults know what a rule is, even if they are unable or unwilling to abide by any rule. This is an egocentric stage, where the person finds it very difficult to put himself into the position of the other, or to sympathize with anyone else's feelings. This is close to the view of Somerset Maugham, who once said that his morality was 'do what you like, with one eye on the policeman at the corner'. There is a great deal of fear: of himself, of other people, of what may happen. This often leads to superstitious practices, designed to ward off disaster of one kind or another.

So much for a very brief outline of the main theory of moral development. Let us now look at the evidence for the theory, and see whether it stands up to criticism. We shall mainly look at the work of Piaget and Kohlberg.

Piaget

It is Piaget who has carried out or inspired most of the research on the moral development of younger children. For fifty years he and his co-workers in Geneva have been bringing out reports on one aspect or another of child development.

A good deal of the research has been concerned with establishing the difference between what we have called stage two (morality as a set of rules) and stage three (morality as social agreement). Some of the research was done by asking questions about the game of marbles, while some of it was done by offering two contrasting tales, and asking about which represented the worse behaviour. Here, for example, are two such connected tales:

I. There was a little boy called Julian. His father had gone out, and Julian thought it would be fun to play with his father's ink pot. First he played with the pen, and then he made a little blot on the table-cloth.

II. A little boy named Auguste once noticed that his father's ink pot was empty. One day when his father was away he got the idea of filling up the ink pot to help his father, so that it would be ready for him when he came home. But while he was opening the ink bottle he made a big blot on the tablecloth.

And children were asked to say whether both children were equally naughty, or whether one was naughtier than the other, and which one should be punished more. Here is one such conversation with a child at stage two, which we said ran from about 4 to about 8 years old: this is a seven-year-old talking:

A little boy sees that his father's ink pot is empty. He takes the bottles, but he is clumsy, and makes a big blot. There is another little boy who was always touching things. He took the ink and made a little blot.

—Well, are they both equally naughty?
No.
—Which is worse?
The one who made the big blot.
—Why did he make the big blot?
To help out.
—And why did the other boy make the little blot?
Because he was always touching things. He made a little blot.
—Then which is naughtier?
The one who made the big blot.

This example clearly shows that the younger child's moral concept does not have to do with inner motivation, but according to outer conduct, to the physical effects of a person's actions. This kind of answer tails off as the child gets to nine years old, and becomes rare in ten-year-olds. Piaget's main book, to which we have been referring all the way through this chapter, was one of his earlier ones, published before much of his later work made much clearer the way in which a child's general cognitive awareness grows, and Roger Brown[6] has a good chapter attempting to bring Piaget's moral findings into line with his later and better developed theory.

Later research has on the whole backed up Piaget's view of the way in which moral awareness develops with age. A good deal of the evidence is reviewed in Kay's book already quoted, but in addition there is work in a number of different countries by Medinnus [7, 8], Najarian-Svajian[9], Breznitz & Kugelmass,[10], Kugelmass, Breznitz & Breznitz[11] and Bull[12] which substantiate the general age trend.

Kohlberg

The work of Kohlberg is more recent, having started only in the 1960's. It was conducted mainly with children between the ages of 10 and 16, but has been extended later to students and adults. The research mainly took the form of giving stories to children, and asking them to answer questions about the stories and their reactions to them. For example:

In Europe, a woman was near death from a special kind of cancer. There was one drug that the doctors thought might save her. It was a form of radium that a druggist in the same town had recently discovered. The drug was expensive to make, but the druggist was charging ten times what the drug cost him to make. He paid £200 for the radium and charged £2,000 for a small dose of the drug. The sick woman's husband, Heinz, went to everyone he knew to borrow the money, but he could only get together about £1,000, which is half of what it cost. He told the druggist that his wife was dying, and asked him to sell it cheaper or let him pay later. But the druggist said, 'No, I discovered the drug and I'm going to make money from it.' So Heinz got desperate and broke into the man's store to steal the drug for his wife.

And the questions then follow – Should the husband have done that? Why? If he is arrested, what action should the judge take? And so on.

After a very thorough and sensitive analysis of the open-ended responses to a number of dilemmas like this, Kohlberg came to the conclusion that there were six stages or levels in moral reasoning, such that the earlier levels tended to be characteristic of the younger children, and the later levels of the older ones, but where some of the older ones never went beyond some of the earlier levels. Here are the six levels which he found:

I. PREMORAL
Stage 1. Obedience and punishment orientation. 'Obey rules to avoid punishment.'
Stage 2. Instrumental Relativism (IR). Naive egocentric orientation, towards personal pleasure. 'Conform to obtain rewards, have favours returned, and so on.'

II. MORALITY OF CONVENTIONAL ROLE CONFORMITY
Stage 3. Personal Concordance (PC). Good-boy morality of maintaining social relations, approval of others. 'Conform to avoid disapproval, dislike of others.'
Stage 4. Law and Order (LO). Authority-maintaining morality. 'Conform to avoid censure by legitimate authorities and resultant guilt.' Doing one's duty.

III. MORALITY OF SELF-ACCEPTED MORAL PRINCIPLES
Stage 5. Social Contract (SC). Morality of contract, of individual rights, and of democratically accepted law. 'Conform to maintain the respect of the impartial spectator judging in terms of general welfare.'
Stage 6. Individual Principles (IP). Morality of individual principles of conscience. 'Conform to avoid self-condemnation.'

Because this research was done in a systematic way, it has been possible for other workers to follow up and test out the details of this schema. One of the most interesting suggestions of Kohlberg was that a child who was at a given level would only be able to comprehend the levels below him and one level above him; he would be unable to reach as far as two levels above his own position. This seems to have been borne out quite consistently, in research by Turiel,[13] Rest,[14] LeFurgy & Waloshin[15] and others.

This is even more interesting because the Kohlberg type of research has been applied to adults as well. For example, Haan *et al.*[16] found, in a large sample of college students and Peace Corps volunteers, that most of them fell into stages 3 and 4. The relatively few people who came out at stages 5 and 6 were independent of their parents, very active in social-political protest movements, thought of themselves as rebellious, and were agnostic, atheist or non-religious.

A good deal of this research has been put together by Hampden-Turner,[17] and it appears that the person who exhibits the higher form of motivation mentioned in Chapter 3, the higher form of perception mentioned in Chapter 4 and the higher form of learning mentioned in Chapter 5 of Volume 1 is also the person who exhibits the higher form of morality which Kohlberg calls Stage 6. Such a person is also likely to be more or less radical politically.

This rather surprising conclusion is also found by Lane[18] in his work, which also tries to link in political science with individual psychology.

What all this research seems to have shown is that the Kohlberg levels do make sense not only with the adolescents who took part in the original research, but also with older people. So let us now put side by side the child development stages with the Kohlberg stages to see the relation between the two.

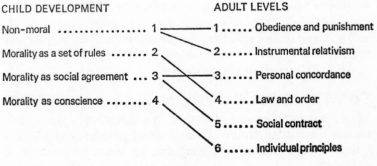

CHILD DEVELOPMENT

Non-moral 1

Morality as a set of rules 2

Morality as social agreement ... 3

Morality as conscience 4

ADULT LEVELS

1 ...... Obedience and punishment

2 ...... Instrumental relativism

3 ...... Personal concordance

4 ...... Law and order

5 ...... Social contract

6 ...... Individual principles

Fig. 1

It can be seen quite clearly now how the non-moral stage of infancy splits into two contrasting types of adult premoral behaviour; how morality as a set of rules based on personality in the young child becomes a morality based on rigid principles in the adult; how morality as social agreement in the child of ten or so splits into a fairly empty conformity and a much more well-thought-out reliance on principles of general welfare; and how the discovery of the conscience during adolescence corresponds with the real working out of individual principles in later life.

It is unfortunately true that it is always possible to slip back in moral matters, into a less adequate form of approach, and it is not being maintained at all that there is anything automatic about moral development. What is said here is that each stage in child development depends upon the stage before, and also on the social environment of the child at the time a particular stage is reached.

We have deliberately not shown child development stage 5 – morality proper – partly because it would introduce more confusion by crossing lines, and partly because it opens up the question of whether there are other stages beyond Kolhberg's stage 6. My own view is that there are indeed other stages beyond Kohlberg's stage 6, and that they have been described by philosophers, political scientists and sociologists.* The problem is, however, that few people indeed have any very sophisticated or well-thought-out morality – far too few to be picked up in any numbers in an ordinary survey.

There is also another possibility, of course, which is that people do, in fact, have very complex and advanced ideas about morality, but that the research instruments employed are too crude and ill-designed to measure them. This seems quite possible, but at present we do not have any better instrument than the Kohlberg stories to compare them with. No doubt over the next few years new methods will be found to deal with this area even better, and the picture may then become clearer. At the moment, the evidence seems to point to most adults sticking at stages 3 and 4.

So What About Socialization?

What are the implications of all this for socialization? It seems that there is this natural process of development going on, which acts as a limit upon whatever the parents can get across to the child or adolescent.

* See for example H. Walsby, the **Domain of Ideologies**, Maclellan 1947.

At the earliest stage, before about 4 years old (and remember that these are not precise age estimates, but statements about what comes earlier and what comes later) the child does not understand what a rule is; there can then be a systematic mismatch between what the parent thinks he or she is doing, and how the parent's action is received and understood by the child. The parent thinks he or she is teaching the child a rule by correct discipline, and the child thinks the parent is being incomprehensibly disagreeable.

At the second stage, it becomes extraordinarily easy for parents to get rules across to a child, and if the parents don't do it, the child will get rules from somewhere else, or make them up himself or herself. During this period, from about four to about eight, the parent is 'spoilt' in the sense that he or she gets a sense of power over the child which is quite misleading for later stages. There is a great sense of 'togetherness' very often, because the child is trying to conform, and this is very comfortable for the standard family situation, giving the parents a very nice sense that they are doing the right thing, because everything is going well.

At the third stage, however, the child starts to look outside the home for models, and begins to argue about what is fair and what is not fair. From about nine to around thirteen, other children start to become an alternative source of influence becoming more and more important in rivalling the parents. The structure which the parents thought they had built (but which they merely exploited, in fact) starts to crumble, and the parents often wonder 'where they went wrong', and why the previous stage doesn't continue, as if they were somehow to blame. But this stage is still a stage of socialization, only now the socializing group is the peer group – the other children of the same age.

The struggle does not become acute, in many cases, until the fourth stage is reached, and the adolescent starts to talk about leading his or her own life, according to the principles of conscience. But we shall come back to discuss this whole area when we come to Chapter 7 of the present volume, where we discuss adolescence specifically.

REFERENCES

1. J. & E. Newson. Four years old in an urban community, Penguin 1970 (1968)
2. J. Piaget. The moral judgement of the child, Routledge 1932
3. L. Kohlberg. Stages in the development of moral thought and action, Holt, Rinehart & Winston 1969
4. W. Kay. Moral development, Allen & Unwin 1970
5. G. H. Mead. Mind, self and society, Univ. of Chicago 1934
6. R. Brown. Social psychology, Collier-Macmillan 1965
7. G. R. Medinnus. Immanent justice in children, J. genet, Psychol. 94, 1959
8. G. R. Medinnus. Objective responsibility in children, J. genet. Psychol. 101, 1962
9. P. H. Najarian-Svajian. The idea of immanent justice among Lebanese children and adults, J. genet. Psychol. 109, 1966
10. S. Breznitz & S. Kugelmass. Intentionality in moral judgement: Developmental stages, Child Devel. 38, 1967
11. S. Kugelmass *et al.* The development of intentionality in moral judgement: Suggestions and initial test, Scripta Hierosolymitana 14, 1965
12. N. J. Bull. Moral judgement from childhood to adolescence, Routledge 1969
13. E. Turiel. An experimental test of the sequentiality of developmental stages in the child's moral judgements, J. Pers. soc. Psychol. 3, 1966
14. J. R. Rest. Developmental hierarchies of comprehension and preference in moral thinking. Paper read at meeting of the Society for Research in Child Development at Santa Monica, California, March 1969
15. W. G. LeFurgy & G. W. Waloshin. Immediate and long-term effects of experimentally induced social influence in the modification of adolescents' moral judgements, J. Pers. soc. Psychol. 12, 1969
16. N. Haan *et al.* Moral reasoning of young adults, J. Pers. soc. Psychol. 10, 1968
17. C. Hampden-Turner. Radical man, Duckworth 1971
18. R. E. Lane. Political thinking and consciousness: The private life of the political mind, Markham 1969

CHAPTER FOUR

Intellectual Development

In the previous two chapters we have been struggling, to a certain extent, to counteract a mistaken impression that socialization is a process where parents and teachers have to impose something basically alien on to a mass of intractable material, licking it into shape and imposing civilizing influences. This has been something of a struggle because all our cultural traditions go the other way. But in this chapter, although we are saying very much the same thing, it is not a struggle any more, because few people think that you can give children intellectual qualities, in the way that they do think you can give children moral qualities.

This is an intriguing difference. Why should the same message be perfectly acceptable in one context, and unacceptable in what seems a very similar context? The reason is probably that intellectual development is not a threat, in the same way that moral development can be. If one's children have brilliant minds, that is a credit to one, and they can get cups for it – or diplomas, degrees, certificates, etc. But if one's children have advanced moral existences, they are likely to be uncomfortable to live with; they may go to jail for their beliefs; they may get involved in attention-arousing political activities, and so on. So in fact a great deal of many parents' and teachers' activities are designed to hold back any moral development, as Kay[1] has pointed out. They are designed to keep children at the level of 'morality as a set of rules'; this is done by making communication mainly a one-way process, where the teacher or parent is in a privileged position, as someone who basically talks but does not listen. As a behaviorist says approvingly:

A teacher teaches in the same sense that a cook cooks. The cook himself does not change state; it is the meal that cooks. So, too, it is the student who changes state – he learns. (Logan.[2])

Now we saw in Chapter 5 of the first volume that this is a very inadequate approach to what is going on in a teaching/learning situation; we can now see that it is a very inadequate approach to the moral situation too. As long as there is one-way communication there is no possibility of really learning the principle of reciprocity on which depends any further moral development.

But parents and teachers who are quite prepared to hold their children back morally would be quite appalled at the idea of holding their children back intellectually. So intellectual development is non-controversial in a way in which moral development is not.

There are several theories of intellectual development, each of which is supported by quite good evidence, and they hang together in much the same way as we found with moral development, not contradicting one another so much as emphasizing different aspects of the same process.

Piaget Again

The best-known of these theories is that of Jean Piaget, whom we have already met in Chapter 3. He maintains that there are four clear and definite stages in the development of children's thinking; though in his later writings he emphasized the essential continuity between the second and third stages. He also made more distinctions within the first stage, finding within it six sub-stages. But the basic four-stage scheme, without these qualifications, runs as follows:

1. *Sensorimotor period* From birth to about two years. The child learns through action that permanent objects exist, and acquires the concept of purposive action. There are rudimentary concepts of classification, of space, time and causality. But there is a lack of ability to believe in absent objects as still existing. (It has six sub-stages.)

2. *Preoperational period* Two to about seven years old. The semiotic function appears, enabling language and other symbols to act as a tremendous intellectual boost. Deferred imitation and symbolic play appear. Drawings and mental images become evident. But this is a period of intuitive thought where the child finds it hard to give reasons for things.

3. *Concrete operations period* Seven to about eleven years old. An increasing ability to reason, but the child needs concrete objects to manipulate, and finds it hard to abstract from them, or generalize from one situation to another. He can, however, take more than one dimension

into account in arriving at a conclusion, which the preoperational child cannot.

4. *Formal operations period* Eleven to about fifteen. The child is fully capable of abstracting, seeing rules and the reasons for them, and generalizing to other situations. He can draw conclusions from pure hypotheses and not merely from actual observation.

As with the stages of moral development we have already looked at, the ages do not matter very much – they are only given to give some sense of what is being talked about. What is being stated is that the sequence of stages is invariant – that is, whatever age the child gets to the formal operations period, he or she must have gone through the three earlier stages (and in the right order) first.

What is also being stated is that it is literally useless to attempt to teach something which depends on Stage 4 thinking to a child who is only at Stage 2. Even if some semblance of correct answering is achieved by sheer drill, there is no insight and therefore no retention. We shall return to this point later in the chapter.

So to sum up in Piaget's own words:[3]

(1) Their order of succession is constant, although the average ages at which they occur may vary with the individual, according to his degree of intelligence or with the social milieu . . . (2) Each stage is characterized by an overall structure in terms of which the main behaviour patterns can be explained . . . (3) These overall structures are integrative and non-interchangeable. Each results from the previous one, integrating it as a subordinate structure, and prepares for the subsequent one, into which it is sooner or later integrated.

What kind of evidence is this theory based on? Basically a number of experiments which must by now represent the most-often replicated series of experiments in the world. Here is an account of one experiment which can be done quite easily in the home, enabling anyone to check what happens for themselves.

Get two tumblers of the same size and shape, and put equal amounts of water (preferably coloured) into each. The child to be the subject in this experiment should agree that there is exactly the same amount in each, and small adjustments may be made until the child is entirely satisfied that the amounts are indeed the same. Then take three small glasses (perhaps small tumblers or wine glasses) which are all the same size as each other, but smaller than the two original tumblers or beakers. Say – 'This is your drink and this is mine, but I prefer my drink in three glasses.' Then pour out the water from one of the beakers or tumblers into the three smaller glasses, making the amounts about equal in each of the three. Place your hand over the three glasses, and repeat – 'This is my drink and that is yours.' Ask the child – 'Who has more to drink, you or me?'

When Hyde[4] did this experiment in Aden, she got these results:

TABLE 4

Results on Water Test at Three Ages

	Age 6+ %	Age 7+ %	Age 8+ %
Answer showing understanding of conservation principle	15	31	63
Answer showing no understanding of conservation principle	85 (n = 48)	69 (n = 48)	37 (n = 48)

Hyde does not give any significant estimate for this result, but if we apply the simple chi-square test which is explained in Chapter 10, we find that this result is very highly significant, at well beyond the ·001 level. It can be seen quite easily that the understanding of the principle of conservation (that the amount of liquid remains the same no matter how it is poured about) goes up by leaps and bounds over this age range. And this was not so only for Europeans, but also for subsamples of Arabs, Indians and Somali children. At eleven years of age, virtually no children go wrong on this test.

This is also a test of reversibility, and again we find that the pre-operational child cannot understand this concept. Another concept he cannot grasp is seriation – that is, a series of things where each one is slightly larger than the earlier members of the series. As Piaget & Inhelder[3] say:

> For example, working with H. Sinclair, we presented ten sticks seriated according to their differences in length, and after a week asked the child to reproduce them by gesture or drawing . . . The most important result obtained is that, with significant regularity, subjects produce a drawing that corresponds to their operatory level (pairs, unco-ordinated short series or III III IIII etc.) rather than to the configuration

presented. In other words, memory causes the schemes corresponding to the child's level to predominate: the image-memory relates to
this scheme rather than to the perceptual model.

This is, of course, exactly what we found with perception generally
in Chapter 4 of Volume 1. When we look at something, we produce
a sort of recognizable caricature of it in our minds, and this is our
idea of it. When we remember it afterwards, it is this caricature
that we will be remembering. (For a restatement of this basic point
in the language of behaviorism, see Atkinson & Wickens.[5]) It just
so happens that the caricature of the preoperational child is different in certain ways from the adult version – and this is the sort
of thing which Piaget more than anyone else has explored.

If the test just quoted is possible, then it should be possible in
theory to produce a series of tests which between them would place
any child on the scale of periods or stages, and act as a check on the
whole system. Such a test is now in existence, and is described in a
preliminary way by Phillips.[6] It is the product of a research programme by Pinard and others at the University of Montreal. In its
original form it took 10 hours to administer, which made it of
limited use in everyday situations, but there is every reason to believe that this can be reduced to reasonable limits. It has confirmed
in all essentials the stages outlined by Piaget.

So if we can now accept that children do in fact pass through
Piaget's four stages or periods, the question immediately arises – can
we accelerate the process? Piaget himself calls this 'the American
question' and attaches little importance to it, but for most parents
and teachers it must at least have some interest.

Accelerating the Process

If Piaget is right, and the ability to perform real abstraction and
combination does not arrive until the stage of formal operations, at
the age of perhaps eleven years old, then most of our attempts to
teach children arithmetic below that age are doomed to failure. All
we will obtain is an easily shaken rote performance, which is not
truly grasped and will be quickly forgotten soon after 'learning'.
No wonder that teachers are baffled by the poor memory of the
child who 'knows' a rule one day and does not know it the next!
And no wonder that so many children feel baffled and messed
about in the mathematics classroom.

But if we want children to be numerate as early as possible, so that they can cope with a culture based on science and technology, is there any way of bringing children on into the stage of formal operations more quickly than they otherwise would?

Opinion on this has changed over the past few years, as more and more evidence comes in. As late as 1968 the general opinion was that conservation, for example, could not be taught with any great success. This view was partly based on experiments like that of Smedslund,[7] who took two groups of children, one of whom had acquired the concept of conversation by intensive training, and the other of whom (being the same age) who gave conservation answers without special training. The experiment was a common Piagetian one of taking two equal balls of plasticine, making one a different shape, and asking if they still have the same amount of plasticine in them. As Roger Brown[8] tells the story:

> In the process of altering the shape of one of the balls of plasticine he would surreptitiously pinch off a bit of the substance and so, when the child weighed the two, they were not equal. The experimenter did this a number of times. The children who had acquired the conservation of weight by special training showed no great surprise at the outcomes and reverted to non-conservation answers. The children who had acquired conservation in the usual way refused to relinquish their belief in it. They argued that a piece of the plasticine must be missing – perhaps it had fallen on the floor.

Well, this all sounds very convincing and interesting. But in fact the group which was supposed to have had the special training was drawn from the experimental group of a previous experiment by Smedslund[9] in which the training procedure *failed* to induce weight conservation. In other words, his trained children came from the same group of subjects who had already been found to be not trained successfully. It is not so surprising that they gave up their beliefs in conservation if they never had them to begin with. And in fact, Smith[10] replicated Smedslund's procedure and found no difference in the reactions of natural and trained weight conservers.

By 1969 a great deal more work had come in, and Brainerd & Allen[11] reviewed it all in a very thorough way, finding that out of 18 studies, 12 had reported successful outcomes; of the 6 studies reporting no success, 3 are by one author, and all but one appeared prior to 1967. Flavell & Hill[12] also concluded that:

The early Piagetian training studies had negative outcomes, but the picture is now changing. If our reading of present trends is correct, few on either side of the Atlantic would now maintain that one cannot by any pedagogic means measurably spur, solidify or otherwise further the child's concrete-operational progress.

And Glaser & Resnick[13] reviewed a further 11 studies published after the other papers mentioned, finding that 9 of them reported successful induction of conservation, while two did not.

It does appear, then, that conservation can be trained, usually by emphasizing the reversibility of the relationships. Does this upset Piaget? We have already seen that Piaget himself is not much interested in this aspect, but does it actually upset the theory which he is putting forward? No, it does not. Already in 1960 Inhelder & Matalon[14] were saying:

> This process of acquisition which can, of course be accelerated by training, corresponds to a general progress towards an 'operational' quality in the thought of the child.

Now if the progress from preoperational thinking to the thinking characteristic of the stage of concrete operations can be speeded up, this brings Piaget's theory much closer to the other theory which occupies the same ground, that of Bruner.

It is important to remember, however, that Piaget's theory is essentially one which says that the child matures in a culture which holds all these concepts in a kind of suspension, so that the child can easily latch on to what he needs when he is ready for it; this is particularly so in this age of television, where the mass culture reaches the literate and the illiterate alike. Piaget is not saying that the modes of thought would develop irrespective of the culture, and indeed some research by Prince[15] in New Guinea seems to show that in a primitive culture some schooling or contact with Western culture is necessary for the later concepts to develop. Apparently in such cultures the base experience is not sufficient to produce spontaneous emergence of operational concepts, while even in relatively deprived Western cultures (Mermelstein & Shulman[16]) or in poor but urbanized cultures (Goodnow[17]) the incremental effect of normal schooling is slight, and the general culture can be relied on to do most of the work, in providing opportunities for the later forms of thinking to be used. But let us now look at Bruner's theory, and see how it differs from Piaget's.

Bruner

Bruner is quite different in his basic approach, but at first sight his formulation is closely similar to that of Piaget. He says that knowledge about anything can be represented in three ways, each of which amounts to a system of processing information:

1. *The enactive system* Information is processed by acting on it. We cannot, for example, give an adequate description of familiar streets or floors over which we often walk, nor do we have much of an image of what they are like; yet we get about them without tripping or even looking much.

2. *The iconic system* Information is processed by perceptualizing it. Images in the mind stand for objects or events in a selective but basically one-to-one way. This is a pretty concrete approach.

3. *The symbolic system* Information is processed in terms of a set of verbal or symbolic propositions governed by the laws of language and logic. This enables reasoning to take place in an abstract way.

These different ways of processing information emerge in the order presented, Bruner believes, and each one is said to depend upon the previous one for its development. But each of them remains intact throughout life.

Now it is tempting to line up the enactive mode of representation with Piaget's sensorimotor stage, the iconic mode with the pre-operational and the concrete operations stage, and the symbolic mode with the stage of formal operations – particularly as Piaget has, in his later writings, tended more and more to see his two middle stages as basically one. It may not be right to do this, however. Rohwer[18] has carried out some fairly extensive research which seems to show that a preference and a capacity for the use of visual representation develops later than verbal modes of information processing – in other words, the symbolic system may emerge, in some ways at least, before the iconic system. Rohwer explains this by saying that at earlier ages language is a coherent, organized system and imagery is not.

While Bruner[19] originally stated that the three systems emerged in the order presented, he has later[20] laid more emphasis on their continuing existence in the adult. And this is not surprising when we remember that he began with a detailed study of an adult's strategies of thought[21] and then looked back, so to speak, to see what influences had been at work to produce those modes of thought.

What comes out of this picture is a view of human beings who have developed three parallel systems for processing information and for representing it—one through manipulation and action, one through perceptual organization and imagery, and one through the symbolic apparatus. It is not that these are 'stages' in any sense, but rather emphases in development: that one in some measure must master the manipulation of concrete objects before there can be perceptual decentration, or in simple terms, that you must get the perceptual field organized around your own person as centre before you can impose other, less egocentric axes upon it, and so on. In the end the mature organism seems to have gone through a process of elaborating three systems of skills that correspond to the three major tool systems to which he must link himself for full expression of capacities – tools for the hand, for the distance receptors and for the process of reflection. (Bruner.[20])

Looking on these three systems as parallel is of course very plausible and interesting, but it is not at all like Piaget. It may, however, illuminate something about Piaget, too; maybe Piaget should also say that his earlier stages are found, in some way, in adult functioning. Let us shelve that problem for the moment, and return to it later.

If it makes more sense to regard these three systems as all working together, from the moment when the child first begins to talk, then perhaps the problem changes from accelerating progress through the stages to orchestrating the systems together in the most helpful ways. This is indeed the point of view of Jones,[22] who criticizes Bruner for overemphasizing the purely cognitive element in the process of development, as if the symbolic mode was somehow simply cognitive and simply superior.

Cognitive Structures
It seems, when we read Piaget or Bruner, that all children are on an escalator which brings them all out eventually at the same point. And yet there is a great deal of evidence to show that adults think very differently from one another – they are not at all uniform in the thinking processes which they bring to the world. And this is quite a distinct point from the merely quantitative position which they may hold on some scale of intelligence. (We shall be discussing intelligence in Volume Four, since we shall see it more as a social problem than as of any interest for the individual aspect of social

psychology.) We are speaking now of the way in which people look at the world in different ways.

Now there have been a variety of attempts to say something about cognitive structures in adults—Rokeach[23] with his concept of the open as against the closed mind, Hampden-Turner[24] with his anomic man and radical man, Pettigrew[25] with his broad categorizers and narrow categorizers, Scott[26] with his six dimensions (which reduce to something like simplicity-complexity), Vannoy[27] with his simplicity-complexity dimension, Harvey[28] with his concreteness-abstractness dimension, Ostrom & Brock[29] with centrality and relatedness, Witkin[30] with his global-articulated dimension, Kagan[31] with his impulsives and reflectives, Stager[32] with his high and low general conceptual levels, and Harvey, Hunt & Schroeder[33] with their four levels of concreteness-abstractness.

Zajonc[34] mentions eight dimensions which have been described and Weick[35] describes nine sources of cognitive linkages, and twelve determinants of ramification. If it is all as complex as this, is it worth saying anything about it at all? I think it is, because there is a very high degree of agreement about one particular point, and that point is an important one.

This point of agreement consists in the fact that all investigators seem to find a large group of people who exhibit a type of cognitive functioning which is much closer to the earlier stages of child intellectual development than to the later. These are people who think in concrete rather than abstract terms, use simple rather than complex categories, use global rather than articulated concepts, have closed rather than open minds, are impulsive rather than reflective, and so on. For example, Brim *et al.*[36] conducted a large survey of the general population, and factor-analysed the results (see Chapter 11 for an account of factor analysis), finding a major first factor consisting of things like:

> Belief in fate
> Belief in supernatural causes
> Dominance in child-rearing attitudes
> Belief in acting before thinking
> Low independence of judgement
> Impulsivity
> Dependency
> Defensive optimism
> Low rationality

In others words, these things tend to hang together, in such a way that a person who has two or three of them is likely to have all the rest, too. This fits in with the summary of laboratory work by Harvey,[37] abbreviated below, which spells out the findings on what concreteness in thinking means:

1. A simpler cognitive structure, particularly in areas of high involvement.
2. A greater tendency to black-and-white thinking.
3. A greater dependence on status cues.
4. Greater intolerance of ambiguity.
5. Greater *need* for cognitive consistency. (Not necessarily greater ability to attain it.)
6. Inability to change set.
7. Lack of clarity between means and ends.
8. Insensitivity to lesser cues.
9. Poorer capacity to act 'as if'.
10. Fixed opinions.
11. Need for authoritarian structure.
12. Low task orientation.
13. Jumps to conclusions about people.

So whether we go into the field with Brim or McClosky,[38] or whether we go into the laboratory with Harvey and others, we seem to arrive at the same point – there are a lot of people about who are still operating in a very concrete way mentally, and have not advanced to the level of rationality which Piaget and Bruner both seem to assume is natural to man.

Now this is exactly what we found in the previous chapter, in regard to moral development – many people lingered at the earlier levels there, too. And one reason is not hard to find, in both cases; it takes a lot of energy and courage to operate at high moral level, and it takes a lot of mental energy to operate at a high intellectual level. With concrete thinking, each subject of thought falls into its own logic-tight compartment, unrelated to any other compartment, and this is very sparing of energy. As soon as one area of one's thinking life is related to another, as soon as the connections are made, it is as if energy had to be spent holding those doors open. It is as if the doors of the mind had springs, and unless they can be held open, they close of their own accord.

Werner[39] has given a brilliant and insightful description of the level of concrete thought, saying that it is syncretic, diffuse, indefinite, rigid and labile; and he has carefully defined these terms.

If this is all true, then it follows that much everyday activity will be based on this very low-level concrete thinking; and indeed this is so. I have shown elsewhere[40] that the company or brand image, which gives a certain character or personality to that company or brand, is essentially an object of physiognomic perception, in Werner's terms, which is used in a very primitive way.

Let us now try, then, to draw up a similar diagram to the one which we used in the previous chapter:

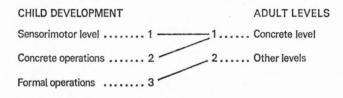

CHILD DEVELOPMENT	ADULT LEVELS
Sensorimotor level 1	1 ...... Concrete level
Concrete operations 2	2 ...... Other levels
Formal operations 3	

Fig. 2

It can be seen that this is neither so interesting nor so satisfactory as the earlier diagram. This is mainly because the adult levels are so ill-described in the literature. The concrete level always works fine; in the Harvey, Hunt & Schroeder book, for example, they lay down their basic argument in Chapter 2, 65% of which is devoted to describing the classic features of concrete cognitive functioning, as laid down by Murphy, Werner, Goldstein and Scheerer. But when they come to their other three levels, they are considerably less convincing, and I find the chart on page 96 totally unbelievable. Walsby[41] again is most convincing on the concrete level, and he points to important features, such as fear of the group, which others have not done so much justice to; but when it comes to the higher levels, what he says is highly plausible and fascinating, but without any empirical evidence to back it up.

Again we have to make the point that stage 3 of child development is *not* necessarily the end – again the horizon may be too low. Formal logic, even of the propositional kind, is not the highest form of intellectual functioning known to man, as Piaget seems to think. Process thinking and dialectical logic are both to be taken into account here, though psychology has not done very much as yet to investigate them.

There is one cautionary note we need to sound about all this. It sometimes sounds as though we are trying to pin a label on to someone, and say that he is a concrete thinker; now obviously in any specific investigation, this is so. But it is not necessarily the case that a person who comes out as a concrete thinker in one investigation does so in all other investigations. As Zajonc says, in the chapter just quoted:

> It will not be an easy task to find aspects of cognitive functioning that remain stable from situation to situation, and yet reliably distinguish between individuals . . . Most individuals are complex in some areas and simple in others, and these areas differ from individual to individual.

What we should really say, therefore, is that in any situation we shall be likely to find a number of people taking up a cognitive stance which is basically concrete, but the actual composition of that number of people is quite likely to alter from one situation to another.

What emerges from this examination is that we know very little about intellectual development – particularly in the transition from child functioning to adult functioning. Why do some people revert to more primitive patterns of mental functioning? Leach[42] suggests that it may be to do with upbringing in the home; Walsby suggests that it may be social forces arising out of fear that too much nonconformity may destroy society, leading to intolerance of any kind of criticism. We do not really know yet.

What also emerges is that we know very little about the relation between intellect and emotion in development. Werner makes it clear that in concrete thought, intellect and emotion are completely inseparable. But does this mean that in abstract thought, emotion should be completely separated and put away? Clearly not. We saw in Chapter 5 of Vol. 1 that in any real learning emotion and intellect must go together, and Jones[43] spells this out in some detail.

It seems amazing that an area like this, so central to education, has been so inadequately tilled. But we shall find again and again that excellence and practicality seldom go together in psychology.

REFERENCES

1. W. Kay. Moral development, Allen & Unwin 1970
2. F. A. Logan. Incentive theory, reinforcement and education, in R. Glaser (ed). The nature of reinforcement, Academic Press 1971
3. J. Piaget & B. Inhelder. The psychology of the child, Routledge 1969 (1966)
4. D. M. G. Hyde, Piaget and conceptual development, Holt, Rinehart & Winston 1970
5. R. C. Atkinson & T. D. Wickens. Human memory and the concept of reinforcement, in same ref. as 2
6. J. L. Phillips. The origins of intellect: Piaget's theory, W. H. Freeman 1969
7. J. Smedslund. The acquisition of conservation of substance and weight in children, III. Extinction of conservation of weight acquired 'normally' and by means of empirical controls on a balance scale, Scand. J. Psychol. 1961
8. R. Brown. Social psychology, Collier-Macmillan 1965. The same experiment is reported in a similar way in Krech, Crutchfield & Livson, Elements of psychology. Knopf 1969
9. J. Smedslund. The acquisition of conservation of substance and weight in children. II. External reinforcement of conservation of weight and of the operations of addition and subtraction, Scand. J. Psychol. 2, 1961
10. I. D. Smith. The effects of training procedures on the acquisition of conservation of weight, Child Devel. 39, 1968
11. C. J. Brainerd & T. W. Allen. Experimental inductions of the conservation of 'first-order' quantitative invariants, Psychol. Bull. 75, 1971
12. J. H. Flavell & J. P. Hill. Developmental psychology, Ann. Rev. Psychol. 20, 1969
13. R. Glaser & L. B. Resnick. Instructional psychology, Ann. Rev. Psychol. 23, 1972
14. B. Inhelder & B. Matalon. The study of problem solving and thinking, in P. Mussen (ed), Handbook of research methods in child development, Wiley 1960
15. J. R. Prince. The effect of Western education of science conceptualization in New Guinea, Brit. J. Educ. Psychol. 28, 1968
16. E. Mermelstein & L. S. Shulman. Lack of formal schooling and the acquisition of conservation, Child Develop. 38, 1967
17. J. J. Goodnow. A test of milieu effects with some of Piaget's tasks, Psychol. Monogr. 76, 1962
18. W. D. Rohwer. Images and pictures in children's learning, Psychol. Bull. 73, 1970. See also, Mental elaboration and proficient learning, in J. P. Hill (ed). Minnesota symposia on child psychology 4, 1970
19. J. S. Bruner. The course of cognitive growth, Amer. Psychol. 19, 1964. This has been reprinted often
20. J. S. Bruner. Education as a social invention, in R. M. Jones (ed). Contemporary educational psychology: Selected essays, Harper & Row 1967. There are many good papers in this book
21. J. S. Bruner, C. Goodnow & G. Austin. A study of thinking, Wiley 1956
22. R. M. Jones. Fantasy and feeling in education, Penguin 1972 (1968)
23. M. Rokeach. The open and closed mind, Basic Books 1960
24. C. Hampden-Turner. Radical Man, Duckworth 1971 (1970)
25. T. F. Pettigrew. The measurement and correlates of category width as a cognitive variable, J. Personality 26, 1958
26. W. A. Scott. Structure of natural cognitions, J. Pers. soc. Psychol. 12, 1969
27. J. S. Vannoy. Generality of cognitive complexity-simplicity as a personality construct, J. Pers. soc. Psychol. 2, 1965
28. O. J. Harvey. Conceptual systems and attitude change, in C. W. Sherif & M. Sherif (eds), Attitude, ego-involvement and change, Wiley 1967

29. T. M. Ostrom & T. C. Brock. A cognitive model of attitudinal involvement, in Abelson *et al.* (eds). Theories of cognitive consistency: A sourcebook, Rand McNally 1968

30. H. A. Witkin *et al.* Psychological differentiation, Wiley 1962

31. J. Kagan. Developmental studies in reflection and analysis, in A. H. Kidd & J. L. Rivoire (eds). Perceptual development in children, Univ. London Press 1966

32. P. Stager. Conceptual level as a composition variable in small-group decision-making, J. Pers. soc. Psychol. 5, 1967

33. O. J. Harvey *et al.* Conceptual systems and personality organization, Wiley 1961

34. R. B. Zajonc. Cognitive theories in social psychology, in G. Lindzey & E. Aronson. The handbook of social psychology (Vol. 1), Addison-Wesley 1968

35. K. E. Weick. Processes of ramification among cognitive links, in same ref. as 29

36. O. G. Brim *et al.* Personality and decision processes. Stanford 1962

37. Same ref. as 28

38. H. McClosky. Conservatism and personality, Amer. Pol. Sci. Rev. 42, 1958

39. H. Werner. Comparative psychology of mental development, Science Editions 1961 (1948)

40. J. Rowan. Perception and the image, Advertising Quarterly 1965

41. H. Walsby. The domain of ideologies, Maclellan 1947

42. P. J. Leach. A critical study of the literature concerning rigidity, Brit. J. soc. Clin. Psychol. 6, 1967

43. Same ref. as 22

CHAPTER FIVE

Personality

Personality, too, develops through various stages. There have been many definitions of personality, but we shall take it as meaning the expression of the self. This means that we shall be particularly interested in the development of the self, along the lines already mentioned in Chapter 3 of Vol. 1.

One of the most influential accounts of the development of the self has been that of Erikson,[1] who outlined eight stages which the person has to go through, with a characteristic developmental task at each stage. We shall not be following this model, however, for two reasons.

First, the model is, in its early stages, obviously based on Freudian concepts which we saw good reason to reject in Chapter 2 of Vol. 1. And the later stages are much less convincing and plausible, having no place, for example, for adjustment to working life, crises in changing jobs, self-esteem in work, and so on.

Second, the model is quite unsupported by research. There have been very few attempts to test out the theory in any way, and none of them has come to my notice. So in spite of its great popularity this theory will be ignored here.

Ego Development

There is, however, a more recent theory of ego development which has very good research backing, coming from Jane Loevinger and her associates.[2] She has used a sentence-completion technique to arrive at the following six levels of development:

1. *Pre-social. Symbiotic* This represents a stage before the child has any sense of self at all.

2. *Impulsive* A very concrete stage, easily dominated by one perceptual stimulus. There is little holding-back or reflection. The person sometimes seems to be acting 'at random'.

   Delta This is a kind of subdivision of stage 2, dominated by *self-protection*. All the person's efforts seem dominated by the need to hold things stable. This may take the form of imposing very strict rules, or behaving in a very repetitive and stereotyped way.

3. *Conformist* Going along with the crowd. Liking to be liked. Sociable, but basically quite anxious about rejection. Ready to reject others who do not conform.

4. *Conscientious* Bound by self-imposed rules, which are much more derived from personal experience. But often a split between what is believed to be right and actual ability to carry it out. Much more feeling of being a real person. Dependence on others is being loosened.

5. *Autonomous* Greater ability to relate to other people as an individual. Greater ability to recognize different aspects of oneself as real. Ability to live with oneself. A good level of self-esteem. Some feeling of achievement or potential.

6. *Integrated* Full selfhood. Flexible and creative. Humorous in unexpected ways. No need to be loved and approved by everyone. No need to be thoroughly competent and adequate. No unrealistic fears about possible catastrophes. Ability to face internal conflicts and the external world.

It can be seen how similar this is to the stages we have already looked at in the fields of intellectual and moral development. And, just like the others, Loevinger finds that most people never reach the higher levels – or if they do, they slip back again into the middle or lower levels which need less energy to sustain, and are less painful. Most of her many subjects operated at levels 3 or 4.

It should be pointed out that Loevinger's research has all been done using women and girls as subjects, and it may well be the case that the developmental stages are different for boys and men. But it seems likely that the differences would be of detail rather than of basic structure.

What is interesting is that Loevinger has gone beyond the other researchers we have examined so far, at the top of the scale. We said earlier that Kohlberg's horizons seemed a bit low, and this seems to confirm that suggestion.

But it must be beginning to dawn on us that there is something going very wrong here. In all three fields of development we have considered, there is a clear line of increasing maturation visible, and confirmed by adequate research checking; and yet when we come to look at the adult world, we find people existing far below their potential. For example, we saw in the last chapter that Harvey outlined the characteristics of concrete thinking (the most inadequate and primitive stage of intellectual functioning); in some further research he and his associates[3] carried out on teachers, he found that out of 67 teachers, 50 of them were functioning at this lowest level – that is, 75% of them! And he got similar results with another piece of research with 3,000 undergraduates. This is a very disturbing thought, which we shall return to later in this chapter.

Theories of Personality

What can we say about the personalities of the people we see around us – or our own personalities, for that matter? Having developed up to a certain point, how are we to describe them?

It has been traditional to plunge straight into a description of trait and type theories, or other classifications, but let us hold off for a minute and look at what we are trying to do, before doing it.

There is a nice saying which has been handed down, that each person is like every man, like some men and like no other man. The ways in which he is like every man correspond to the general laws of psychology and other human sciences. The ways in which he is like no other man are individual and idiosyncratic, and we can't say very much about them. So it is the ways in which he is like *some* other men that form the subject-matter for personality theories, or so it would seem.

But there is an infinite number of ways in which he is like some other men, and this depends only upon the ingenuity of the observer and what he wants to find out. There is no possibility of ever coming to the end of ways in which we can slice the similarities and differences between people. So any classification of people is either good only for some particular stated purpose, or is arbitrary.

It may well be that in a particular culture, there are important stereotypes which people are willing and able to fit into, and it seems that there are just those types of people existing; or it may be that in a certain culture or subculture some qualities are highly valued and others are disapproved, and again some people may cultivate such qualities so that their salience is reinforced. But all this is very culture-bound, and says much more about the demands of society than it does about personality.

So there seems good reason to be sceptical about the value both of trait theories like those of Murray[4] or Cattell,[5] and of type theories like those of Sullivan,[6] Fromm[7] and Maddi.[8] The sort of theory which could be useful would be developmental theories; and we have already rejected the most obvious one, that of Freud and Erikson. What is left? Let us look at Maslow's theory.

We came across Maslow's theory briefly in Chapter 3 of Vol. 1. It says that there are five levels or stages of development, and that the relative satisfaction of one level makes possible the emergence of the next.

1. *Physiological* Hunger and thirst, sensory stimulation, temperature adjustment, etc.
2. *Safety* Defence against danger, fight and flight responses, fear, etc.
3. *Love and belongingness* Wish for affection, for a place in the group, tenderness, etc.
4. *Self-esteem* Mastery, competence, reputation, recognition, avoidance of failure, etc.
5. *Self-actualization* To become everything that one is capable of becoming, to be that self which one truly is, etc.

Now these look familiar, but there are bits missing, in terms of our previous looks at development. And when we come to look at it, we find that there has been very little research done on Maslow's theory. Just as Erikson's ideas have been very attractive to teachers, so Maslow's ideas have been very attractive to management training experts, but in neither case has the interest been supported by any very good research.

The importance of Maslow's theory is that it is quite explicitly a growth theory, implying that to reach the self-actualization stage (level 5) is something which is normal for everyone. What is this stage, then, that is normal for human beings to reach? It cannot be summed up neatly, and Maslow[9,10] has spent many pages writing about it, but let us try to summarize briefly, just to give the overall gist and flavour of it:

1. *More efficient perception of reality and more comfortable relations with it* An ability to detect the fake and the dishonest in people, art, politics, etc. Perception based on reality rather than on hopes, fears and fantasies. No fear of the unknown. No obsessive need to impose structure on the world.
2. *Acceptance* Not crippled by guilt, shame or anxiety. Accepting the self, and others, and nature, for what they are. Liking for food, sleep, sex and other satisfactions. Lack of defensiveness. But no acceptance for evils which can easily be changed.
3. *Spontaneity* Genuinely not bound by convention inside, though may

observe the conventions to please others. Never allows convention to stop him doing what he considers important or basic. High internal standards of ethics. Very open to his own impulses, desires, feelings – fully aware.

4. Problem centering Strongly focused on external problems, perhaps some mission in life. Wide horizons rather than narrow ones.

5. The quality of detachment and the need for privacy Can be solitary without harm or discomfort. Ability to concentrate intensely in any surroundings. Can take personal misfortunes without being thrown. Able to retain their dignity in trouble.

6. Autonomy Independence from many of the pressures of the culture and the environment. Relying on their own potentialities and their own resources. Rewards less important than self-development and inner growth.

7. Continued freshness of appreciation The capacity to experience ordinary things with awe, wonder and even ecstasy. Nature, children, sex, music can all be revivifying and inspiring; nothing seems to be stale or boring.

8. The mystic experience The oceanic feeling at times of limitless horizons opening up; the feeling of being at once more powerful and also more helpless than one ever was before. Complete fullness and complete emptiness at the same time. The peak experience, occurring quite often in varying degrees.

9. Gemeinschaftsgefühl A deep feeling of identification and sympathy with the whole human race, as if all were members of the same family. Even when people are weak, foolish or nasty, they are still brothers or sisters.

10. Interpersonal relations Tending to find other self-actualizing people, and have deep ties with them. Kind or patient to almost everyone, and easily touched by children. Ability to be hostile in a realistic way when appropriate. Tendency to attract admirers, without really wanting to.

11. Democratic character structure Unaware of differences in class, colour, etc. Can learn from anybody who has something to teach. No attempt to maintain status or prestige. Unwilling to do anything which would rob someone else of his or her dignity. Humility about what they know.

12. Discrimination between means and ends Tend to be clear about ethical choices, and choose means which fit with ends. Often regard things as ends which other people think of as means only. The most trivial and routine activity can be turned into a game or dance.

13. Unhostile sense of humour Tending not to laugh at jokes involving hostility, superiority or envy. May not like formal jokes at all. But strong sense of the absurd, of man's pretensions in the world. May be seen by others as rather serious.

14. Creativity Always seen as a strong characteristic. Not a narrow and specialized creativity, but more like the creativity of children before they have been spoiled. It just pours out effortlessly in everything the person does, in a human, natural way.

15. Resistance to enculturation Not well adjusted, in the sense of approval of an identification with the culture. Healthy people in an unhealthy culture. Tending to take a long-term rather than a short-term view of what changes can be made in the culture. Not against fighting but only against ineffective fighting.

16. Typical imperfections Can be very strong and ruthless. Can be embarrassing to have around when they are expressing hostility. Can become absent-minded and lacking in ordinary politeness. May marry out of pity or get too closely involved with unhappy people or scoundrels, through not rejecting those whom others reject. May become too detached and unsociable. By no means free from guilt, anxiety, sadness, self-criticism, internal conflicts.

These 16 points are based on a research study which Maslow carried out on a small number of people – about 50 altogether. Those who exhibited the full pattern were usually over 60 years old, but in many of the younger people the same pattern could be seen emerging.

It is fascinating to see how these 16 points, arrived at in a totally different way, seem so much like the opposites of the 13 points we saw in the last chapter as characteristic of the concrete thinker. And this may make us think back to Chapter 4 of Vol 1, where we saw how Hampden-Turner[11] outlines the difference between anomic man and radical man in terms of the same kinds of contrasts.

Now it is obvious that most people are not self-actualizing, in the sense of matching Maslow's 16 points. And the question we now want to ask is – Why?

What Goes Wrong ?

We have seen that there is a normal moral development, which somehow goes wrong – instead of arriving at the higher moral levels which it looks as though children are tending to rise towards, adults appear mostly to function at the lower levels.

We have seen that there is a normal intellectual development, which somehow goes wrong – instead of arriving at the higher intellectual levels which it looks as though children are tending to rise towards, adults mostly appear to function at the lower levels.

And we have now seen also that there is a normal ego development, whether described in Loevinger's terms or in Maslow's, which again goes wrong, so that the genuinely open and free human personality which children look to be developing towards is somehow defeated; and we find adults functioning at low, narrow and even harmful levels.

What is happening here?

This is a difficult question to answer, because the pattern is so consistent. In other words it is something which we are all immersed in, to the extent where we see it as 'just the way things are'. Someone once said that the last creature to discover water would be a fish.

But if this is the case, it may not be just an individual thing. We have said that the higher moral levels, the higher intellectual levels, the higher ego levels take more personal energy to maintain, but if the culture set great store by these things, and was organized in such a way as to foster them, these demands might well provide the motivation to expend the necessary energy. So perhaps we should look at the culture and see what effect that actually does have.

And as soon as we do this, we find that, far from valuing and fostering these higher levels of functioning, the society in which we live at present systematically denies them.

This happens first of all in the family. We have already noticed that parents like very much the relationship which exists when children think of them as all-powerful and completely right. Now as Ausubel[12] has pointed out, this is essentially a relationship in which the parents represent the major planet, and the children represent satellites.

> In a satellizing relationship the subordinate party acknowledges and accepts a subservient and deferential role, and the superordinate party in turn accepts him as an *intrinsically* valuable entity in his personal orbit. The satellite thereby acquires a vicarious or derived biosocial status (a) which is wholly a function of the dependent relationship and independent of his own competence or performance ability, and (b) which is bestowed on him by the fiat of simple intrinsic valuation by a superordinate individual or group whose authority and power to do so are regarded as unchallengeable.

In some ways this development may be inevitable and even desirable at a certain stage, because it gives the child of three or so a way of 'climbing down' from a feeling of omnipotence which is now more and more evidently unjustified. He can transfer the omnipotence to the parents before getting rid of it altogether. But what so often happens is that far from seeing it as a regrettable temporary necessity, parents see it as the normal and desirable permanent state of affairs which ought to exist between them and their children.

And this is not the worst that can happen. It may be the case that parents do not even give the child the benefit of valuing it intrinsically, but instead value it only extrinsically. In other words, they value the child only when it conforms to their expectations. The parent only values the child in terms of his potential eminence, his potential capacity for gratifying frustrated parental ambitions. This can be an even worse stranglehold. As Laing[13] says:

> Love and violence, properly speaking, are polar opposites. Love lets the other be, but with affection and concern. Violence attempts to constrain the other's freedom, to force him to act in the way we desire, but with ultimate lack of concern, with indifference to the other's own existence or destiny.
>
> We are effectively destroying ourselves by violence masquerading as love.

This does seem to be literally true, to some degree, as we are now seeing. So the family is one of the places where children are held back from developing in any adequate way.

The school is another. We have already remarked on this in Chapter 5 of Vol. 1 and at the beginning of Chapter 4 in this volume. Earlier in this chapter, we also mentioned a piece of research by Harvey *et al.*[3] which found a high proportion of teachers functioning at a low intellectual level. What effect do teachers like this have in the classroom?

They are more punitive, more dictatorial and less resourceful than teachers at a higher level. And the effect this has on pupils (the research covered 118 classes of children mostly between four and six) is to make them less active, more inclined to narrow, parroted answers, lower in achievement and lower in classroom involvement. So this is a vicious circle. Teachers who are themselves operating at a low level treat children in such a way that the children are not encouraged to go beyond it. Their development, far from being hastened (in terms of the Piaget controversy we noted earlier) is actually being held back.

And this is not just something about the psychology of the teachers. The teachers themselves are influenced by the whole atmosphere and ethos of the school. And in the vast majority of cases this is itself a regressive force. The paper by Hoy[14] makes it clear that there is a pupil control ideology in schools generally, which is very close to the outlook of those who run prisons and mental hospitals:

> Teachers who hold a custodial orientation conceive of the school as an autocratic organization with a rigid pupil-teacher status hierarchy; the flow of power and communication is unilateral downward. Students must accept the decision of their teachers without question. Teachers do not attempt to understand student behaviour, but instead view mis-behaviour as a personal affront. Students are perceived as irresponsible and undisciplined persons who must be controlled through punitive sanctions. Impersonality, pessimism, and 'watchful mistrust' pervade the atmosphere of the custodial school.

This was contrasted with a humanistic orientation, in which teachers see the school as an educational community in which students learn through co-operative interaction and experience. Open channels of two-way communication lead towards increased self-determination.

What Hoy found was that teachers during training moved to-wards the humanistic orientation, but that after a year in an actual school, they moved substantially over into the custodial orientation. This was a longitudinal study, confirming an earlier cross-sectional study.[15] Research in Britain by Morrison & McIntyre[16] confirms the generality of this picture. As Hoy says:

> New, idealistic teachers appear to be confronted with a relatively cus-todial control orientation as they become a part of the organization; in fact, the vast majority of teachers in the present study at both elemen-tary and secondary levels described their school subculture as one in which good teaching and good discipline were equated.

By 'good discipline' here is meant a heavy control which ensures a quiet classroom with little movement. So most schools, then, seem to have an ethos, dominated by experienced teachers, which as a matter of course regards children as basically dangerous forces which have to be held down for their own good. Obviously this makes it hard for new teachers to do anything other than fit in with the prevailing view.

It would be possible to go on and show that not only in the home and the school, but also in work situations, in leisure situations, in politics, in the mass media, people are systematically narrowed and reduced to less than what they are capable of being. We shall be looking at many of these areas in chapters to come. So this holding back of children's capacity for self-development is not unique to children – it happens to adults too. Laing again says it well:

> Personal action can be creative or destructive.
> In a world where the normal condition is one of alienation, most personal action must be destructive both of one's own experience and of that of the other.

It is the second part of this quotation which strikes us now. Laing is saying that alienation is normal in our society. And we have seen something of what this means. In particular, it means that we are systematically alienated from our own potential as human beings. We still live in a divisive and constricted society, which deforms our development in every sphere.

To follow up this line of thinking in detail would take us far into sociology and politics. It will perhaps be enough to say, for the moment, that this position seems to be changing. We saw in Chapter 5 of Vol. 1 how this is happening in education, and the more general picture is outlined in books by Reich,[17] Marcuse,[18] McLuhan[19] and others. How fast it changes depends on each one of us taking part in the change in some way.

The view we have taken of personality is one of a developmental process, which will progress if not stopped, but which is apparently quite easy to interfere with and spoil. A person's personality is not likely to determine so much what he does, but rather the way he does it.

Personality Assessment

A great deal of the literature on personality deals with ways of assessing personality. Now what does assessing personality mean? In terms of trait and type theories, it must mean that we are able to say of a person—'He is aggressive', 'She is sexy'; or 'He is an anal type', 'She is an introvert'. But since all these classifications have get-out clauses, such that it is always possible for someone to fall into more than one category, we can say of any man that he is aggressive, and of any woman that she is sexy – it is simply a matter of degree. So we now need to give some sort of score, or point on a scale. But any scale must be arbitrary, and one scale does not correspond with any other scale, so such a score would have no meaning except in terms of the one scale. (And similarly, everyone is a bit of an anal type, everyone is a bit of an introvert, etc.)

So much for pure logic. But what about actual practice? Is it not a fact that personality tests are used in industry, in clinics, in vocational guidance – surely they must be some use? Everyone has heard of the Rorschach test, and the Thematic Apperception Test (TAT) – surely they must be well attested? There is a regular publication called the **Mental Measurement Yearbook**[20] which carries detailed reviews of all the commercially available achievement, aptitude and personality tests in print. Each test is reviewed by a highly qualified expert in the field, in terms of the experiments carried out to confirm its validity. And so far as the personality tests are concerned, each review which is published comes to the conclusion that there is no validity for any of the personality tests now in existence – whether projective tests like those already mentioned, or so-called objective tests like the 16PF or the MMPI.

So even the scales which one might use to try to measure something have not been shown to measure what they are supposed to measure. And it is well known that it is, in fact, quite easy to fake responses on any personality test to get the answer which the subject thinks the tester wants. There is even an excellent little book[21] which tells you exactly how to beat personality tests. As the author says:

> It may startle you to hear that all personality tests which you may be compelled to take are of no value, but it is a fact. They do not measure your personality or your personal characteristics or give a picture of your psychological structure. Over a hundred million tests are given each year and all of them are valueless.

If personality tests worked, what they would do would be to give a label which could be pinned on to somebody. He would not only be John Smith, he would be 'a cyclothyme'; she would not only be Jane Doe, she would be 'an extravert'. Now pinning labels on people is a dangerous practice; it is one of the prime ways of turning people into things. Maslow points out that this turning of people into things by labelling (many people call this reification; Maslow calls it rubri-

cization) is something which is very easy to do in everday life. Instead of reacting to someone as himself, we label him as 'a student',
or 'a businessman' or 'a Jew', and from then on react largely in
terms of the label, rather than in terms of the uniqueness of the
person. But when we catch ourselves or others doing this, we catch
ourselves up, or criticize the other person, because we know it is
inadequate.

And Maslow also says that one of the things which the self-
actualizing person resents most is being labelled in this way. Even
in therapy, he wants to be looked on as an individual, not an interesting example of some diagnostic category. (See also Chapter 12
on this.)

Not only is this kind of labelling dangerous and resented, it is also
unlikely to be accurate or useful. The reason for this is that human
behaviour is more dominated by situational constraints, for the most
part, than by personal dispositions. We saw this very clearly and at
some length in Chapters 6 and 7 of Vol. 1. Most of our activities are
dominated by the requirements of the real situation in which we
find ourselves. Getzels & Thelen[22] have a very good statement of
this, which makes very clear the way in which role and situational
needs and internal personal needs relate to one another.

What we are saying, then, is that even if personality tests worked,
and even if they were not dangerous, and even if they were not resented by healthy people, they would still not be worth using, for
the most part.

There may well be highly specific circumstances where a test of
some kind is useful, just as we saw in the first volume that there
were times when an attitude test could be useful – but these will
usually be in experimental situations where we want two contrasted
groups, or something of that kind.

If we are to reject psychological tests of personality, what about
the research we have mentioned with approval, by Harvey, Brim
and others, which have used various tests – how about Piaget,
Bruner, Loevinger, Kohlberg and all the rest? These are not personality tests – they are tests of the level of mental functioning in
various ways. And it is quite explicit that there is nothing final about
anybody's level in this sense. Further growth is always possible. In
fact, one of the main points of telling someone where he came on
the scale would be to let him know how much work had still to
be done.

Of course, if one simply told someone that he was at Stage 2 out of six stages, and left it at that, it could be just cruel. But there is now a whole movement dedicated to enabling people to become more adequate in these ways, as can be seen in books by people like Otto,[23] Blank *et al.*,[24] Otto & Mann[25] and Schutz.[26] We know how to do this now – we know how to lift people up the levels – and the social implications are huge.

Some Recent Developments

This chapter may have been somewhat disconcerting for anyone who expected a comfortable trot round some representative theories in the manner of Hall & Lindzey,[27] or a detailed examination of personality theories in a comparative way in the manner of Maddi,[28] a sure-fire set of examination answers in the manner of Lazarus[29] or a sensitive look at some detailed problems in the manner of Roger Brown.[30] But there is really no point in repeating these excellent efforts.* What may be of some use is a quick look at two current controversies, one in the field of theory and the other in the field of assessment.

Robert Carson's book[31] took up a new approach to personality which looked at first sight as a very promising one. He looked at all the forms of interpersonal behaviour, and ordered them (with the help of a lot of empirical work) into a simple formula: all inter-personal behaviour, he said, could be ordered into a framework with two dimensions—dominance and submission, as against love and hate.

More elaborately, the dominance pole was labelled 'managerial-autocratic' and the submission pole 'self-effacing – masochistic'; if one person in a two-person interaction (dyad) acted in terms of the one pole, the other person would be expected to act in terms of the opposite pole – otherwise the interaction would be likely to break down. The love pole was labelled 'co-operative – overconventional' and the hate pole 'aggressive-sadistic'; here each pole would invite a response in its own terms, not in terms of its polar opposite. The diagram below fills in some more details:

---

* A book which chimes in a great deal with this chapter, and goes much deeper into some important aspects, is Ralph Ruddock (ed), **Six Approaches to The Person** (Routledge 1972), particularly the chapters by Shaw and by Ruddock himself.

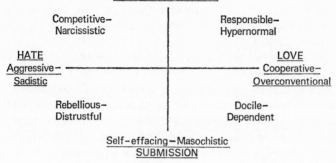

Fig. 3

In each of the pairs of words, the first word indicates a mild form of the behaviour in question, while the second refers to its extreme form. In terms of what elicits what, responsible behaviour tends to invite co-operative or docile behaviour in return. Docile behaviour invites behaviour of a managerial or responsible kind. Rebellious behaviour tends to inspire behaviour in the aggressive or competitive ranges. And competitive behaviour tends to elicit rebellious or self-effacing responses.

Carson goes on to develop these ideas in terms of the kind of interaction matrices which Thibaut & Kelley introduced, and gives a number of examples of ways in which his kind of analysis could be used. What Carson is suggesting is that someone's personality is evidenced mainly in terms of 'a person's prevailing interpersonal style (Competitive, Responsible, Docile, Rebellious, and so on)'.

What are we to say of a theory like this? There is a lot of evidence that these forms of behaviour do exist, and do have the kind of relationships which Carson says they do. But the whole thing describes a sick society, a society where all human relationships are structured in terms of dominance and submission. To a large degree, this is true of our society – but even in this society, many of the relationships I value most are not like this. And if we go back to the Triandis diagram in Chapter 6 of Vol. 1, we can see at once that it is only relatively formal relationships which are structured in a dominance-submission (respect – subordination) fashion; more intimate relationships are not structured in this way at all. So Carson is really caricaturing human relationships, rather than describing them.＊

The caricature may be valuable if it draws our attention to the danger that our relationships could become like he says they are, if we are not careful.

The other point we want to cover is a new idea in the field of personality assessment. Goldfried & Kent[32] make a contrast between 'traditional' and 'behavioral' approaches to assessment. The traditional approaches are those we have looked at so far, and the behavioral approach involves things like: observations of individuals in naturalistic situations; experimental analogues of real-life situations by role-playing; reported responses to given situations. The purpose of the behavioral approach is quite specific – it is to give information to the behaviour therapist. And the orientation of the behavioral approach is quite specific – it takes for granted that behaviour is due as much to the situation as to events or structures inside the organism. As Mischel[33] says:

> . . . behaviors which are often construed as stable personality trait indicators actually are highly specific and depend on the details of the evoking situations and the response mode employed to measure them.

In constructing their tests, exponents of the behavioral approach take account of the basic distinction drawn by Goodenough[34] between the 'sign' and 'sample' interpretations of test responses. The sign approach assumes that the response may best be taken as the expression of some underlying personality characteristic. The sample approach, on the other hand, assumes that the test responses form a subset of the actual behaviour that is of interest. Traditional testing takes the sign approach for granted, while behavioral testing assumes that the sample approach is right.

Accordingly the behavioral approach takes role-playing as being an important way of finding out how people normally behave in certain situations. For example, Stanton & Litwak[35] found that responses to interpersonal stress in a role-playing situation correlated to the extent of 0·82 with independent ratings by informants who were familiar with the subjects' behaviour in this type of situation.

Another method which has been used a good deal is self-ratings.

＊ Everett Shostram, in his **Man the Manipulator** (Bantam 1968) uses the same data in a much more positive way.

And it turns out that when one simply asks people about such things as their achievement motivation, hostility, body concern, religious concern, dominance, sociability, responsibility, etc., their self ratings have far higher predictive power than the Rorschach, the TAT, the Rotter Incomplete Sentences Blank, the Guilford-Martin Personnel Inventory and numerous other scales. And Goldfried & Kent remark:

> Even when linear regression equations were used to capitalize on the optimal combination of scales, self-prediction proved to be more accurate.

Their conclusion is, of course, that these methods should be used instead of traditional personality tests. But of course if they were used instead of the usual tests for the usual purposes—vetting for jobs, clinical diagnosis, etc. – they would be just as open to faking and distortion as the others. If tests are used in an oppressive way, to label a person, they become oppressive, no matter how technically superior they may be.

But from a practical point of view, it seems that the newer approach has much to recommend it. If you want to predict a person's behaviour, it seems very fair to ask him to co-operate and take whatever comes. And because the testing must be very close to the actual criterion behaviour, checking for validity must become very much easier. This is exactly the same movement we saw in the attitude field in the previous volume – towards much closer contact with the situation at issue.

REFERENCES

1. E. H. Erikson. Childhood and society, Penguin 1965 (1950)
2. J. Loevinger *et al.* Measuring ego development (2 vols), Jossey-Bass 1970
3. O. J. Harvey *et al.* Teachers' beliefs, classroom atmosphere and student behaviour, Amer. Educ. Res. J. 5, 1968
4. H. A. Murray. Explorations in personality, Oxford 1938
5. R. B. Cattell. Personality: A systematic, factual and theoretical study, McGraw 1950
6. H. S. Sullivan. The fusion of psychiatry and social science, W. W. Norton 1964
7. E. Fromm. Man for himself, Holt, Rinehart & Winston 1947
8. S. Maddi. Personality theories: A comparative analysis, Dorsey 1968
9. A. Maslow. Motivation and personality, Harper & Row 1954
10. A. H. Maslow. Toward a psychology of being, Van Nostrand 1962
11. C. Hampden-Turner. Radical man, Duckworth 1971
12. D. P. Ausubel. Theory and problems of child development, Grune & Stratton 1957
13. R. D. Laing. The politics of experience, Penguin 1967
14. W. K. Hoy. The influence of experience on the beginning teacher, School Review

76, 1968. Reprinted in A. Morrison & D. McIntyre (eds). Social psychology of teaching, Penguin 1972

15. D. J. Willower *et al*. The school and pupil control ideology, Pennsylvania State Univ. Studies Monogr. 24, 1967

16. A. Morrison & D. McIntyre. Changes in opinions about education during the first year of teaching, Brit. J. soc. clin. Psychol. 6, 1967

17. C. Reich. The greening of America, Penguin 1969

18. H. Marcuse. An essay on liberation, Penguin 1971 (1969)

19. McLuhan. Understanding media: The extensions of man, Sphere 1967 (1964)

20. O. K. Buros (ed). Personality tests and reviews, Gryphon 1970

21. C. Alex. How to beat personality tests, Arc Books 1965

22. J. W. Getzels & A. W. Thelen. A conceptual framework for the study of the class-room group as a social system (1960). Reprinted in same ref. as 14

23. H. Otto. Guide to developing your potential, Charles Scribner's Sons 1967

24. L. Blank *et al*. Confrontation: Encounters in self and interpersonal awareness, Collier-Macmillan 1971

25. H. Otto & J. Mann (eds). Ways of growth, Pocket Books 1971 (1968)

26. W. Schutz. Joy, Grove Press 1967

27. C. S. Hall & G. Lindzey. Theories of personality, Wiley 1957

28. Same ref. as 8

29. R. S. Lazarus. Personality (2nd edition), Prentice-Hall 1971

30. R. Brown. Social psychology, Collier-Macmillan 1965

31. R. C. Carson. Interaction concepts of personality, Allen & Unwin 1970

32. M. R. Goldfried & E. N. Kent. Traditional versus behavioral personality assessment: A comparison of methodological and theoretical assumptions, Psychol. Bull. 77, 1972

33. W. Mischel. Personality and assessment, Wiley 1968

34. F. L. Goodenough. Mental testing, Rinehart 1949

35. H. R. Stanton & E. Litwak. Toward the development of a short form Test of Inter-personal Competence, Amer. Social. Rev. 20, 1955

CHAPTER SIX

Person Perception and Interpersonal Relations

When we meet a person we form an instant impression of his or her personality. This may change as we get to know them, but it is almost impossible to prevent it happening in the first instance. And it seems that this kind of impression of another person tends to take the form of some kind of judgement of the person's personality.

In the previous chapter, we saw how professional psychologists, using the most advanced tests, can say very little about personality. One research study[1] showed, for example, that clinical experts could not tell from blind personality test results whether the tested person was male or female, nor whether the person was homosexual or heterosexual. If even such gross differences, which affect so much of our social life, cannot be picked up by experts, what chance does the average person stand of picking out more subtle things, doing the job instantly and without training? And if our amateur efforts at personality reading are so ineffectual, why do we keep on with them so consistently?

Perceptual Categories

In the second chapter of Volume 1, we saw how perception works generally, and found that people, as well as things, are instantly summed up in terms of the Osgood factors[2] of Evaluation, Activity and Potency. The Evaluation factor split into two sub-factors:

Evaluation A	*Evaluation B*
Moral	Broadminded
Reputable	Relaxed
Obedient	Sense of Humour
Trustworthy	Individualistic
Predictable	Tolerant
Good	Flexible

We suggested that these represented two contrasting ways in which a person could win our liking or respect, which could be complementary or conflicting. The Activity dimension was unitary:

Activity
Fast
Agile
Courageous
Inventive

This was a factor which was independent of the two previous ones: a person could be active and liked, or active and disliked – Till Eulenspeigel is the activity dimension come to life.

And the Potency factor again fell into two sub-factors:

Potency A	*Potency B*
Sturdy	Proud
Large	Sophisticated
Heavy	Rich
Strong	Self-confident
Courageous	Unyielding
Unyielding	Knowing

These gave us the two kinds of power – physical power and the power of influence, including knowledge. And we said that left out of this research by Kuusinen[3] was any real attention to sexual attraction, which would also need to be taken into account, as a third kind of evaluation. Surprisingly little research has been done in this area, except among adolescents.

It looks, then, as though there are some very general categories which are used by virtually everyone in summing people up. But there are also more specific categories which become used in appropriate situations. For example, in the conventional classroom situation, it is hard not to classify people into 'bright' and 'dim', simply because the competitive situation there tends to bring out this distinction more than any other. In the public-house situation, where rounds of drinks are being bought, it is hard not to classify people into 'generous' or 'stingy' categories, because that is the salient category there. In the discussion-group situation, it is hard not to categorize people as 'talkative' or 'quiet', because that is the most generally visible characteristic. These characteristics, however, are all misleading in various ways. Most people are neither very bright nor very dim, in any objective sense, and can function as either, depending on how they are treated in a given situation. Most people are neither very generous nor very stingy, but can appear to be either, depending on a whole range of factors. And most people are talkative in some situations, quiet in others. We saw in the previous chapter how Mischel[4] had found this to be true very generally, over a wide range of personality characteristics.

This also fits in with our findings about the importance of roles. When in church, we behave church. When in a shop, we behave like a customer, or an assistant. When being interviewed, we behave like an interviewee. We can play certain variations on these roles, but to an outside observer, the similarities are much greater than the differences. What is interesting, however, is that our impression of someone's personality is affected considerably if that person says or does things which go against the expectations of the role he or she is supposed to be playing. Research by Walster *et al.*[5] has shown that someone we would not normally trust – a professional criminal specializing in smuggling and selling heroin – can be extremely convincing if he is arguing in favour of stricter, more powerful courts; we take more notice of it because it appears to be going against his role interests. And the person then appears to be more moral, reputable, trustworthy, etc., which we have seen to be so important. Similarly, in the 1972 Olympic Games, two black American athletes were involved in the very simple and strict role of being awarded gold and silver medals; the normal expectation is that the athlete turns towards the national flag as it is being raised, and stands at attention while the national anthem is played, sometimes weeping with emotion at the same time. In this case, however, the gold medal winner lifted the silver medal winner up on to his own plinth, they both turned sideways on to the flag and appeared to ignore it, and stood in a relaxed and slightly bored way; one of them scratched himself. The stadium crowd reacted badly to this, and there was much whistling and catcalling while the athletes were returning to their rooms; one of the athletes gave the Black Power salute just as he left the stadium. This relatively small role infraction, which might not even have been noticed by a casual observer, resulted in the International Olympic Committee banning the two athletes for life from ever taking part in the Olympics again. All this adds up to a great respect for the power of role expectations, whether one goes with them or goes against them. Counter-role behaviour, in particular, seems to tell us a lot about a person, in a quite exaggerated and sometimes unrealistic way.

One method which has been used a great deal in finding out how people sum up and judge other people is the Kelly repertory grid technique[6] which is specifically designed to get at people's own categories.

Implicit Personality Theory

The repertory grid is a method which takes twenty people close to the subject person – mother, father, best friend, etc. – and presents them in threes. The subject person is then asked to say how any two of the three differ from the third. Whatever he says, he is then asked – what is the opposite of that, for you? Then another three are presented, and this time he cannot repeat the same distinction which he used before. This goes on until he runs out of further categories.

After an hour or so of this, the subject often has twenty or thirty categories. These can then be factored down[7,8] to show the main broad dimensions which the person is using in summing up the people he meets. Because this is a very individual thing, it is hard to compare one grid with others, and to extract any general categories in the manner of the semantic differential. Instead, we find that we can study things like the content of the categories, the complexity of the factor structure, and the tightness or looseness of the structure. Since these are unfamiliar ideas, let us look at each of them in turn.

The content of the categories has been found to change as children get older. Brierley[9] did the test on ninety boys and girls from a range of social class backgrounds at three different ages. She found the following six types of categories being used:

1. Kinship (these are not in our family, etc.).
2. Social role (these are children, etc.).
3. Appearance (these are on the skinny side, etc.).
4. Behaviour (these play musical instruments, etc.).
5. Personality (these are nosy, etc.).
6. Literal (these have the same Christian name, etc.).

The following table shows what happened as the children matured.

TABLE 5

Percentage of six types of category used by children in three age groups.

Type of category	Percentage at age		
	7	10	13
Kinship	3	3	1
Social role	30	27	9
Appearance	32	31	9
Behaviour	24	31	41
Personality	10	18	40
Literal	0·2	0	0

It can be seen that both behaviour and personality-type categories increased in number with age, and all others decreased – kinship and literal categories, never very important, virtually vanished altogether. The most impressive increase is in personality categories – partly due, no doubt, to the pressure of an individualistic culture, and partly to the increasing emphasis on individuality which comes with adolescence. It was interesting, too, that girls used more personality categories than boys at all ages. Similar results were found by Brian Little[10] in later research on adolescents.

The complexity of the factor structure has to do with the number of categories which do not overlap or repeat each other in just slightly different words. But a person can have highly complex categories in one area of his life, and very simple and crude ones in another area. For example, in our society it is common for men to have a complex structure for things and a simple structure for people, while with women it is the other way round. It appears to be the case that in any area it is important for success to have categories which are adequately complex. McComsky and his associates[11] found that architectural students who had many ways of categorizing buildings did much better in examinations than others, and that this was not related to intelligence. Attempts to treat cognitive simplicity/complexity as a static and general personality trait seem to be misplaced, as we suggested in Chapter 4. Even if we treat the judgement of people as a single area, this seems to be unrewarding: it seems to be very hard to show that a person can be a generally good judge of people, as Brown[12] points out: it may make sense only to say that a person can be a good judge of people only in certain restricted circumstances.

The third point we wanted to say something about was the tightness or looseness of the structure. Kelly defines a tight structure as one which leads to unvarying predictions, while a loose structure is one which leads to varying predictions, but which can, all the same, be identified as a continuing interpretation. Most technical distinctions, for example, are tight; while many evaluative distinctions appear loose. We have seen in the last volume that in the idea-generating phase of science, it is best to have a very loose structure, so that one's expectations do not dominate one's view of the facts and thereby distort them; while in the idea-checking phase of science, it is best to have a much tighter structure, to enable reasonably precise statements to be made. In science, therefore, there is a necessary circular movement from loose to tight, tight to loose, loose to tight again; and Kelly sees each person as being much like a scientist in this respect.* The pressures of group membership can affect this process of tightening and loosening one's cognitive structures. A study concerned with group interaction in terms of construct theory and grid method[13] found that loosening and tightening took place at the same time for most of the members of the group, over a twelve-month period; and an observer who was supposed to be observing but not participating showed exactly the same pattern of responses, in terms of judgements of all the other group members. This shows how very intimate psychological process can be influenced powerfully by group pressures, even when one may consider oneself to be outside the group, and merely observing it objectively.

All this work with the repertory grid seems, therefore, to have shown that we do carry around with us certain cognitive structures which we use in perceiving people, but that these are not so much in the nature of firm personality theories as used to be thought. It may certainly happen that a person has a simple, tight and rigid structure – we saw in Chapter 5 that this could certainly be so – but that even when this happens, we should not regard it as a fixed and permanent trait of the person. Social influences can either confirm

---

* This is parallel to the difference between convergent thinking (tight) and divergent thinking (loose) as described by Getzels & Jackson in their book **Creativity and Intelligence** (Wiley 1962).

and exaggerate such rigidities, or operate in the direction of enabling people to use more flexible and complex strategies.

Inference Processes

How do we actually go about forming impressions of the people we meet? Mainly, it seems, by exaggerating the importance of the few clues we can pick up. We then ignore further clues which do not confirm our first impressions, and notice only those which reinforce them. An interesting exception to this is found when we know we are going to have to stay with a person for quite some time – and in that situation we tend to exaggerate all their good points and overlook their bad points.

We exaggerate clues in ways which are sometimes obvious and sometimes obscure. The obvious ways include temporal extension (if someone is smiling a lot, to see him as a generally sunny person), resemblance to a familiar person, categorization (labelling, reification, rubricization), inference through analogy (someone with a squint is suspicious, someone with a high forehead is clever, someone with generous lips kisses a lot, etc.) and so on. The more obscure ways usually involve some form of reintegration.

Reintegration is a term introduced by Madison[14] to express a very common phenomenon. We all know how sometimes a person or a statement can call forth an emotional reaction which seems to an outside observer quite inappropriate; past emotional experiences have built up something like a resonating echo–chamber, and if the new experience 'hits the right frequency', as it were, the echo–chamber comes into action and turns a whisper into a shout. When someone 'says the wrong thing' this is often what is happening. A face, a voice, a phrase can be enough to set off a whole train of responses whose origins may be quite hidden from us. Madison follows through a great many examples which show clearly how these processes take place.

Another inference process which is very important in practice is the halo (or horn) effect. If we like a person, we tend to attribute to that person all the other good qualities which he may or may not possess. But we also tend to impute to that person a greater similarity to ourselves – both good and bad qualities. A study by Bramel[15] showed that if one believes oneself to have latent homosexual tendencies, then one will believe one's best friend to have them too; this was an experimental manipulation, and not a field study. Similarly, an investigation by Secord *et al.*[16] showed for fifteen different traits that if they changed for oneself, then they also changed for one's best friend.

As already mentioned, it is interesting that this process also seems to come into effect when we know we cannot avoid someone else's company. Darley & Berscheid[17] conducted a study where female students were told that they were going to participate in a series of discussions about anxiety-provoking material with another female student whom she didn't know. In order to prepare them for the meetings (which never in fact took place) they were given two folders containing personality information about other girls who had supposedly also volunteered for the study. The descriptions contained a mixture of pleasant and unpleasant characteristics, and were intended to produce a very ambiguous picture of the person described. Half of the subjects were told that they were going to interact with the young woman described in folder A, and the other half that they were going to meet the one described in folder B. Before actually meeting the one person they were going to discuss with, subjects were asked to read through both folders, form a general impression of both girls, and then rate each of them along a number of dimensions, including liking. Those subjects who felt that it was inevitable that they were going to be sharing their intimate secrets with the young woman described in folder A found her much more appealing as a person than the one described in folder B, whereas those who believed that they were going to have to interact with the young woman described in folder B found *her* much more appealing. The authors account for this in terms of cognitive dissonance, but its seems more appropriate to think of the explanation in terms of role expectations and membership groups, in the manner of Chapter 7 in Volume 1.

One very important and well-attested inference process is to see people as causal. If a person does something, we always tend, apparently, to see it as proceeding from somewhere inside him, rather than as the result of social pressures or situational constraints. We tend to see even his minor movements as expressing an inner nature.* The dangers of this are seen in the following example quoted by From:[18]

* For some important variations and qualifications, see H. H. Kelley, **On Attribution Theory in Psychology**, Nebraska Symposium on Motivation 1967.

A young lady has told me the following observation, which is a nice example of how strongly the experienced behaviour can be shaped according to the pattern to which it belongs. The young lady saw Professor X, whom she dislikes, walk on the pavement in front of her and in the same direction as she was walking, and she thought: 'This man does walk in a very theatrical and pompous fashion; he clearly thinks very highly of himself.' When she got a little closer to the man, she saw that it was not at all Professor X but her beloved teacher, Doctor Y, whom she thought was not rated according to his deserts because of his humility. And now, walking just behind Doctor Y, she thought: 'This man's whole appearance shows his humility; his walk is so straightforward and humble.' Only then did she realize the curious fact that the same person had made two such different impressions on her.

This example makes it clear how dubious is the direction of the inference process. Do we see an action and make inferences about the person from it, or do we come to a global reaction to the person, and then see his actions as expressing that consistently? All the research seems to be quite consistent with the view that in many and perhaps most cases, the inference process is from the conclusion to the 'evidence', rather than from the evidence to the conclusion.

Expression of the Emotions

One quite important area, however, where we do go by the evidence quite readily, is in the judgement of emotional reactions. We mainly go by facial expressions in judging such reactions, and are normally fairly accurate in doing so. Schlosberg[19] found that there is a circular order in the expression of the emotions through facial expressions, such that two main dimensions are involved, with a third also needed to make the whole picture clear. The two main dimensions are PLEASANTNESS/UNPLEASANTNESS and ATTENTION/REJECTION, and the third is LEVEL OF ACTIVATION. This results in the following circumplex ordering of the expressions. See page 98.

If photographs of emotional expressions are shown, then those which are closest on the circle are easiest to confuse together, while those which are furthest away are hardly ever confused.

There used to be some doubt as to whether this expression of the emotions was cross-cultural, but more recent research by Ekman[20] has shown that it is. Not only has he made films in culturally isolated New Guinea, showing that the expressions of the natives there are quite understandable by Western observers, but he has also done

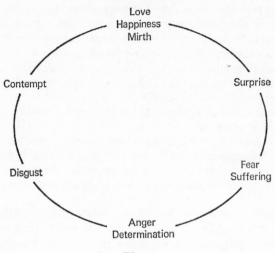

Fig. 4

work in Japan showing that while in social situations the Japanese strongly control their facial expressions, when they believe they are alone they exhibit just the same reactions which Americans also show in public. In other words, there are cultural conventions surrounding the expression of the emotions, but these are superimposed on a groundwork of expressive responses which are universal. And these cultural conventions do not in fact run very deep; it takes very little to remove them. As Danny Kaye was once reported as saying:

> I find I don't have to vary my act in the slightest, no matter where I am playing. Audiences are composed of people, and, deep down underneath, people are the same the world over. They come into the theatre covered in a few veneers of their own peculiarities and prejudices.
>
> American audiences like to think they are tough and hard to get. A myth has developed that English audiences are cold, unemotional and unenthusiastic. In fact, they are not, but they like to believe they are.
>
> You have to get out on the stage and start peeling off those veneers until you get at the people underneath. Sometimes it takes a little longer than others, sometimes there are a few more veneers to remove, but when you finally get down to the people underneath, they are the same the world over.

But it perhaps is time to come down from the universal nature of the

expressions of emotion to the more specific and small-scale interactions which can be much more easily studied.

The Dyad

Much of the reasearch which has been carried out on inter-personal
relations has used the situation of the dyad – two people relating to
one another.

There are, for example, a whole series of findings about eye-
contact, many of which are recorded in Argyle's two books[21],[22]. It
appears that mutual eye-contact is maintained in the dyad for about
half the time – though the range of variation is very large. People
try to maintain eye-contact while they are listening to someone, but
the speaker will look away during much of the time he is speaking,
only returning the glance briefly at ends of sentences, and for a
longer time at the end of his utterance. If a speaker maintains eye-
contact all the time he is speaking, this is experienced by the other
person as unusual and significant, and a sexual interpretation may
be put on it. And if the listener fails to maintain eye-contact, this
is experienced as lack of interest. If either person's pupils are seen
to open wider, this is a particularly important expression of interest
– perhaps sexual interest – because this reaction is not normally
under conscious control, and therefore indicates a 'deep' attraction
which cannot be hidden.

Power relationships can be expressed through eye-contact. It can
be demonstrated that if B looks away while A is speaking, it makes
B seem more powerful in A's eyes. There is a certain dependency
expressed in eye-contact, and power is the opposite of dependency,
as we saw in Chapter 5.

A great deal of eye-contact implies a wish for intimacy, and this
may be felt as threatening by people who are low in self-esteem. To
such people, eye-contact can easily become unpleasant and embarrassing. People with a very low opinion of themselves may
experience eye-contact as expressing power or criticism – as being
watched. The wish for intimacy expressed by much eye-contact
obviously implies self-disclosure, as Jourard[23] has shown in many
investigations, and one does not wish to disclose oneself if one sees
oneself as unworthy or guilty.

Proximity also expresses a wish for intimacy – the closer a person
stands to another, the greater the liking and wish for further closeness is expressed. And it can be shown that for a given relationship,

these indications of closeness are complementary, in such a way that if the distance is arbitrarily increased, then the rate of eye-contact goes up, in order to maintain equilibrium, and vice versa.

It may be doubted whether any of these findings about the dyad really tell us very much which is either of theoretical interest or of human value. Investigators in this area sometimes tell us that they are doing work on 'non-verbal communication'; let us now look critically at this contention.

Non-Verbal Communication

At first, the idea of non-verbal communication seems an exciting one. Here we were, all the time saying things we never intended to say, or never knew we were saying, but which could be clearly interpreted and understood by brilliant investigators like Hall,[24] Birdwhistell,[25] Fast[26] and others. If only we could understand this, we too could learn how to understand what other people were saying about themselves without their knowledge.

But the excitement soon subsided when it became obvious that there was a systematic ambiguity about what these investigators were saying. Non-verbal communication, it turned out, could mean one of two things:

1. A skilled observer can pick up and interpret certain signs and states, in a diagnostic way. This says nothing about what is going on in the focal person. It could also apply to animals or inanimate objects – e.g. the vat is ready to be poured out, the rope is strong enough to bear the weight, etc.

2. A person can express some of his thoughts and feelings in words, but others he may express covertly, because they are unacceptable to him and perhaps others. He may or may not be fully conscious of what he is expressing in these other ways. But these pieces of symbolic behaviour can be picked up by anyone sensitive enough to look for them.

Now these two statements are very different from each other. But they are also very different from what we would normally mean by the word 'communication'. Communication normally means a *shared* system of symbols, which are coded and decoded according to explicit rules. In both of the versions noted above, it is quite on the cards that each person's expressive movements are unique and idiosyncratic. There is nothing to say that there is any kind of a common language. And if there is no common language, then what kind of communication is that?

Hebb & Thompson[27] in their excellent chapter on animal studies, distinguish three levels of communication:

    A. Reflexive (not true communication).
    B. Purposive but nonsyntactic.
    C. Syntactic (and usually purposive) or true language.

Neither version of non-verbal communication says anything about being purposive – the only purpose mentioned is in hiding the communication, not in expressing it. It seems, then, that what is being talked about is something like the warning cry of birds, which is emitted automatically at the approach of danger, but does not appear to be purposive in any individual sense. Even this case seems nearer to true communication in one way, since all the other members of the species understand this warning cry. So it seems that much 'non-verbal communication' can hardly be counted as communication in any real sense at all.

We must also be aware by this time that the diagnostic process described in (1) above is extremely risky. Expressive movements, whether captured in formal tests like the Rorschach, or less formal but highly structured disciplines like graphology, or in even less formal and structured situations like that of From's young lady who we met earlier in this chapter, are notoriously hard to validate. It seems awfully easy for even experts to go wrong. And it brings in all the dangers of labelling, self-fulfilling prophecies and so on, which we have already found cause to suspect very strongly.

The version outlined in (2) above deserves a little more study. It certainly does seem possible for people to communicate one thing verbally and something else with their voice or their movements. Bateson *et al.*[28] give this example of a young man visited in a mental hospital by his mother:

> He was glad to see her and impulsively put his arm round her shoulders, whereupon she stiffened. He withdrew his arm and she asked, 'Don't you love me anymore?' He then blushed, and she said, 'Dear, you must not be so easily embarrassed and afraid of your feelings.' The patient was able to stay with her only a few minutes more and following her departure he assaulted an aide . . .

This sort of thing is very common, particularly in families. It merely becomes more obvious when one of the family gets diagnosed as mentally ill, and an outside observer comes in for the first time. Laing & Esterson[29] mention this example, of a woman of 28, living with her family, who was convinced that something she could not fathom was going on between her parents, seemingly about her:

> Indeed there was. When they were all interviewed together, her mother and father kept exchanging with each other a constant series of nods, winks, gestures, knowing smiles, so obvious to the observer that he commented on them after twenty minutes of the first such interview. They continued, however, unabated and denied.

Much more common are the everyday examples of the husband who says that he wants to take his wife out to the theatre, but never gets around to buying the tickets; the girl who refuses intercourse, but who snuggles closer to her boyfriend; the man whose life ambition is to be an artist, but who never actually gets down to painting. These are all conflict situations, where it really does make sense to say, 'Part of me wants to do it, and part of me does not want to do it at all.' One effective form of psychotherapy developed by Fritz Perls[30] involves bringing out these conflicts and becoming more conscious of what these 'parts of ourselves' are really like.

So there does seem to be at least some point in non-verbal communication considered as something really very obvious and easy to pick up once we start looking for it. Many psychotherapists have talked about this, as of course it is something they become aware of very quickly. Perls calls it listening to the tune, rather than the words; Reik[31] calls it listening with the third ear, and so on. But it is something we can all do, if we have any sensitivity; and it is something we can in most cases check out with the person concerned, to see whether we are right in our guesses. Sometimes, of course, we cannot; and in these cases we should have great reservations about the probable correctness of our interpretations.

There is a very good discussion of this whole very difficult area in an article by Wiener *et al.*[32] which should be consulted by anyone who wishes to pursue it further. It is interesting, however, that even this article says nothing about non-verbal communication by touch. It seems clear that touch is a very powerful source of messages from one person to another, and this area needs much more investigation.

Situational Identity
All through this chapter we have been concerned with personality

as it comes across in everyday interactions. But if our earlier conclusions are justified, personality itself is a somewhat problematical
concept.

If we are so much influenced by the roles we take up, and the
situations we find ourselves in, and the groups we move in, does it
make sense to try to see people in terms of their personality at all?
Do we just consist of all the roles we play, and that is it?

This does seem to be close to the view of McCall & Simmons,[33]
who see personality solely in terms of interactions, and also to the
view of Harré & Secord,[34] who see personality as a cluster of powers
and liabilities, which are called into being by situational factors. In
fact, the whole sociological emphasis is on people as nodal points
of social pressure lines, to the exclusion of any positive content.

But having rejected the 'empty organism' of the behaviorists,
and the 'black box' of the information theorists, we are not going to
accept the 'nodal point' of the sociologists.

Our view is still as stated in Chapter 3 of Vol. 1 – that the main
motive behind all human action is the preservation and enhance-
ment of the phenomenal self. And personality is regarded as the
expression of the self. What we need to do justice to, in the light of
our whole discussion of personality and our impressions of personality, is that the self is something subtle and elusive, rather than
a heavy structure with hard edges. Just as Maslow saw instincts as
something very weak, in human beings, and easily overlaid, so the
self is something easily shaken, easily confused, depending a lot on
social recognition and social help in its development. There is a
tremendous tendency to see the good things that happen as coming
from the self, and bad things as coming from the environment. The
reason for this is the tremendous fear we feel about the self being
attacked, and the feeling which comes from this that we have to see
the self as good exclusively. A few people take the other tack, and
see themselves as wholly bad – this is a form of self-defence which
has gone wrong; the idea was that if one imagined the worst had
already happened, then nothing worse could in fact happen – but
the effect is that even when one does good things, one can get
neither pleasure nor profit out of them. And the bad things can still
happen.

There is a good description of Rogers' account of the self in Hall
& Lindzey,[35] which fits in very well with what we have been saying
here.

The point for the present chapter is that the self is not easily visible, even to ourselves. The self is something we have to find out about, rather than having automatic access to every part of it.

Personal Encounter

One of the best ways of discovering personality – one's own or someone else's – is to get into situations where a variety of reactions are possible and encouraged, and where the expression of genuine reactions is facilitated. This happens in T-groups, sensitivity groups and encounter groups, as Aronson[36] has said:

> 'Trying things out' not only helps the individual to understand his own feelings, it also allows him the opportunity of benefiting from learning about how his behaviour affects other people. If I want to know whether or not people find me to be a manipulative person, I simply behave – and then allow others in the group to tell me how my behaviour makes them feel.

It is in the encounter group, in fact, that many of the concerns of this book so far come into a common focus. We found in the last chapter that people seldom reached up to their full potential, largely due to the social pressures found in the family, in schools and workplaces in our culture. The encounter group can form a cultural island of a temporary nature where some of these pressures can be taken off for a while, and where personal growth can take place, as Egan[37] has shown in great detail. And we now find that the encounter group can also be a place where we can get to know our own personality, and the personalities of others, in an atmosphere of trust where we do not have to raise all the defences which normally distort our perception. It is also a place where interpersonal relations can be explored in ways which may be far more relevant to our real existence than the conventional studies on eye-contact and the proximity of seating.

REFERENCES

1. N. Weisstein. Psychology constructs the female, in R. Morgan (ed.) Sisterhood is powerful, Vintage Books 1970
2. C. E. Osgood *et al*. The measurement of meaning, Univ. of Illinois Press 1957
3. Kuusinen. Affective and denotative structures of personality ratings, J. Pers. soc. Psych. 1969
4. W. Mischel. Personality and assessment, Wiley 1968

5. E. Walster *et al*. On increasing the persuasiveness of a low prestige communicator, J. Exper. soc. Psych. 2, 1966

6. D. Bannister & F. Fransella. Inquiring man, Penguin 1971

7. D. Bannister & J. M. M. Mair. The evaluation of personal constructs, Academic Press 1968

8. D. Bannister (ed). Perspectives in personal construct theory, Academic Press 1970

9. D. W. Brierley. The use of personality constructs by children of three different ages, unpublished Ph.D. thesis, London University 1967

10. B. R. Little. Factors affecting the use of psychological v. non-psychological constructs on the Rep. Test, Bull. Brit. Psych. Soc. (abstract) 70, 1968

11. J. McComsky *et al*. An experimental investigation of some basic concepts in architecture, Int. J. Educ. Sci. 3, 1969

12. R. Brown. Social psychology, Collier-Macmillan 1965

13. F. Fransella & M. P. Joyston-Bechal. An investigation of conceptual process and pattern change in a psychotherapy group over one year, Brit. J. Psychiat. 119, 1971

14. P. Madison. Personality development in college, Addison-Wesley 1969

15. D. Bramel. A dissonance theory approach to defensive projection, J. abnorm. soc. Psychol. 64, 1962

16. P. F. Secord *et al*. Effects of imbalance in the self concept on the perception of persons, J. abnorm. soc. Psychol. 68, 1964

17. J. Darley & E. Berscheid. Increased liking as a result of the anticipation of personal contact, Human Relations 20, 1967

18. F. From. Perception of other people, Columbia University Press 1971

19 A. Schlosberg. The description of facial expressions in terms of two dimensions, J. Exper. Psychol. 44, 1952

20. P. Ekman & W. V. Friesen. Constants across cultures in face and emotion, J. Pers. soc. Psychol. 17, 1971

21. M. Argyle. The psychology of interpersonal behaviour, Penguin 1967

22. M. Argyle. Social interaction, Methuen 1969

23. S. Jourard. Self-disclosure, Wiley 1971

24. E. T. Hall. The silent language, Doubleday 1959

25. R. L. Birdwhistell. Kinetics and context, Univ. Penn. Press 1970

26. J. Fast, Body Language

27. D. O. Hebb & W. R. Thompson. The social significance of animal studies, in G. Lindzey & E. Aronson (eds). The handbook of social psychology (2nd ed), Addison-Wesley 1968

28. G. Bateson *et al*. Toward a theory of schizophrenia, Behav. Sci. 1, 1956

29. R. D. Laing & A. Esterson. Sanity, madness and the family, Penguin 1970 (1964)

30. F. S. Perls. Gestalt therapy verbatim, Real People Press 1969

31. T. Reik. Listening with the third ear, Farrar Strauss 1940

32. M. Wiener *et al*. Nonverbal behaviour and nonverbal communication, Psych. Rev. 79, 1972

33. J. L. Simmons & G. J. McCall. Identities and interactions, Collier-Macmillan 1966

34. R. Harré & P. F. Secord. The explanation of social behaviour, Basil Blackwell 1972

35. C. S. Hall & G. Lindzey. Theories of personality, Wiley 1957

36. E. Aronson. The social animal, Freeman 1972

37. G. Egan. Encounter, Brooks/Cole 1970

CHAPTER SEVEN

Adolescence

There is no time in our lives when we are more interested in our personalities, and the impression we make on others, than in adolescence. As Ausubel[1] has pointed out better than anyone, in our culture adolescence can be most usefully regarded as a crisis of ego revaluation. In this chapter we shall be exploring some of the things which this might mean.

It has been questioned whether adolescence has, in fact, any special characteristics at all. The continuity of development in most respects has been pointed out, and it has been suggested that the problems of adolescence are no more pressing or peculiar than comparable problems which occur at other times in the life of an individual, such as getting married, or starting his first job. An investigation by Kuhlen,[2] for example, showed that in his sample, boys as they grew older gave fewer answers indicating emotional stress; also boys and girls showed increasing stability of friendships with advancing age. It is well known that IQ scores rise steadily throughout the period of maturation, tailing off very gradually only in the twenties. Adolescence is a time of greater commitment to mental hospitals and of more suicides, but in both these instances the rates increase further with the coming of the early twenties, indicating that at any rate pubescence is unlikely to be a precipitating factor.

It is certainly true that adolescence is a peculiar 'period', because it has no definite end. It would be neater if adulthood began as precisely as childhood ends. But to show that a developmental period is unique it is only necessary that a distinctive cluster of changes, which play a meaningful role in the total developmental cycle, tends to occur consistently within a given age range. Depending on which sex we are referring to and which aspect of development is under consideration, the adolescent phase can start as early as eight years old (early maturing girls) to as late as twenty

years old (late maturing boys). But some rough norms can be established. Douglas *et al.*[3] used the following: (age when girls had their
first period)

    a. Very early (before eleven years ten months).
    b. Early (11 : 10 and before twelve years ten months).
    c. Late (12 : 10 and before thirteen years ten months).
    d. Very late (13 : 10 or later).

There is no corresponding set of norms for boys, because there is
no event for boys which is as well remembered and easy to pin down
as the first period is for girls. The Douglas *et al.* survey found the
following proportions at age fifteen in boys:

    a. Mature (24·5% of sample) fully broken voice, hair under arms,
       profuse pubic hair, mature genitals.
    b. Advanced (30·0%) genitals assessed as mature, but one of the other
       maturity signs absent.
    c. Early signs (35·1%) intermediate between advanced and infantile.
    d. Infantile (10·4%) infantile genitals, no pubic or axillary hair, voice
       unbroken.

It can be seen from both these sets of criteria that the range of
variation is very wide, both for boys and for girls. Adolescents frequently worry whether they are normal, and these figures show that
reassurance is usually in order.

Theories of Adolescence

There have been a great many theories of adolescence, but it does
not seem that there is very much point in going over them, since
most of them are pretty stupid, and they have been well summarized
in a book by Muuss[4] which is generally available.

It seems more profitable to put together the theoretical position
which has been put together by two or three generations of social
psychologists, and get some clarity about that. It was originally got
off the ground mainly by Robert Havighurst[5] who talked in terms of
the developmental tasks of adolescence. What is a developmental
task? Havighurst says that it is 'midway between an individual need
and a societal demand'. Such a task is achieved through physical
maturation, social expectations and personal efforts. This links up
with the previous chapters, in which we saw how development takes
place in various areas – but now the process is complicated by the

far greater part which is taken by the person's own self-conscious self.

The success with which these tasks are undertaken depends very largely upon how successfully (and in what way and by what means) previous developmental tasks have been accomplished. The tasks have been variously defined, and some of the lists are rather long; there seem to be at least four which are generally agreed upon.

1. Achieving some adequate sexual identity
2. Becoming emotionally independent of parents
3. Becoming responsible for self
4. Finding a job in life.

All these tasks involve conflict and resistance in the early stages at least, and sometimes one, or two, or all four, are never satisfactorily completed. We shall have more to say about the first task in the next chapter.

The theory says that there are two primary ways of achieving success in these tasks in most of the cultures which have been studied.

One of the primary ways is to become accepted by the like-sexed peer group. This involves boys, for example, in gaining acceptance as a young man by other young men. To the extent that this is successful, it helps in the first task by initiating the newcomer into all the folklore of manhood, or at least that portion of it which is current in his class, locality and generation. It helps in the second task by offering an alternative reference point for anchorage; but this is a much less unquestioned anchorage point than the parents were in the palmy days of the ten-year-old, and offers sufficient freedom to experiment in various forms of defiance of the peer group itself, leading to full emancipation in the ideal case. It helps in the third task by providing a framework in which the individual stands or falls by his own personality and ability rather than his parents'.

This is a terribly important concept, and there is a lot of evidence to support it, much of it summarized in the excellent little book by Mays.[6] It ties in with the concept of desatellization, which we met in Chapter 5: the adolescent has to learn how to stop being a satellite, whose only source of personal meaning was in the family, and particularly in the parents, and how to start being a person in his or her own right. But as soon as the adolescent starts to do this, trouble comes through the door. He or she is seen as 'disobedient' or even 'naughty'. These words are quite inappropriate, because they assume a satellite status which it would be harmful to maintain; in other words, they are calculated to hold the adolescent back in development.

There are, of course, problems with the peer group. Many of them centre round the question – which peer group? Hargreaves[7] and Partridge[8] have shown with a wealth of painful detail that the school tends to have at least two different subcultures – one supporting the aims of the school, and the other opposing them. And the important survey by Bynner[9] shows in detail how the subculture of opposition is constructed in psychological terms. What is not clear in Bynner but quite plain in Hargreaves and in Partridge is the way in which the school actually created the subculture of opposition.

But however it is created, it remains true that parents often get worried about what group their adolescents are mixing with, and may choose a school – if they have any choice in the matter – with this very much in mind. This seems perfectly valid in terms of the evidence we have adduced. There is, however, no guarantee that any school will be 100% safe, and it may be better to take some risk if one believes in values such as equality or self-development. What adds to the problem, however, is that just at the moment when the adolescent is starting to get some feeling of his or her own membership of alternative groups – whether aligned with the values of the school or not – the father of the family is likely to be experiencing career failure, and sexual inadequacy. Most males in our culture, at the age of forty or so, come to the realization that they have not 'made it' in their own terms, and that they are virtually stuck in a rut for the rest of their lives; and they are getting less satisfaction from sex with their wives, but haven't the courage to go out and look for it anywhere else. So they are in a state of defensive and rather passive frustration, complicated in many cases by all sorts of regrets about actions not taken because of wife or children. This means that 'the adolescent problem' should often be renamed 'the middle-age problem'.

One of the greatest worries which parents have is about drugs. They did not have such things when they were the same age, and do not read the underground magazines where such things are discussed at length; neither do they read such excellent sources of information as **The Little Red Schoolbook**[10] or **Alternative**

London.[11] And so they panic at the very thought of their adolescent smoking cannabis or taking LSD. It seems, on the whole, that while concern is in order, panic is not. The details about LSD, for example, are to be found in such easily available books as the one by Stafford & Golightly,[12] or the earlier one edited by David Solomon.[13] This problem will of course change in a few years' time, when those who have grown up in a world where cannabis is relatively normal (as much as anything can be which is forbidden by law) become parents of adolescents themselves.

The other primary way of achieving success in the four tasks is by inflation of the self-concept. Different writers put this point in different ways, depending on their theoretical framework, but they seem agreed that adolescence is a period when the individual is preoccupied with his own personality. Adolescents are characteristically much occupied with self and the symbols of self. There is a lot of evidence for this, from Kuhlen,[14] Stone & Barker,[15] Jersild,[16] Stolz & Stolz,[17] Coleman[18] and Rosenberg[19] among others.

Another way of putting the same point is to say that adolescents are concerned about their own identity. 'Who am I?' is the universal question. And this can become such a pressing problem that it may seem better to accept a negative identity than to have no identity at all.

> At any rate, many a sick or desperate late adolescent, if faced with continuing conflict, would rather be nobody or somebody totally bad or, indeed, dead – and this by free choice – than be not-quite-somebody. (Erikson.[20])

The danger of this negative identity* is that all human beings need some kind of social support in order to function well; usually this means some kind of relationships with other people. It is possible for the rare person to do without this, and become a hermit for short or long periods, but normally this can only be done in later life, when a great deal of social support has become internalized; this is a part of what self-actualization is about, as we saw in Chapter 5. But the adolescent is not in this position at all; as we have just seen, the peer group is crucially important to him or her, and if it is

* In adopting a negative identity, the person comes to get greatest emotional satisfaction from activities that are the most disturbing to those whose support is essential to him or her. Madison says of one of his students – 'She knew she was destroying herself in the process, but satisfying her hatred was more important than protecting her own welfare.'

suddenly or gradually lost, very serious consequences may follow. As Madison points out on the basis of a very thorough investigation into the life of college students:[21]

> A fundamental separation of self from others is, for western man at least, an intolerable state. The vicious thing about a negative identity is that the person is emotionally driven to do the very acts which will bring about such a separation . . . But success in a negative identity role destroys the person through creating an unbridgeable separation from society.

The relationship of negative identity to the abuse of alcohol, drugs, sex and so forth is an important one – it is only when there is this connection that these pleasures become harmful in any drastic way.

All the problems connected with identity become more difficult in a society where adults have identity problems, too. And our society is like this, as Klapp[22] has documented very convincingly. He has pointed out that, growing up all through the 1960's, there has been a whole syndrome of associated phenomena, all to do with the collective search for identity:

1. The sheer variety of 'looks' (types) available to the common man.
2. The explicitness of identity search (for the 'real you').
3. Ego-screaming: the plea 'look at me!'
4. Style rebellion (style used as a means of protest or defiance).
5. Theatricalism and masquerading in the street.
6. Post as a way of getting to the social position one wants.
7. Dandyism: (living for style, turning away from the hard-work model of success).
8. Dandyism of the common man as well as of the aristocrat.
9. Pronounced escapism in many styles (such as those of beatniks, hippies, surfers, and in language such as 'cool' and 'freak out').
10. A new concept of the right to be whatever one pleases, regardless of what others think 'the new romanticism'.
11. The breakdown of status symbols, the tendency of fashions to mix and obscure classes rather than differentiate them.
12. The pursuit of status symbols reaching the dead end of a vicious circle breaking down meaning and making it harder to tell who is who.

In a society where all this is going on, and much of it in areas which affect the adolescent more than most others – but which ultimately affect everyone more or less – it is only to be expected that any identity problems which plague the adolescent normally will be made very much worse. Instead of sliding neatly into some role slot which has been already prepared, there is a huge agony of choice facing the adolescent. But it is not even a choice between clear alternatives – where there is such confusion, the very meaning of one's choices becomes doubtful. As Klapp puts it:

> Such a malady is not just a failure of particular interactions and personal efforts but a blight on the forest of meanings which a child needs to grow up into a man, a grandparent, finally an ancestor. Many of its causes are difficulties in the way of a person in a mass society finding meaning to, for, and in himself: dehumanized work, extreme impersonality, destruction of places, social mobility, lack of identifying ceremonies, pile-up of objective (meaningless) information, mediocrity of bureaucratic and white-collar self-images, explosion of expectations from impact of mass communications and increasing leisure, and fragmentation of identity from multiplicity of personality models.

In a society like this, there is little of what Gross *et al.*[23] call role consensus. Even about common roles like son, daughter, boy-friend, girl-friend, friend, there is little agreement as to what this entails; each relationship has to be worked out anew. And looking ahead to such relationships as husband and wife, there is little consensus there, as we shall see in more detail in the next chapter.

So just at the time when the person is feeling the first and greatest urge to know himself and understand who he is, the social supports which once made that a relatively understandable task are progressively being withdrawn.* The messages about what other people expect him to be are contradictory and often hypocritical: because the people advocating certain standards frequently do not live up to them themselves.

The Self in Adolescence

We have seen how the social-psychological theory of adolescence says that there are four main developmental tasks to be undertaken, and that the two main means by which they are to be achieved is through acceptance by the peer group and through inflation of the self-concept. And we have seen that there is not just one peer-

---

* Chickering, in his book, **Education and Identity** (Jossey-Bass 1969) has some counter-arguments to show that maybe it is not quite as hard as all that.

group, but two or more; and that the possible ways of inflating the self-concept have all become much more problematical because of changes in the whole social fabric.

What we have now to consider is whether in fact this is not a much healthier situation for the development of the self. The old ideal of definite and understandable roles on which there was high consensus may in fact be a false ideal. In any case it has been under fire for something like two centuries, ever since the ideas of romanticism became popular.

In an age when established role structures are crumbling and new and more flexible ones being set up, it may actually be an advantage to postpone 'settling down' into a single identity for as long as possible. A role can be a very narrowing thing, as well as a source of strength, and the more it is taken for granted, the more narrowing is it likely to be. There are, it seems, at least seven kinds of peer groups which the adolescent can identify with at present – I have adapted and updated these from Mays:

Group 1. The roughs. Rejecting and rejected. Prone to physical aggression and petty crime.

Group 2. The fixers and wanglers. Non-violent, but involved in activities around the edges of the law.

Group 3. Low-level conformists. Acute sense of their own limitations – often a wish to impose limitations on others.

Group 4. The freaks. A mixture of seekers, retreatists, risk-takers, withdrawers, positive and negative identities, united by a common rejection of conventional society, and by what Klapp has called 'the new romanticism'. Unusual clothes.

Group 5. The political. Leftist, humanitarian, emotionally extremely sore and sensitive. Often both intelligent and creative.

Group 6. The cowboys. Often working-class, positively oriented towards the affluent society, interested in fashion and possessions. Distinguished from 'the Indians' in Group 4, but equally interested in appearance.

Group 7. High-level conformists. The public school type. Not so clear nowadays what to conform to.

How does this help us? It seems clear now that it is only Group 4 which has the potential for accommodating someone who is totally confused, until he can sort himself out. This is why Group 4 is so important, in spite of its small size. It offers a myth, an ethos which is propagated through the media – and particularly through the underground media – and can be picked up by anyone. It is a genuinely non-elitist group, which has no mechanism for ejecting or excluding anyone.

But does Group 4 offer any possibility for self-development? Or is it too careless, too non-supportive? Does it really exist, in any usable form, or is it *just* a myth? Answers to questions like this are very variable, depending on what part of the country we are talking about, what year it is, how persistent one is, and so on. It may often mean creating such a group, rather than joining it. But insofar as it does exist, it can provide some very important things. These include:

a. An atmosphere of acceptance. This is very important for ego-development: Rogers calls it 'unconditional regard'.

b. An intolerance of sham. A norm of doing without masks and clichés – of making sure that my experience is real for me. This is close to what Rogers has described as 'genuineness' – a key requirement for good ego-development.

c. A deep respect for the separateness of people. Phrases like 'doing his own thing', and the important moral insight that 'you can't lay your trip on someone else' testify to the centrality of this value. It has been stated by Perls and others that this, too, is crucial to the development of a strong self.

d. A readiness to take risks. People in this group will often take off for foreign parts, without any real preparation; or go in for some new religion in a deep way; or learn the mysteries of the Tarot cards. This ability to take risks has been remarked on by Hampden-Turner as one of the most characteristic things about the healthy personality.

Those who are familiar with encounter groups, or with the literature on T-groups, sensitivity groups and the rest, will recognize at once that these are four of the most typical background values to such groups, which are themselves all about ego-development and the releasing of human potential. Among the freaks, therefore, we find a sort of naturally-occurring encounter group setting.*

Let us look in more detail at each of these four values, and see how they work in encouraging someone up the ladder which we took a look at in Chapter 5; the ego-developmental ladder of Jane Loevinger.

* It is important to remember the qualifications which were stated earlier. This is not a universal statement endorsing one group, merely an attempt to indicate something rather rare anywhere, but practically nonexistent in any of the other groups the adolescent may come across.

a. The atmosphere of acceptance is one of the most often re-marked-on features of the freak culture. In place of the world seen as a jungle, with every man for himself, or the world seen as a merito-cracy, where each man seeks position in a rigid hierarchy, the world is seen as a community. As Reich says:[24] 'People all belong to the same family, whether they have met each other or not.' Here is an example from Abbie Hoffman:[25]

> ... rememberin the great scene that Anita told me about how this bus was comin up the Thruway and how it was all freaks and everyone laughin, singin and passin around dope, and the bus stalled in traffic and the kids saw this cat standin in the road and needin a ride and they all started jumpin up and down and yellin 'Pick him up! Pick him up! Pick him up!' and the bus driver began sweatin all over and shoutin out things about company regulations and other kinds of horseshit. A sort of instant people's militia was formed and they started up the aisle when all of a sudden the bus doors opened and this freak with a knap-sack on his back came aboard. Everybody was jokin and clownin and even the bus driver felt better. He didn't accept the joint a cat tried to lay on him but he scratched the guy's shaggy head of hair and smiled.

Often this acceptance is merely a kind of stoned tolerance, but as can be seen in the example above, it can go much further than that. What is so sad is that this acceptance is often met with hostility and rejection from other people, who are so upset by oddity and dirt and cannabis that they refuse to see anything else. However that may be, it is important to recognize that for the freak himself, the acceptance is unconditional. This is what is important from an ego-developmental point of view – because a person can grow in such an atmosphere; as Carl Rogers[26] puts it: 'To the degree that the therapist can provide this safety-creating climate of unconditional positive regard, significant learning is likely to take place.'

The atmosphere which many parents provide, however, is en-tirely opposite: conditional regard. The adolescent is only accepted to the extent that he keeps in line with parental demands. The moment he goes beyond that, he is made to feel unwanted and under fire. Factors of social status enter into the picture, so that Koskas[27] found in France, for example, that middle-class parents are slower to relinquish control of the adolescent than their working-class counterparts, and instigate therefore a correspondingly greater amount of rebelliousness in their offspring. Similarly, schools and places of work offer only conditional regard, and therefore hold back the ego-development of the adolescent. We have only recently begun to explore the implications of all this, but books like the ones by Rogers[28] and by Postman & Weingartner[29] are showing that schools do not have to be run in the old way; while books like those by Argyris[30] and Herzberg[31] are showing that companies do not have to be run in the old way either. In a way, it might be thought that it would be easy to change the family, because there are no high structures of commercial interests to hold up change; but on the other hand there are such things as refresher courses for teachers and managers, but none for parents. And we have seen that the parents are having their own troubles in any case.

b. The intolerance of sham seems to arise very naturally in adolescence. One starts suddenly to see through the pretences of everyday life. There is an enormous gap, for most of us, between our opinions and our lives, touched on in the saying – 'Do as I say, not do as I do.' And we lead our lives out in this way. But what Rogers has found in the practice of psychotherapy is that personal growth is stunted by such behaviour.

So when the adolescent finds, in the freak group, precisely this value of genuineness cultivated and appreciated and given free rein, he finds not only something congenial but also something nutritive. In the ideal therapist relationship, Rogers says, 'the therapist is genuine, hiding behind no defensive façade, but meeting the client with the feelings which organically he is experiencing. And in the freak group, as Reich has said:

> It is a crime to allow oneself to become an instrumental being, a projectile designed to accomplish some extrinsic end, a part of an organization or a machine. It is a crime to be alienated from oneself, to be a divided or schizophrenic being, to defer meaning to the future . . . The commandment is: 'Be true to oneself.'

And what this does is to lay a heavy responsibility on the person to lead his or her own life in an authentic way. David Wood[32] has defined authenticity as a combination of self-respect and self-enactment. He says that self-respect includes: the awareness of one's subjectivity; the awareness of one's freedom; and the acceptance of responsibility for oneself. And he says that self-enactment includes: that one must always try to act consistently; that one must try to enact what one believes; and that one must be prepared to avow or own one's actions. From an ego-development point of view, this kind of atmosphere is optimal – it enables a person to get to grips with the internal and external problems which are most salient at any given moment.

But what do we find in the family, or in other, more usual situations? We find a great tendency to falsify experience, to put up defensive façades and to set up systems of communication which are ambiguous. This again is calculated to hold back development of the self, not to assist it.

c. A respect for the separateness of people is central to any adequate concept of the healthy self. This message has come out of nearly every system of therapy, no matter how different they may be in other respects. The problem is so frequent in clinical practice, of people trying to live someone else's life for them, or suffering from someone else trying to live their life, that it must be one of the most crippling ailments of our civilization. The antidote to it is well summed up by the great therapist and teacher, Fritz Perls, in his 'gestalt prayer':[33]

> I do my thing
> And you do your thing
>
> I am not in this world
>   to live up to your expectations
> And you are not in this world
>   to live up to mine
>
> You are you
> And I am I
>
> And if by chance we find each other
>   it's beautiful
> If not
>   it can't be helped

Perls shows that if the therapist maintains this attitude, he can produce important and lasting changes in the other person, in the direction of personal growth and increasing self-direction.

In the freak group, this value is acted upon every day. The very phraseology of the gestalt prayer comes out of this soil. And Reich says: 'No one judges anyone else. This is the second commandment.'

In the family, this value is so rare that one sometimes feels that the family itself may be incompatible with it, in which case, the worse for the family as an institution. In education, Rogers says:

> I am inwardly pleased when I have the strength to permit another person to be his own realness and to be *separate* from me. I think this is often a very threatening possibility. In some ways I have found it sort of an ultimate test of staff leadership and of parenthood. Can I freely permit this staff member or my client or my son or my daughter to become a separate person with ideas, purposes and values which may not be identical with my own?

In industry, it is rare, too. The typical manager wants people to be assimilated to the purposes of the organization, so that he can deal with them as mere incarnations of that purpose. In an age when the purposes of organizations are changing so quickly, this is not only harmful as ethics and inadequate as psychology, but is actually antagonistic to business success into the bargain.

Again we see that the freak group is providing something which is hard to find in the rest of society, but something which is essential to healthy ego development in the adolescent.

d. The readiness to take risks is not so much a source of ego development as evidence that it is happening. One of the most important risks, because it is a risk which goes to the centre of one's being, is the risk of going mad. Those who take LSD and mescalin are prepared to take this kind of risk, because they trust in themselves sufficiently to feel that no matter how deranged they may feel, it is still *their* experience, *their* fantasy, *their* trip, be it good or bad. It is real for them.

Recent research has shown that LSD experiences are not in fact equivalent to madness, but just the opposite: ingenious experiments by Aaronson,[34] using hypnotized subjects, have shown that one set of instructions produces a schizoid experience, while precisely the opposite instructions produce a psychedelic experience. But the risk seems equally important, however we describe it. It does involve a loss of immediate self-control which is certainly experienced as risky. It is this ability to risk one's very *self* which therapists see as evidence of psychological health; Lynd[35] for example says:

> Confronting, instead of quickly covering, an experience of shame as revelation of oneself and of society – facing 'actual life' – requires an ability to risk, if necessary to endure, disappointment, frustration and

ridicule . . . Engagement with life and with history – self-discovery and further discovery of the world – has always involved such risks.

It is this experience of self-discovery which we have seen all along that the adolescent needs most. Without the other values – acceptance as a person, the intolerance of sham and the respect for separateness – the adolescent may well not have the strength to take the necessary risks, and may be pushed back into a life which is relatively meaningless.

It may be thought at the end of this examination that what is being offered is merely a paean of praise for the freak group. This is far from being the case – one must recognize that this group contains too many people who are existing on the basis of a negative identity, with all the very real dangers which that brings with it. What we are really saying is that the greater part of society does not offer what the adolescent needs. At the moment, the freak group does offer at least some of that, along with many real dangers. It would be better for society if it could introduce some of these values into its major structures, so that the adolescent would not have to go elsewhere for them.

REFERENCES

1. D. P. Ausubel. Theory and problems of adolescent development, Grune & Stratton 1954
2. R. G. Kuhlen & G. C. Thompson (eds). Psychological studies of human development, Appleton-Century-Crofts 1952
3. J. W. B. Douglas *et al.* All our future, Panther 1971 (1968)
4. R. E. Muuss. Theories of adolescence, Random House 1962
5. R. J. Havighurst. Human development and education, Longmans Green 1953
6. J. B. Mays. The young pretenders, Sphere 1969 (1965)
7. D. H. Hargreaves. Social relations in a secondary school, Routledge 1967
8. J. Partridge. Life in a secondary modern school, Penguin 1968
9. J. M. Bynner. The young smoker, HMSO 1969
10. S. Hansen & J. Jensen. The little red schoolbook, Stage 1, 1971
11. N. Saunders. Alternative London 3, Nicholas Saunders 1972
12. P. G. Stafford & B. H. Golightly. LSD: The problem-solving psychedelic, Award Books 1967
13. D. Solomon (ed). LSD: The consciousness-expanding drug, Berkley Medallion 1966 (1964)
14. R. G. Kuhlen. The psychology of adolescent development, Harper 1952
15. C. P. Stone & R. G. Barker. The attitudes and interests of pre-menarcheal and post-menarcheal girls, J. Genet. Psychol. 54, 1939
16. A. T. Jersild. The psychology of adolescence, Macmillan 1957

17. H. R. Stolz & L. M. Stolz. Adolescent problems related to somatic variations, in Adolescence, Yearbook of the National Society for the Study of Education, 1944
18. J. S. Coleman. The adolescent society, Free Press 1961
19. M. Rosenberg. Society and the adolescent self-image, Princeton 1965
20. E. H. Erikson. Identity: Youth and crisis, W. W. Norton 1966
21. P. Madison. Personality development in college, Addison-Wesley 1969
22. O. E. Klapp. Collective search for identity, Holt, Rinehart & Winston 1969
23. N. E. Gross *et al.* The postulate of role consensus, in P. B. Smith (ed), Group processes, Penguin 1970
24. C. A. Reich. The greening of America, Penguin 1972 (1970)
25. A. Hoffman. Woodstock nation, Vintage Books 1969
26. C. R. Rogers. On becoming a person, Constable 1961
27. R. Koskas, *L'Adolescent et sa famille*, Enfance 2 1949
28. C. R. Rogers. Freedom to learn, Charles E. Merrill 1969
29. N. Postman & C. Weingartner. Teaching as a subversive activity, Penguin 1971 (1969)
30. C. Argyris. Intervention theory and method, Addison-Wesley 1970
31. F. Herzberg. Work and the nature of man, Staples Press, 1968 (1966)
32. D. Wood. Strategies, in S. Godlovitch *et al.* (eds). Animals, men and morals, Gollancz 1971
33. F. S. Perls. Gestalt therapy verbatim, Real People Press 1969
34. B. Aaronson, chapter in C. Tart (ed.) Altered states of consciousness, Wiley 1969
35. H. M. Lynd. On shame and the search for identity, Harcourt Brace 1958

CHAPTER EIGHT

Sex Differences

Up to this point we have avoided talking about any differences between boys and girls, men and women, except insofar as they arose in talking about some specific topic. Now it is time to look at this as a topic in itself, because it is extremely important, not only as an adolescent developmental task, but as an issue in the life of each of us. Men and women in our culture dress differently, behave differently, are treated differently.

And it has to be said straight away that this chapter is being written by a man, subjected for years to a whole series of socialization processes which have the effect of tending to make him blind to a great deal of female experience. In other words, I am prejudiced against women, in a million tiny ways which I am not even conscious of, much of the time. Like most prejudice, it is well hidden from my conscious mind, and well defended from examination, but easily detectable from outside.

Let us start, then, by getting as far outside as we can.

Cross-Cultural Evidence

Margaret Mead[1,2] was able to show, in two famous books, that the turbulence of adolescence was a cultural thing – that there were other cultures where adolescence was a smooth and natural growth into adulthood with no giggles, no suicides and no generation gap. This was a tremendous slap in the face for the theorists of adolescent development, who had adduced all sorts of highly impressive evidence about glands and hormones, which proved conclusively that adolescents were bound to have severe psychological problems, simply because of biological facts. Interestingly enough, this view has still not died out altogether: a recent book says:[3]

This dependence of affective states upon endocrine function very probably accounts for some of the turbulence of the adolescent period:

both boys and girls have to adapt, fairly suddenly, to high levels of circulating sex hormones. Whereas with oestrogens the situation may only be depressive, with androgens it is likely to be explosive!

Old psychologists' tales die hard, it seems. But most social psychologists today would hold that it is not biology, but cultural expectations and pressures, that make adolescence a time of stress and storm.

A rather similar picture emerges in relation to sexual differences. We tend to assume without thinking, and biologically-minded psychologists seem to confirm, that all sexual differences are basically biological. But let us look at some of the cross-cultural facts. Margaret Mead[4] again draws our attention to four societies – the Mundugumor, the Arapesh, the Tchambuli and modern America. In America, she says, the men are supposed to be aggressive and active, the women dependent and passive. Among the Tchambuli, it is the other way round; the men are expected to be dependent and passive, the women aggressive and active. Among the Arapesh, both men and women are normally dependent and passive. And among the Mundugumor, both men and women are usually aggressive and active. Brown[5] has a nice exposition of the ins and outs of this analysis, but the point is that in all four of these societies, most people fit in to the norms, while a minority find it hard to live up to these expectations, and find ways of living differently from the others. The main effects are strong. Mead says of the Tchambuli:

> This is the only society in which I have worked where little girls of ten and eleven were more alertly intelligent and more enterprising than little boys . . . the minds of small males, teased, pampered, neglected and isolated, had a fitful, fleeting quality, an inability to come to grips with anything.

There is a great deal of cross-cultural evidence which supports the general view that what seems like basic temperament or character is often carefully implanted by socialization processes. For example, Barry *et al.*[6] have the following table, based on a survey of 110 different cultures:

TABLE 6

*Differences between cultures in
encouraging certain qualities in boys
and girls*

	BOYS	GIRLS	NEITHER
Nurturance	0	82	18
Responsibility	11	61	28
Obedience	3	35	62
Achievement	87	3	10
Self-reliance	85	0	15

Main figures are percentages in which qualities were
systematically encouraged in socialization.

If all these qualities came naturally, it does not seem as though
there would be such a need to bring them on by social means. But
why should it be that it is usually the boys who are given the active
role, and the girls the co-operative, caring and dependent role? Is it
really because men are bigger and stronger than women, or because of women's child-bearing capacity? Some light is thrown on
this point by a study of 224 cultures carried out by Murdock[7]:

TABLE 7

*Some activities mainly or always carried out by males
or females*

MALE ACTIVITIES	FEMALE ACTIVITIES
Metal working	Water carrying
Weapon making	Burden bearing
Manufacture of musical instruments	Gathering of shellfish
Work in wood and bark	Crop tending and harvesting
Work in bone, horn and shell	Fuel gathering
Trapping of small animals	Gathering of herbs, roots and seeds
Manufacture of ceremonial objects	Fire making and tending

The full list is much longer, and these items are picked out to illustrate the point that many of the activities which men do in a wide variety of cultures are not particularly related to size or strength, and many of the activities which are most often done by women are not related either to this or to child-bearing. And these are not just odd happenings – Murdock found *no* culture in which women did metal working, and only 7 where men did water carrying. These are massive patterns, growing up independently in small cultures all over the world. It is just *as if* they were biological; yet it is hard for me to see how they can be.

And if substantial patterns like this can arise without much in the way of biological foundations, it does raise the question of how much else that is regular is necessarily anything to do with biology. D'Andrade[8] has a very full and interesting discussion along these lines, concluding that sex roles are very much influenced by 'which sex controls economic capital, the extent and kind of division of labour by sex, the degree of political "authoritarianism" and family composition'.

The possibility seems to arise, in fact, that in each culture one sex seems to become dominant (usually, though not always the male sex) and to take the most prestigeful jobs to itself, leaving the less prestigeful jobs to the opposite sex. 'The manufacture of ceremonial objects' is perhaps particularly revealing here. This is not a task requiring great speed or strength, nor does it lead in any way to such tasks – but it is a task with great honorific value and high status.

What we seem to have now come out with, then, from the cross-cultural data, is that in many cultures the male sex has become dominant, and has put down the female sex into an inferior position.*

Biology Versus the Culture

Having got this far with the telescope, let us now take up the microscope. Cross-cultural studies seem to say that men and women differ in ways which seem to be largely shaped by the culture: what do genetical and physiological studies say?

It is extraordinarily difficult to be sure. Let us take one example

---

* It is interesting to speculate why it is usually the male sex which comes out on top in this way. Perhaps it is simply that men can concentrate on power all the time, while women have to think, at least part of the time, about babies.

to illustrate the difficulties. Weller & Bell[9] made an interesting discovery that newborn female babies are significantly higher in basal skin conductance than newborn male babies. Their skin conducts electricity more easily; they are more sensitive to pain; they show more immediate and marked responses to unpleasant stimulation. Now at first we may immediately jump to conclusions, and say that this proves that females are biologically different from males – this accounts for their greater sensitivity to pain in adult life, as found for example by Notermans & Tophopf.[10]

But further research on newborns found that second and later children have a significantly higher basal skin conductance than firstborn children, regardless of sex. Now we know that there cannot be any genetic difference between firstborns and later children – there is no known mechanism in genetics which could produce such an effect. But we do know that parents handle second and later children very differently from firstborn – they are more used to the situation, and they have learned from experience more about handling children. So the conclusion seems at first hard to accept, but unavoidable, that even something so basic and seemingly biological as basal skin conductance may have more to do with the way the baby is handled than to do with anything inborn and inevitable.*

An example like this shows how cautious we have to be in interpreting all the research which has been done on biological sex differences. We saw in Chapter 1 how social expectations can influence behaviour as early as nine hours old.

There is another difficulty, concerned with the juke-box theory of the emotions which we met in Chapter 5 of Volume 1. It seems to be a fact that our emotions have a two-stage structure: there is a physiological arousal which is fairly indefinite and vague, plus a sense of the situation which may be very well defined. For example, if we are a sentry at night in enemy territory and feel our heart beating, we may take it as a sign of fear; if we are in a tense argument with someone we dislike and feel our heart beating, we may take it as a sign of anger; and if we are coming close to someone we love and feel our heart beating, we may take it as a sign of passion. The symptom is the same: but the way we interpret it is different.

In the light of this, what are we to make of such an argument as that of Welch[11] who says that male hormones in the blood make

---

* There is also the possibility that the womb environment and the birth process are different for later-born children – two other external sources of influence.

males more aggressive than females? All he can actually show is that these hormones increase the general level of arousal in the brain – but the way the child is treated must determine the *meaning* of this arousal. Meaning is a social creation, not a biological one, as we saw throughout the first volume. Arousal is physiological, aggression is cultural.

What we are saying, then, is that not only do cultural influences start very early, but also it is cultural influences which give meaning to biological/physiological facts. This means that, so far as human beings are concerned, it is very hard to separate the two things – the biological and the cultural. It is for this reason that psychologists have had recourse to animal studies, where it is easier to separate the two things one from another.

Experimental Evidence

One of the studies which is most often quoted as evidence for the biological necessity of active maleness and passive femaleness is that carried out by Harlow[12] on sexual behaviour in rhesus monkeys. You may remember from Chapter 1 that he was rearing young monkeys with a mechanical mother, so that there could be no cultural transmission of expectations from the mother to interfere with the process of development, and no imitation of the mother's or father's actions. (Though it is not altogether clear at exactly what age the babies were removed from the mother – even a few hours could have some effect in this direction.)

These young monkeys, when allowed to mix with each other, showed the following behaviour: males did more threatening actions than did females; females did more rigid and passive withdrawal; males indulged in more rough-and-tumble play than females; females did more grooming than did males.

Assuming that there really was no teaching by the mother in the early hours of the baby monkeys' lives, what are we to make of this kind of information? First of all there is a certain gap between the rhesus monkey and man: it is true that they both have mammalian brains, and that the body chemistry is much the same, but there are still vast differences which make it unwise to rush directly to conclusions of a one-to-one kind. But let us assume again that it *is* close enough to be relevant – what then? Surely the question for us must be – can the culture reverse this pattern or can it not?

What we are now asking is not – 'Will sex differences show themselves, other things being equal?' Our question is a much more real and relevant one – 'How unequal do other things have to be before this tendency can be reversed?'

We already have some information on this from the cross-cultural work. Cultural influences can either reinforce women's passivity and men's activity, or reverse them. So it seems that whatever the latent tendencies may be, we do have the power of choice as to whether to encourage them or discourage them.* And we have this power of choice at several levels. We saw in the first volume that there are three basic influences on human action – heredity, environment and the self. Heredity seems to give us only rather vague and ill-defined states of arousal; the environment can work at the level of the small group, the organization, the local community, the nation, the historical culture, and so on; and the self does have at least some power (which can be increased) to initiate action from the inside.

It comes back, now, to a question of values. What do we want?

Sex Roles and Gender Identity

It seems that more and more women are beginning to question the whole question of their automatic passivity over against men's activity. They have noticed that all the elements of the feminine stereotype have rather odd overtones, when you put them together and really look at them coolly: distinctive appearance, colourful dress, not very bright intellectually, inconsistent, emotional, weak, all right in their place, contented as long as well treated, inoffensive, anxious to please, guile rather than directness, appearance of help-lessness . . . these all sound very much like a description of a slave – the stereotype of the nigger on a Southern plantation, as Hacker[13] has pointed out at length.

And this is rather insulting, once perceived in this way. It is not something nice and comforting – it is systematic devaluation. And as soon as one sees it in this way, one cannot any more feel happy about a culture which emphasizes this image of women, reinforces it, plays it up in every way, teaches it to children – and blames it all on biology, as Hutt does in her very misleading book:[14]

* It is important to see that, for man, the natural does not equate with the biological. As Stuart Hampshire once said – 'It is "natural", in the sense of necessary, to man to be a social being, and "social" implies convention-observing, and "conventional" is ordinarily opposed to "natural".' (**Thought and Action**, Chatto & Windus 1959.)

The essentially feminine coffee-mornings, as well as the more ritualized Rotarian nights, Freemasonry and Forestry of the males are simply adult human manifestations of natural proclivities which are already manifest in our ontogenetic kith and phylogenetic kin!

What is the reason why women, after excelling all the way through school life, fall back intellectually at and after university? Hutt cites a study by Maccoby[15] where a sample of female academics was compared with a male sample of equal status, qualification and experience. Irrespective of discipline, and of number of children, marriage, etc., the women published substantially less than the men. What neither of them quote is the old and well-known study of Komarowsky,[16] which explains why this is likely to be so. About 40% of her sample of women students reported that they pretended to be stupider than they really were in order to please the men they went out with:

> I am engaged to a southern boy who doesn't think too much of the woman's intellect. In spite of myself, I play up to his theories because the less one knows and does, the more he does for you and thinks you 'cute' in the bargain . . . I allow him to explain things to me in great detail and to treat me as a child in financial matters.
>
> One of the nicest techniques is to spell long words incorrectly once in a while. My boy friend seems to get a great kick out of it and writes back, 'Honey, you certainly don't know how to spell.'
>
> When my date said that he considers Ravel's 'Bolero' the greatest piece of music ever written, I changed the subject because I knew I would talk down to him.

Some later research found the same thing, more systematically, on following up a sample of 140 adolescents of high intelligence. They found that, at a certain point, many of the girls' records showed a sudden sharp drop in IQ scores. When these girls were questioned, over and over again they said things like – 'it isn't too smart for a girl to be smart.' As Friedan[17] remarks:

> In a very real sense, these girls were arrested in their mental growth, at age fourteen or fifteen, by conformity to the feminine image.

This picture does not appear to be changing very quickly, if at all. Each new piece of research which comes out seems to confirm that the expectations which surround girls and women act very powerfully to narrow and constrain their picture of themselves. Even in today's student world, where men and women live with each other, marry each other, even have children while at college (either in or out of marriage), the same thing is going on; the sexual freedom, such as it is, makes no real difference. One of the students in the excellent research study of Madison[18] has this to say:

> My attitudes, although unverbalized to a large degree, were essentially these: that I didn't need to prepare for a specific career because career girls were essentially girls who had to do something themselves because they had no immediate prospects for a husband and could not look forward to the security and happy housewifeship that I felt were implied in marriage. I had never lacked for a husbandly prospect or two . . . Theoretically I was on campus to study and learn. I would have been very indignant if someone had told me I was there to earn or catch a husband, or even because going to college was expected of me (especially by my parents). I would have been ten giant steps ahead if I'd only just honestly realized that these two things probably each had some measure of validity. Then maybe I could have dealt with them in some more constructive way.

What is wrong here is that 'career girl' has one image – a hard, bitchy, man-hating, money-oriented, selfish, dominant image – and 'housewife' has another – a soft, loving, nurturant, helpless, self-sacrificing, dependent image – both equally false and harmful, and both set up by a culture which is basically dominated by men. It cannot escape notice that both of these images benefit men considerably: the one enables them to put down possible competitors with a good conscience, because they are so nasty; while the other enables them to walk unopposed over all the rest.

The amazing thing is that these images have been accepted for so long by women themselves. Women themselves believe that women are intellectually inferior. In a well-known experiment,[19] women students were given a number of essays on various subjects to evaluate on a number of criteria, including intellectual excellence. Half the sample, chosen at random, were given the essays signed with men's names, and half the same essays signed with women's names. And the same article received significantly lower ratings when it was attributed to a female author than when it was attributed to a male author; irrespective of what subject it was written on. And if this takes place in the university, where people have very little investment in perpetuating the established way of looking at

E

social issues, how much more is it likely to be so in the everyday life of most people?

Women have been conned, so to speak, into accepting the career-girl image, the housewife image, the intellectual inferiority image, the general incapacity image, and keeping it going by surrounding their daughters with all the same expectations which did it for them. How has this been done? Are men conspiratorially plotting to keep women in their place, and devising ever more cunning psychological means of doing so? The Bems[20] suggest that what is involved here is a *nonconscious ideology*:

> A society's ability to inculcate this kind of ideology into its citizens is the most subtle and most profound kind of social influence. It is also the most difficult kind of social influence to challenge, because it remains invisible. Even those who consider themselves sufficiently radical or intellectual to have rejected the basic premises of a particular societal ideology often find their belief systems unexpectedly cluttered with its remnants.

Where this is the case, there seems to be a clear case for making a first priority of making the nonconscious conscious. And this is precisely the view which has been taken by the Women's Liberation Movement in its consciousness-raising groups. One of the purposes of such groups is to enable women themselves to get clearer about what is involved in this ideology of domination which is the dominant ideology.

And out of this movement, and its surrounding publicity, has come a very clear and consistent picture of a system in which women are regularly put down by men for their own benefit. Take something as simple and basic as housework. Mainardi[21] has given some horribly convincing examples of what happens when a woman asks a man to help by doing his share of the housework:

> I don't mind sharing the housework, but I don't do it very well. We should each do the things we're best at.
> I don't mind sharing the work, but you'll have to show me how to do it.
> We used to be so happy! (Said whenever it was his turn to do something.)
> We have different standards, and why should I have to work to your standards. That's unfair.
> I've got nothing against sharing the housework, but you can't make me do it on your schedule.

I *hate* it more than you. You don't mind it so much.

Housework is too trivial to even talk about.

The problem of housework is not a man-woman problem! In any relationship between two people one is going to have a stronger personality and dominate.

In animal societies, wolves, for example, the top animal is usually a male even where he is not chosen for brute strength but on the basis of cunning and intelligence. Isn't that interesting?

Women's liberation isn't really a political movement.

Man's accomplishments have always depended on getting help from other people, mostly women. What great man would have accomplished what he did if he had to do his own housework?

These quotations are amplified in the article with a full account of what each one really means in practical terms. But all of them boil down to just one thing – I'm on top and I'm going to stay there. And this leads to the thought that maybe the ideology is not so non-conscious after all. Maybe men have a fairly shrewd idea of what benefits them and what doesn't.

But is it so shrewd? What is happening to the male all this time? This is a more difficult subject, because there is much less literature to fall back on. What seems to have happened is that the male in our culture has put *everything* into a master-slave mould, involving separation and isolation. And in doing so he has cut himself off from a great deal of his own reality.* Even inside himself the same separation takes place – it is one of the main findings of modern Gestalt and existential psychotherapy that people carry around with them a whole system of phoney roles, which often contains a pair of roles which Perls[22] calls the top dog and the underdog; and a great deal of energy is spent in phoney struggles between these two separated parts of the personality. It is a whole system of 'shoulds' – I should be this, I should do that – but there is a kind of unreality about it all. There is a separation of opinions from behaviour, such that it is easy for men to sympathize with women and 'see their point' without changing their conduct in any way.

In this way men's heads somehow get separated from their living. A woman once wrote to me:

---

* This is particularly so in the area of sex. The male way of dealing with sex normally involves separating it from everything except the act itself, as Kate Millett has spelt out in scholarly detail in her book **Sexual Politics** (Doubleday 1970).

A lot of the time what happens in your head is what you think is happening. This is to do with being an intellectual and to do with being a man . . .

A lot of the time you don't hear what a person is saying, you hear what you think they are saying. This also is related to being an intellectual . . . This needn't be authoritarian, it just mightn't leave the right space for the person to grow into.

I am a man. This is not just some other people I am writing about in this chapter – it is me, too. And you, the reader, are involved. This chapter is about me, and about you. We are all in this mess. Is there any way of climbing out of it?

How do we get out of a situation where men are discouraged from developing certain traits such as tenderness and sensitivity, just as surely as women are discouraged from being assertive and 'too bright'; where young boys are encouraged to be incompetent at cooking and child care just as surely as young girls are urged to be incompetent at mathematics and science?

First of all we have to become conscious of what is going on. And secondly we have to recognize that however much men's lives are distorted by the culture which we share, women's lives are very much more distorted and cramped. As the Bems say:

Consider the following 'predictability test'. When a boy is born, it is difficult to predict what he will be doing 25 years later. We cannot say whether he will be a doctor or an artist or a college professor, because he will be permitted to develop and to fulfil his own unique identity, particularly if he is white and middle-class. But if the new-born child is a girl, we can usually predict with confidence how she will be spending her time 25 years later. Her individuality doesn't have to be considered because it will be irrelevant.

And this throws a very different light on the biological arguments which we started with. If indeed heredity does mean anything, it means that every child is born different, with the possible exception of identical twins. And it must certainly mean that some children are born more dominant and some more submissive, as Gottesman[23] claimed to find. But he found that this potential was realized more frequently in males than in females. It seems that only the males in our culture are raised with sufficient flexibility, with sufficient latitude given to their biological differences, for their natural potential to come through. The females are subjected to such a heavy dose of socialization that even the effects of biology are swamped. They are just reduced in any case to what Greer[24] has called the female eunuch.

But is it enough to become conscious of all this? The answer seems to be No. One of the problems, as we have already seen, is that it is so easy for people in our culture to assent to something consciously, but still go on acting in basically the same old way. How can we modify this?

We saw at the end of the previous section of this chapter that there are a number of different levels which can be brought into play for any psychological change. First of all there is the level of the self; to the extent that a person is self-aware, and has insight into his or her own emotions and wishes, he or she has greater self-control and self-determination.[25]

At the level of the family, parents can try to bring up their children in a way which does justice to their individual differences, without worrying too much over whether the children are ultimately going to be 'normal' and 'fit in'. There is some evidence that this can be successful, as Oakley[26] shows in her book.

At the level of the small group, people can share experience, either just by talking, or by engaging in action of various kinds. Women have found it valuable to have their own groups, closed to men, in order to find themselves and define their own reality, as Morgan[27] describes. Women's encounter groups have also been very successful, as Meador *et al.*[28] have described:

> Until coming to the group, Liz saw no alternatives, but by the end of the eight weeks there were visible changes in her. Her face and body seemed more relaxed and she had lost all traces of her tight, clipped speech. She said calmly, and with confidence, 'I think the two of us may make it now. But if we can't, I feel like I can make it alone.'
> Liz had begun to feel her own potency.

Something can be done at each level, and all these efforts make some difference to some part of the structure. Just because this is a culture-wide phenomenon, there can be no reliance on any one method: employment policies of individual companies, admission policies of universities, medical schools, etc., legal changes in taxation, social security benefits, etc., all need to be worked on at the same time. Once we begin to look around with open eyes, the arbitrariness of gender expectations cannot fail to strike us with great force. We find out that in Russia 75% of the doctors are women, 35% of the engineers are women, and only one married woman in twenty is a full-time housewife. This may not be any kind of an ideal, but it does indicate that there is nothing inevitable about our own mix, where women are prevented from going to medical school by discriminative quota arrangements, only a tiny percentage of women go in for engineering, and being a full-time housewife is the norm.

Similarly for men – all the indications are that we are moving into a situation where men may not only have three or four different careers in a lifetime, but where they may take time off from the whole idea of a career, for six months, a year, five years or more at a time. This would involve a whole different feeling about dedication and commitment to one thing. There are some indications, too, that the whole idea of 'success' may be changing. This may take some of the pressure off men to be aggressive and pushing, hard and tough and impervious.

Other things are happening too. If McLuhan[29] is right, we are moving out of a visual and linear age into an aural and tactile age. This changes the way in which we use our senses – but it has never been pointed out that it changes the balance of the sexes as well. J. S. Watson[30] wanted to condition babies to look at a spot of light whenever it appeared. The remarkable thing was that he was only able to do this if he used sounds as reinforcement for the girls and lights as reinforcement for the boys. The training was not successful if he used visual reinforcement for the girls and aural reinforcement for the boys. This links with the statement of Casanova that while men are seduced through the eyes, women are seduced through the ears. If the whole culture is moving away from the visual sense to the senses of hearing and touch, this marks a movement away from the dominance of male patterns of experience. The whole concept of female beauty, fashion, make-up and all the rest, may be in the melting-pot here. The female experience may have a chance to emerge and attain a more realistic place in the whole process of cultural change.

But let us make no mistake that the female experience at present has been seriously damaged, and damaged by men. As Janet Gooch has put it in a poem:

when all is said, and though
I have avoided seeing it
and saying it, for so long,

my experience of being
a woman is that
we are a colony.

We have valuable things
to send or bring,

we can be visited,
we may be pacified

and should we choose
to learn about the world
that they have made
(as they have made it)
(and they will teach us)

then we may share in it
as much, as fast
as we can learn.

My experience of being
though, is that
something inside me
refuses to learn
about the world they go on making
the way they go on making it,

something inside me that knows
your tears and pain, my tears
and pain, are the centre
of whatever it is
we live and make

and anything I try and say
is too elaborate already.

I don't know how a man can add anything to that. Perhaps everything I have said in this chapter is too elaborate already.[31]

The Social Individual

REFERENCES

1. M. Mead. Growing up in New Guinea, Penguin 1942
2. M. Mead. Coming of age in Samoa, Penguin 1943
3. C. Hutt. Males and females, Penguin 1972
4. M. Mead. Sex and temperament in three savage societies, Apollo 1967 (1935)
5. R. Brown. Social psychology, Collier-Macmillan 1965
6. H. Barry *et al*. A cross-cultural survey of some sex differences in socialization, J. abnorm. soc. Psychol. 55, 1957
7. G. P. Murdock. Comparative data on the division of labour by sex, Social Forces, 15, 1937
8. R. G. D'Andrade. Sex differences and cultural institutions, in L. Hudson (ed). The ecology of human intelligence, Peng 1970
9. G. M. Weller & R. Q .Bell. Basal skin conductance and neonatal state, Child Devel. 36, 1965
10. S. L. H. Notermans & M. M. W. A. Tophopf. Sex difference in pain tolerance and pain apperception, Psychiatria, Neurologia, Neurochirugia 70, 1967
11. B. L. Welch, quoted in ref. 3
12. H. Harlow. Sexual behaviour of the rhesus monkey, in F. A. Beach (ed). Sex and behaviour, Wiley 1965
13. H. Hacker. Women as a minority group, Social Forces 1951. Compare also the statement—'Woman is the nigger of the world' (Yoko Ono)
14. Same ref. as 3
15. E. E. Maccoby. The development of sex differences, Tavistock 1966
16. M. Komarowsky. Cultural contradications and sex roles, Amer. J. Sociology 52, 1946
17. B. Friedan. The feminine mystique, Penguin 1965 (1963)
18. P. Madison. Personality development in college, Addison-Wesley 1969
19. P. Goldberg. Are women prejudiced against women?, Transaction 5, 1968
20. S. L. Bem & D. J. Bem. Case study of a nonconscious ideology: training the woman to know her place, in D. J. Bem, Beliefs, attitudes and human affairs, Brooks/Cole 1970
21. P. Mainardi. The politics of housework, in R. Morgan (ed). Sisterhood is powerful, Vintage Books 1970
22. F. S. Perls. Gestalt therapy verbatim, Real People Press 1969
23. I. I. Gottesman. Heritability of personality: A demonstration, Psychol. Monogr. 77, 1963
24. G. Greer. The female eunuch, MacGibbon & Kee 1970
25. C. R. Rogers. On becoming a person, Constable 1961
26. A. Oakley. Sex, gender and society, Temple Smith 1972
27. R. Morgan. Introduction: The women's revolution, in ref. 20
28. B. Meador *et al*. Encounter groups for women only, in L. N. Solomon & B. Berzon (eds). New perspectives on encounter groups, Jossey-Bass 1972
29. M. McLuhan. Understanding media, Sphere 1967 (1964)
30. J. S. Watson. Operant conditioning of visual fixation in infants under visual and auditory reinforcement, Devel. Psychol. 1, 1969
31, Some of it is said much better in Angela Hamblin, Ultimate goals, in Women's Liberation Review No. 1,

CHAPTER NINE

Ageing

Social psychology is very weak in the area of describing adult life generally – the few studies of middle life are usually not done by psychologists or even sociologists, but by odd people who have happened to have some interest in the area, or as a by-product of some other kind of research, such as family therapy.

It is for this reason that we move suddenly to a consideration of old age and the problems associated with the ageing process. Why there should be this gap we do not know – perhaps we could speculate that it is for the same reason that there are so few studies in industry of the board of directors – the people who run things do not like their own behaviour to be examined too closely, though they are willing to sponsor research into everyone else. Or perhaps it is simply that normal adults are not a 'problem' to anyone – it is the squeaky wheel which gets the oil. Be that as it may, it remains true that in social psychology, the adult in middle life forms a silent majority.

Psychological Effects of Ageing

One of the most depressing facts which comes out of any examination of the psychological effects of ageing is that it is all a downward path. The following functions get steadily worse as one gets older:

> Conduction velocity of nerve fibre
> Basal metabolic rate
> Male strength of grip
> Cardiac output (heart)
> Vital capacity
> Reaction times to light or sound
> Stated frequency of sexual intercourse
> Brain weight
> Liver weight
> Comprehension
> Arithmetic

Similarities test
Object assembly test
Digit substitution test
Block design test
Sorting test
Visual recognition
Rote learning

And the sad thing is that these things do not start falling off at the age of 60, but at the age of 20. From the age of 20 onwards there is a steady decline.

For many people, particularly in the upper income groups, this is disguised by success experiences of one kind or another, which give an illusion of unimpaired faculties. It may only be at a certain point where failure is experienced that 'it all comes home' and adds to feelings of depression and identity crisis. We saw in Chapter 7 how having an adolescent in the family often adds again to this kind of problem.

If the older man falls out of work, it is extremely difficult, in most cases, for him to get as good a job as the one he fell out of. Wolfbein[1] has pointed out that:

At the upper end of the age spectrum (e.g. men aged 45 years old and over) unemployment rates are relatively favourable; but once out of a job, older men encounter difficulty in becoming re-employed as many find their skills obsolescing in the face of technological change.

And this makes for psychological difficulties which are well described by Chown & Heron,[2] who summarize evidence showing that older people tend to clamp down on their emotions, but are strongly disturbed by unexpected disasters.

This connects up with a good deal of work on rigidity, which seems to show that older people revert more to concrete thinking, in the sense we laid down in Chapter 4. Looft[3] has an interesting paper on egocentrism across the life span, which seems to show some support for this notion, and Hooper et al.[4] spell it out in terms of a framework integrating Piagetian theory and the fluid versus crystallized intelligence distinction. It seems as though the ability to do the Piagetian conservation tasks disintegrates in reverse order of their formation in childhood.

It is important, however, not to exaggerate the way in which ageing affects people. It is often stated, for example, that people become more conservative politically as they get older. When one looks carefully at the evidence, however, it appears that this is not so, Campbell *et al.*[5] found that 80% of the U.S. electorate claimed they had never changed party preference; Key[6] found that people were no more likely to abandon the party their parents had voted for at any one age more than another; and Crittenden[7] found that any given group of people born in the same four-year period remained constant, on balance, in its party preference. These are American findings, but there is no reason to suppose that Britain is any different in this particular respect. It seems both that most people vote as their parents voted, and also that most people vote the same way all their lives; and the exceptions balance out in their political direction.

Many of the changes which people notice in old people, such as increased cautiousness and conservatism (with a small c), are apparently due to decline in intelligence. Research studies by Chown[8] and by Edwards & Wine[9] seem to show rather clearly that when intelligence is held constant these characteristics do not appear in any significant way.

What changes do appear, then? Some very thorough research by Neugarten[10] shows that adult men in their forties are preoccupied with the idea of virility and resistance to coercion. They see themselves as able to cope with the environment and get what they want from it. Those in their fifties show a mixed pattern of reactions, part way between the forty-year-old and the sixty-year-old approaches. And those in their sixties emphasize friendliness, conformity and adaptation to what comes – moved by the environment, rather than moving it. They are much more interested in their own internal lives than in dominating the world outside. But with all these changes, Neugarten makes it clear that these men differed hardly at all in the way in which they could cope with their worlds. They were not lacking in social skills, even at the older ages. And the Edwards & Wine research, which held intelligence constant, found the same thing – that older men moved very definitely into an area of wanting to be liked, and to be seen as warm and friendly.

All these changes seem to point in the same direction – a gradual disengagement of the man from active social involvement of a kind which may involve conflict.

Disengagement Theory

Cumming & Henry[11] have put forward a theory which states that older people tend to cut themselves off from social interaction more and more. These writers see the person as being at the centre of a network of contacts, which gradually constricts. This process is seen further as inevitable, universal, willingly accepted by the person, and good for individual and society alike.

Now it seems that it can at least be shown that most older people do withdraw in this way. What is not quite so clear is whether this process is either inevitable or desirable.

Cumming *et al.*[12] say that this disengagement gives the old person a certain freedom to be different, to be eccentric even, and is therefore desirable. But whether this is enough to make disengagement a desirable outcome is a matter of how we value this kind of freedom in relation to other values, individual or social.

As for being inevitable, Lowenthal & Boler[13] found that four groups of old people could be distinguished:

1. The voluntarily withdrawn.
2. The involuntarily withdrawn (through retirement, viduity or physical disability).
3. Not withdrawn and not deprived.
4. Deprived but not withdrawn.

And they suggest accordingly that it is the three deprivations mentioned which affect morale more than withdrawal itself. The largest group was in fact group 3, which seems to show that there is nothing inevitable about disengagement.

There are some subtle ways of disengaging, however, which resist being picked up in this sort of questionnaire. Birren[14] found that older lawyers and doctors protect themselves from emotional overload by not becoming as involved with their clients as they used to do.

Another interesting finding is that of Riegel,[15] who asked people for a list of people they had met in their lives. Younger people showed a recency effect – most of those remembered had been met fairly recently. But the older people (around the age of 73) remembered more people from the past. He suggested two possible reasons for this – either the person meets fewer people when he gets old, or the people he does meet don't seem to be very important to him.

It looks, then, as if disengagement theory is right insofar as it is merely descriptive, but more doubtful in an evaluative sense. And it is not at all clear where the main influences are coming from – the demands of society or the needs of the individual.

Personality and Disengagement

One way of going further into this question is to look at the way in which different people react to old age – what is the range of variation in ways of withdrawing or adapting in other ways?

An important piece of research in this area is that of Reichard et al.[16] on 87 men aged between 55 and 84, half retired and half in full- or part-time employment. They were divided on the basis of how well they had adjusted to the problems of old age, and then the two sets of data (115 personality variables) were subjected to cluster analysis. Five clusters emerged, revealing five different ways of coming to terms with old age:

1. The mature (constructive).
2. The rocking chair (dependent).
3. The armoured (defensive).
4. The angry (hostile).
5. The self-haters.

Of these, the first three were well-adjusted, and the last two poorly adjusted. So there are at least these three ways of being well-adjusted to old age – there is not just one way.

The *mature* group were well-integrated, enjoyed life and were able to form warm relationships with other people. They had had fairly normal work careers, childhoods and marriages, and did not have serious financial worries. They were not likely to be racially prejudiced, and were tolerant of faults both in themselves and in others. They had accepted the fact of death calmly and undespairingly.

The *rocking-chair* group tended towards passivity and dependence rather than activity and self-sufficiency. They relied on others to provide for material things and emotional support. They ate and drank a little too much, gambled and tended to live beyond their means. They tired easily and often had dominant wives. They did not make good relationships with other people. They were satisfied and even over-optimistic.

The *armoured* group were overcontrolled, habit-bound, conventional and compulsively active. They were very self-sufficient. They avoided retirement if possible, and resented any enforced idleness. They were hard to interview, because of their suspiciousness and defensiveness. They had a good deal of prejudice against minority groups. They were pessimistic about the future, and avoided thinking about it by keeping busy.

These three groups all functioned very well, in their various ways. But the other two did not.

The *angry* group were less well off, and blamed circumstances or other people for their downward movement. They usually had a mixed occupational history, without any successful pattern. Their wives and children were seen as demanding and unreliable. They were extremely suspicious and competitive, but did not have the ability to compete successfully, and protected themselves from this realization by unrealistic expectations of themselves and others, sometimes amounting to paranoia. They were strongly prejudiced. They could see nothing good in old age, and were afraid of death.

The *self-haters* had turned their hostility in upon themselves, and were critical and contemptuous of the lives they had led, which had in fact been unsuccessful, leading them downwards in the socio-economic scale. They were somewhat depressed, and had unhappy marriages. They were pessimistic and unpractical, and welcomed death as a promise of release.

It can be seen from this account that the rocking-chair group and the armoured group, both of which seemed to have adjusted well to old age, had found opposite ways of doing so. The rocking-chair group had disengaged, in just the way that the theory said, but the armoured group had not – they were as active and involved as ever.

We cannot say very much about the number involved, because of the small and unrepresentative sample, which makes it impossible to extrapolate to the population as a whole, but there is no indication that the armoured people are any fewer than the rocking-chair people. So this is something of a blow for disengagement theory.

A similar conclusion emerged from the Kansas City studies on adult life, which covered women as well as men. Havighurst[17] distinguished eight different types of adjustment to ageing, some of which involved disengagement, and some of which did not – both approaches being about equally satisfactory or equally unsatisfactory, depending mainly upon the personality of the person to be considered.

But we seem now to be in a contradictory position. In Chapter 5 we poured a certain amount of cold water on the concept of personality as a very helpful concept in psychology – yet here we are apparently finding it very valuable in studies of ageing!

In order to be consistent, I would have to say either that Chapter 5 was unduly pessimistic, or that the studies just quoted are misleading in some way. In fact, I incline towards the latter. It has been found so often in personality studies that one great pioneering study seemed to open up a whole new area, and throw a flood of light on what was going on, yet when other people came along to try and consolidate the gains and build on these foundations, it has all somehow disappeared into the statistical sand. This seems to be the case here. No one seems to have taken the Reichard *et al.* findings, and made the items into neat scales, and gone out and found more people like those studied already. And if this can't be done, the results immediately look much more dubious. All that they could then demonstrate is that no simple theory of ageing, which ignores the way in which different people react to what seems from outside the same situation, can account for all the facts. And that is just how we have used the results here.

What seems to emerge is that we have some choice in finding our own response to ageing.

Ageing and Self-Actualization

It may have struck the reader how similar the description of the 'mature' type was to the earlier description of the self-actualizing person. And Maslow, in some of his later writings particularly, did suggest that fully self-actualizing people did not develop until mid-life:

In a (letter to D. T. Hall dated 9 March 1967) Maslow has indicated that he conceives of a long time period between the emergence of the various need levels. He suggests that in the fortunate life history the safety needs are salient and satisfied during childhood, the affiliation needs during adolescence, and the esteem needs during early adulthood. Only as a person nears his 50's, generally, will the self-actualization needs become strongly salient. (Hall & Nougaim.[18])

We have already seen a good deal of other data which suggests that older people are more likely to want to do justice to their internal lives. And it is highly characteristic of self-actualizing people that they have no fear of looking inside themselves and facing what they find there.

So the thought emerges that perhaps ageing gives us an opportunity to 'decenter' (in Piagetian terms) from the immediate concerns of our lives up to that point, and rethink our life style in a broader perspective. This seems both possible and desirable.

Ageing and Roles

But it is time to introduce a concept which we shall be using a great deal in the next volume – the concept of a role. There are five main age-roles in our culture:

a. Babyhood or infancy – unable to use language.
b. Childhood – great period of learning and dependence.
c. Adolescence or teenage – period of four developmental tasks.
d. Maturity – period of marriage, work, parenthood.
e. Old age.

Each of these is associated with a whole set of expectations, about which there is more or less consensus – we saw what a problem this can be when we considered the question of gender roles in Chapter 8.

So far as old age is concerned, there is a set of expectations which are mainly negative. Old people are often expected to be poor, narrow-minded, intolerant, interferers, gossipers and so on. This is one reason why charities for the aged find it so hard to get support. A recent report said:

> . . . old people are not felt to be very appealing. It's easier to nurse a child than an old person – they are more attractive, even if they are a bit mental. It's a bore to talk to an old person for an hour about nothing in particular, especially if you're of a different generation. Children are urgent, but old people are not urgent. Old people are seen as ugly, and weak, and likely to be sick. They can be abusive. They can be incontinent. All these are points which came out in these conversations.

This is, of course, naked prejudice emerging, and if we look for it, it is easy enough to find equivalent prejudices emerging for infancy, childhood and adolescence. Babies are messy and scream all the time; children are noisy, thoughtless and destructive; adolescents are disrespectful, conceited and ineffectual. And who are the people who have all these prejudices? Why, the other four groups, with the possible exception of the babies.

But, as with all other forms of prejudice (as we shall see in more detail in Volume 4), these views are also accepted, in many cases, by the old people themselves. In other words, they reject the age-role which they now inhabit. They feel that they have, with retirement, been put into an age-ghetto, and they resist this strongly.

And it certainly is true that most people, with retirement, do experience a drop in income, with all that that means in our culture, in terms of loss of power and effectiveness. Together with that goes, for men particularly, a process of role relinquishment which may bring back memories of all the other times in life when one has had to be separated from something familiar, going right back to the anxiety of being separated from one's mother and getting lost. Going from one central role to another always involves some anxiety and some crisis of identity, and here there is more often than not a real sense of going downwards rather than upwards.

There are social-class differences here, too. Kerkhoff[19] found that:

> (a) upper-level husbands and wives do not welcome retirement, but they are likely to plan for it. Their experience in retirement is comparatively favourable and their reactions to the experience are generally rather positive . . . (c) lower-level husbands and wives are much more passive in anticipation of retirement and have few plans and no outstanding expectations: they evidently do not experience retirement as a particularly pleasant change in their lives and they tend to be much more negative than the others in their reactions to it.

For a variety of reasons, retirement is more of a blow to the manual worker – and these still constitute the greater part of the British work force.

It seems clear, then, that to consider old age as a time of severe role change makes a lot of sense, and Brown[20] confirms this view in his discussion of the importance of having a definite work status in our culture.

But it is not only the work roles which change. The parental role now virtually reverses. Children, once a liability, now become a dubious and undependable asset. If the husband spends more time at home, the whole husband-wife relationship changes, and may become much more difficult. As Miller & Form[21] say:

We know that the dwelling must substitute for the work plant in retirement and that the line between living and working almost disappears.

And it may be just at this time that the dwelling has to change. Maybe one wants to move out of a house which is now too big, with children having left, and a rent which is now too high, or with repair bills which are too heavy. Or maybe one is sick, and cannot run a house properly. Maybe one is a widow, with even more crushing role changes to cope with; one's man having been in some cases one's whole definition.

So the old person moves to a child's house, living in the spare room or a child's old bedroom. Or to a friend's house. Or to an old people's home of some kind – see the Carp[22] article for one way of doing this well. In all these cases, huge changes in one's whole role structure are entailed, no matter how smooth and inevitable the changes may seem to be. And all this at a time in one's life when one finds change most hard to take, as Friedsam[23] has shown.

It may well be, in situations like this, that one looks around for something permanent, which is not going to change, and which can be depended on absolutely. Religion often fills this bill and offers an unchangeable God or access to unchangeable spiritual truths. It can easily be seen that most of the people attending church services are older, as are those who attend spiritualist meetings and buy church magazines, etc. Research by Fukuyama[24] confirms this impression in a more rigorous way.

Turning to religion in this way has another benefit – it helps in dealing with the fear of death.

Death and Mourning

Death is the last separation, as birth is the first. So the separation anxieties connected with retirement not only look backwards, they also look forwards to death. And old age is, of course, a period during which one hears of more and more deaths of those one knew when younger. Some one just reads about in the newspapers – others one knows still, and one goes to their funerals. Some of the funerals are particularly close, and raise uncomfortable emotions; others are mere occasions for meeting old friends and relatives one has not seen for years. But they soon begin to seem like a rising tide approaching one's own rocking-chair.

This is more likely to affect women, since women tend to live longer than men – hence there are more widows than widowers. And there is likely to be a long period of mourning when the husband dies, as Marris[25] has found. Mourning is a particularly important concept, as Bowlby & Parkes[26] have shown, since it links all the types of separation anxiety together.

And so we return to the theme of the first chapter of this book where we saw that the child deprived even temporarily of his or her mother at the age of two or three experiences something very much akin to mourning.

There is much more to say on this subject, but it has been greatly neglected in social psychology, and there is very little in the way of documentation in any rigorous way. In the five-volume **Handbook of social psychology**, there is only one entry in the index for death, and none for funerals. This is a remarkable demonstration of the fact which is often remarked, that in our culture there is an amazing aversion to any discussion of death. We hide it away, just as in Victorian times, sex was hidden away.

This is all the more extraordinary since we have inflicted more death in this century than in any other since the dawn of history. We should be interested in it, if only as a form of self-criticism.

But there is more to it even than that. We need to come to terms with our own death, because it makes a difference to the way we live. As Sam Keen[27] puts it:

> It is in discovering death that joy becomes possible. Ecstasy, like love, is born in the act of dying. And he who would keep his life forever does not escape death. He only evades something of the poignancy of dying by never having known the ecstasy of being alive.

REFERENCES

1. S. L. Wolfbein. Labour trends, manpower and automation, in H. Borrow (ed). Man in a world at work, Houghton Mifflin 1964
2. S. M. Chown & H. Heron. Psychological aspects of ageing in man, in P. R. Farnsworth (ed). Annual Review of Psychology 1965
3. W. R. Looft. Egocentrism and social interaction across the life span, Psychological Bulletin 78, 1972
4. F. H. Hooper, J. Fitzgerald & D. Papalia. Piagetian theory and the ageing process: Extensions and speculations, Ageing and Human Development 2, 1971
5. A Campbell, P. E. Converse, W. E. Miller & D. E. Stokes. The American voter, Wiley 1960
6. V. O. Key. The responsible electorate, Harvard Univ. Press 1966

The Social Individual

7. J. Crittenden. Ageing and party affiliation, Publ. Opin. Quart. 26, 1962. See also his Ageing and political participation, West. polit. Quart. 16, 1963

8. S. M. Chown. Rigidity and age, in C. Tibbitts & W. Donahue (eds). Social and psychological aspects of ageing, Columbia Univ. Press 1962

9. A. E. Edwards & D. B. Wine. Personality changes with age: Their dependency on concomitant intellectual decline, J. Gerontology 18, 1963

10. B. L. Neugarten. Personality and the ageing process, in R. H. Williams, C. Tibbitts & W. Donahue (eds). Processes of ageing (Vol. 1), Atherton Press 1963

11. E. Cumming & W. E. Henry. Growing old: The process of disengagement, Basic Books 1961

12. E. Cumming, L. R. Dean, D. S. Newell & I. McCaffrey. Disengagement: A tentative theory of ageing, Sociometry 23, 1960

13. M. F. Lowenthal & D. Boler. Voluntary versus involuntary social withdrawal, J. Gerontology 20, 1965

14. J. E. Birren. Toward an experimental psychology of ageing, Amer. Psychologist 25, 1970

15. K. F. Riegel. Time and change in the development of the individual and society, in H. W. Reese (ed). Advances in child development and behaviour (Vol. 7), Academic Press 1972

16. S. Reichard, F. Livson & P. G. Peterson. Ageing and personality: A study of eighty-seven older men, Wiley 1962

17. R. J. Havighurst. Personality and patterns of ageing, Gerontologist 8, 1968

18. D. T. Hall & K. E. Nougaim. An examination of Maslow's need hierarchy in an organizational setting, Org. Behav. & Hum. Perform. 3, 1968

19. A. C. Kerckhoff. Husband-wife expectations and reactions to retirement, J. Gerontology 19, 1964

20. J. A. C. Brown. The social psychology of industry, Penguin 1954

21. D. C. Miller & W. H. Form. Industrial sociology, Harper & Bros. 1951

22. F. M. Carp. The impact of environment on old people, in S. M. Chown (ed). Human Ageing, Penguin 1972

23. H. J. Friedsam. Reactions of older persons to disaster-caused losses: An hypothesis of relative deprivation, in same ref as 22

24. Y. Fukuyama. The major dimensions of church membership, Rev. religious. Res. 2, 1961

25. P. Marris. Widows and their families, Routledge 1958

26. J. Bowlby & C. D. Parkes. Separation and loss within the family, in E. J. Anthony & C. M. Koupernik (eds). The child in his family, Wiley 1970

27. S. Keen. To a dancing god, Fontana 1971 (1970)

CHAPTER TEN

The Language of Psychology

All through this book, there are experiments quoted. It is through experiments that we test theories and establish facts. One of the differences which arise in practice between social psychology and sociology is that the social psychologist is always willing to dash back to the laboratory and see if some small-scale experiment can be used to check out an hypothesis which may sound interesting.

But as soon as you do this, you run into the whole set of problems about method. How can we know that the results we have obtained in the laboratory are applicable in any way to the real world outside? The next three chapters are all devoted to an examination of various aspects of this problem.

The first area we shall look at is apparently very simple, but contains some very interesting points on the way. In the journal articles which one consults in writing a book like this, or in writing an essay on a typical course in social psychology, one comes across tables of figures.

Your Feelings About Maths

Now it is a fact, checkable by empirical observation, that many of us, when we come to a table of figures, skip it, and go straight on to see what the author of the paper says about it. After all, we reason, he knows more of what the figures mean than we do – he must have checked them and been through them umpteen times, so what is the point of our bothering? In most cases this is a rationalization, hiding our real hostility to figures and mathematics, but it may still be worth exploding. It is not at all the case that the tables in research reports are unassailable. A statistician once went through a whole sheaf of reports and came up with the finding that most of them had elementary errors of calculation in them. An economist was reported recently as saying that he made a mistake in one of his fundamental formulae which lay undiscovered until he uncovered it himself twenty years later! So it is by no means useless to check whether the figures add up, whether they say what the author says they say, and so on.

But why is it that so many of us skip the tables? I think it is partly, at least, because we tend to hold certain stereotyped notions which are actually false, and I would like to try to spell these out:

1. Mathematics is a fixed body of knowledge which never changes.
2. Mathematics is mainly about calculation.
3. Calculation is very boring – and the answer is very likely to be wrong.
4. People who are good at calculation are very boring people.
5. So to be good at mathematics is to be boring.
6. I don't want to be boring or bored, do I?

What is wrong with these arguments, or with this train of thought? Let us look briefly at each of the points in turn.

1. One of the most soul-destroying things about the way in which mathematics is still taught in many schools is that it gives the impression that maths is just *there* in some way, and all one has to do is to learn it. But mathematics is really one of the freest and most imaginative subjects there is, and there are now a whole range of books which prove this, by Kasner & Newman,[1] Danzig,[2] Adler,[3] Bross,[4] Bell[5] and others. Discoveries are being made every day in mathematics, and there are stirring controversies which divide mathematicians into warring camps. Even in the strict area of small-group statistics, which mainly concern us, there have been a lot of changes in the past few years. So maths is actually a very open subject, in which discoveries are still to be made.

2. In my own voyage of discovery into the excitement of maths, one of the most inspiring statements I came across was this one by Whitehead[6] – 'Many mathematicians dislike all numerical computation and are not particularly expert at it.' What mathematicians are interested in is not calculation, but ideas. What a liberating thought this is! And once one has it, confirmation comes from every angle; Schrödinger[7] says – 'I do not refer to the mathematical difficulties,

which eventually are always trivial, but rather to the conceptual difficulties.' Here Schrödinger is meaning by the word 'mathematical' those things which have to do with actual calculations. Again the thought is that maths is about ideas. And Einstein[8] says:

> Fundamental ideas play the most essential role in forming a physical theory. Books on physics are full of complicated mathematical formulae. But thought and ideas, not formulae, are the beginning of every physical theory. The ideas must later take the mathematical form of a quantitative theory, to make possible the comparison with experiment.

So all this seems to add up to the fact that calculation is actually rather a minor part of maths, and that most of it is concerned with ideas.

3. It is probably true, for most of us most of the time, that calculation is boring. But looking at a table and evaluating it requires very little calculation, in most cases, as we shall see later – particularly if one knows how to approach it and how to gut it most efficiently. What one is looking for in a table is the truths which emerge from it, and these are never boring, if one is interested in the subject-matter at all. If you skip the tables and ignore the figures, you are at the mercy of the author, who may be trying to maintain his thesis at all costs. The figures are the evidence, and you are supposed to weigh the evidence yourself, not let some other person do it for you. And because it is easy to go wrong with calculations, you may very easily discover some error which throws doubt on what the author says.

4. It may or may not be true that people who are good at calculation are boring, but we can now see that this is more or less irrelevant anyway. We are now interested in the figures as a means to an end, not as an end in themselves. We are interested in the facts which underlie the figures. And we are interested in the facts because they are the evidence for or against an idea which is genuinely interesting to us. If the idea is not interesting, we shouldn't be reading the paper at all.

5. Seems to be false, or at any rate not closely tied up in any way with the truth.

6. May probably be true, but could be irrelevant.

So what I am trying to say is that some of these stereotypes are wrong, and some of them are irrelevant, when we are reading a paper in psychology.

It may not do much good to say this – in some cases real therapy may be needed – but one or two of the books mentioned many help in breaking down misconceptions.

From now on we shall be actually doing mathematics, and what I shall try to do is to explain each thing from the point of view of what use it is, and why one should bother to understand it. Some of the things are supposed to be very simple, and some of them are supposed to be very difficult, but in my experience most of these distinctions are false. 'Can I use it?' or 'How can I use it?' seem to me to be the relevant questions.

Percentages

First of all then, percentages. Percentages are used a lot in tables, and there are few books which tell you why percentages are used so much, and how to read a table which has percentages in it.

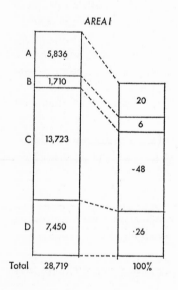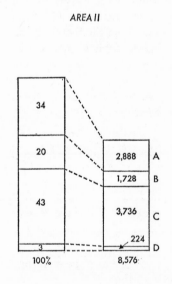

Fig. 5

The main point of percentages is to reduce uneven quantities to a common base. At first it seems as though the votes are much the same for Party B in the two areas, but the percentage is much higher in Area II, because it is a much smaller area.

It is much easier to compare the two columns in the middle than the two outer columns. What we have done is to take a common measure – the figure 100 – and shown the divisions of the areas as a proportion of that. If the areas were divided in half, the percentages would be fifty-fifty.

There is really no catch about percentages – no cunning points you have to remember. The only difficulty can sometimes arise if you forget what the figures are percentages *of*; this happens sometimes if you have a lot of different tables based on areas and sub-areas, or subgroups within areas. It would obviously be a mistake to find, say, that 10% *of students* were studying psychology, and then to say that 10% *of the whole population of the country* were studying psychology. But this is not often a problem.

Often, for clearer presentation, percentages are rounded, as they have been in the example above. A percentage calculation might come out at 37·736%, for example. This could be rounded to 37·74%, or 37·7%, or 38%, depending on the justifiable accuracy, or the purpose involved.

We shall be talking about justifiable accuracy later on. For the moment it is enough to point out that if we are using a ruler marked in tenths of an inch, we can't be accurate to a hundredth of an inch in any calculation based on such measurements. It would just not be realistic.

As far as the purpose involved is concerned, we may need a lot of digits after the decimal point if we are going to do further calculations based on the figures obtained; but for the final display of the results, it is much clearer to drop all decimal figures completely, and deal only with the integers. This is what happens automatically in most computer programs. There is a good discussion of all these questions in Zeisel,[9] a most helpful book.

Percentage Tables

Now let us look at a specimen percentage table, taken from Wallis & Roberts:[10]

TABLE 7

Age (years)	Percent Illiterate								
	White			Nonwhite			Both colours		
	Male	Female	Both	Male	Female	Both	Male	Female	Both
14 to 24	1·2	0·5	0·8	7·2	1·4	3·9	1·8	0·6	1·2
25 to 34	0·8	0·6	0·7	9·7	3·8	6·4	1·6	0·9	1·2
35 to 44	1·2	0·5	0·8	7·5	5·9	6·6	1·7	1·0	1·3
45 to 54	2·2	1·4	1·8	12·8	10·4	11·5	3·2	2·3	2·7
55 to 64	3·6	3·4	3·5	19·4	16·9	18·1	4·7	4·4	4·5
65 and over	5·6	4·4	5·0	35·8	31·2	33·3	7·6	6·2	6·9
All 14 and over	2·1	1·5	1·8	12·7	8·2	10·2	3·0	2·1	2·5

Now why should we be interested in this table? Well, race is an interesting subject, and this tells us how blacks compare with whites – or does it? 'Nonwhite' is a catch-all category which presumably includes Asians, Mexicans, Puerto Ricans and so on. Maybe there are problems as to which category quite large numbers of people belong to. Is a Cypriot white or nonwhite? Is an Arab white or nonwhite? Is an Israeli white or nonwhite? What about half-breeds, quadroons, octoroons, Creoles, and who was *your* great-grandfather? But it is obvious from the table that whoever nonwhites may be, they are in a minority, outnumbered about ten to one. (The exact proportion doesn't matter for the moment.) And also illiteracy is an interesting subject – one of the first things a revolutionary regime does is to have a literacy campaign so as to make it possible for everyone in the country to read and to criticize. People who can't read tend to be apathetic and accepting, waiting to be told what to do by those who are educated and know what to do. (Television may well be changing this picture, but it is too early to be sure.) So there should be some interest somewhere in this table, if we can only track it down. So how do we track things down in a table like this? There are ten operations which one should do; ten may sound like a lot, and the first time we do it properly, it is a lot, but if we do it several times, it soon comes quite naturally.

1. Read the title carefully
The title here is 'Illiteracy rates, by age, colour and sex, 1952' and
we know that it refers to the USA. So this tells us that it refers to a
particular country at a particular time, and it tells us what it is
about.

2. Read the headnote or other explanation carefully
In this case the headnote says – 'Based on a sample of about 25,000.
Persons unable both to read and to write in any language were
classified as illiterate, except that literacy was assumed for all who
had completed 6 or more years of school. Only the civilian, non-
institutional population 14 years and over is included.' We are not
told the type of sample it was, but we can probably assume that it is a
representative sample. It does not include those in the armed
forces, in hospitals, in prisons; does it include those in universities?
We do not know unless we can see what the definition of an institution is. The sample size looks large enough to make it sensible
to show figures to one decimal point, but it would be good to check
that there was no systematic bias in the way the sampling was
carried out.

3. Notice the source
Here the source is the U.S. Bureau of the Census, Current population reports, series p-20, No. 45, as summarized in the Statistical
Abstract for 1955, Table 132, p. 115. This tells us that the source is
large and has the resources to carry out a survey of this kind; it also
tells us that there could be some bias in the direction of Government
policies. If there were any such bias, it would be so well hidden that
we would be unlikely to discover it at this late date, though not
impossible. But let us assume that all is in order for the moment.

4. Look at the footnotes
In this case there are no footnotes, but these very often carry details
about the interpretation of any symbols which may appear in the
table, or any peculiarities which affect any of the cells. (A cell is any
point in the table where a figure could appear; some tables have one
or more empty cells.) The term 'cell' arose in the days when people
used to put neat lines up and down and from side to side.

5. *Find out what units are used*
This is most important, and is also very important when looking at graphs. It is possible to be very misled by not noticing what units are used. In the present case it is percentages, which makes it easy.

6. *Look at the overall average*
The overall average – in this case $2\frac{1}{2}\%$ – is the basic norm to which everything else can be compared. Any group which has an illiteracy rate of less than $2\frac{1}{2}\%$ is better than average, and any group which has a rate of more than $2\frac{1}{2}\%$ is worse than average. Now this is not an easy point to see when one first looks at the table, and it may take quite a bit of looking before one realizes that the lowest line represents the whole population, and that the right-hand column also represents the whole population, so that the cell where they join must be the percentage of illiteracy for the whole population. This must, then, represent the average of all the subgroups in the population, since the whole population is made up of all the subgroups put together. So this 2·5% is, as it were, the centre of gravity of the population – any deviation on one side of it must be made up by an equal deviation on the other side. It is the population mean, and a very useful thing to have at the back of one's mind when considering the meaning of any of the individual figures. All the time it is the *meaning* of the figures which we are trying to extract.

7. *See what variability there is*
The next thing is to get a feeling for how big a swing there is between the highest and the lowest figures. In this case, the lowest figure is 0·5%, and the highest is 35·8%. The former figure refers to young white girls, and the latter to old nonwhite men. This immediately tells us that we are looking at something very big; these are not just tiny variations which can safely be ignored, but huge and very marked differences. Something important and interesting is going on here.

8. *Check the main breakdowns against the overall mean*
A breakdown is any classification used to make a distinct set of columns in the table. The title told us that there were three breakdowns – age, colour and sex. We find that illiteracy rates are higher for nonwhites, for males and for older people. To get this informa-

tion, we compare the figures for the whole white group (1·8%) with those for the whole nonwhite group (10·2%); for all males (3·0%) as against all females (2·1%); and for all younger people as against all older people – here we cannot quote any specific percentages, but merely note that there is a consistent age gradient in the last column. If we wished, we could compare the youngest age group with all the others, or the under-45s with the over-45s, or whatever, but to do this we would have to recalculate the percentages.

9. Examine the consistency of the effects and the interactions among them
Here is where we really start looking into the details of the figures. One of the first things you may have noticed in the previous paragraph was that the sex difference seemed to be much smaller than the other two. But do note that it is completely consistent – every single comparison between the sexes goes the same way. So although it is relatively small, it is highly meaningful and reliable. Now going further, see how the excess of the male over the female rate is higher for nonwhites than for whites, particularly in the younger age groups.

The increases in illiteracy associated with increases in age are greater for nonwhites than for whites.

The difference between the colours is larger for males than for females.

These are all different ways of saying something meaningful based on the figures in the table. What is obvious is that something has been going on which has prevented the older nonwhites – or some majority group within them – from getting a proper education. There has been some improvement in the youngest age group, so far as the girls are concerned, but hardly any for the men. There is something very wrong here, and we can see from the events of the 1960s that these particular pigeons did in fact come home to roost.

10. Finally, look for things you weren't looking for – aberrations, anomalies or irregularities
This takes even more familiarity with the table, and maybe with the underlying facts as well. One which might be worth looking into here is the unexpectedly high figure for white male illiteracy between 14 and 24.

So these are the ten steps to take with a table. As we have seen, they do eventually reveal quite a lot – more than one might think from a quick look at the mass of figures originally presented. And this is a skill which can be very easily learned.

It is interesting that you have now learned also what a contingency table is. A contingency table is any table with breakdowns.

Graphs

Now let us look at another frequently-used method of presenting results – the graph.

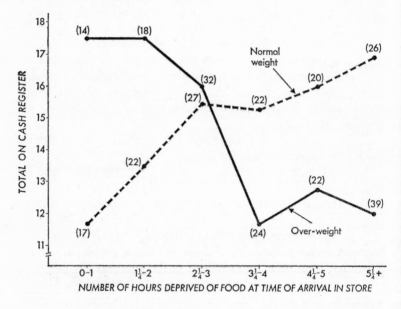

Fig. 6

This is an interesting graph derived from some research[11] done on obese people. What does it show?

First, the title is 'Total on cash register as a function of degree of food deprivation.'

Second, there is no headnote, but we can supply the information that this was based on data collected in a New Haven supermarket from 9·00 to 18·00 on a single day. The population which the supermarket serves is predominantly working-class, and the largest single group in a diverse community is Italian-American. Four-fifths of the sample were women, with ages around the 45 mark. The designation 'Overweight' is derived from an observer's esti-mate, based on the criterion that the person would look better if he or she lost 15 pounds or so. The time since the last meal was derived from a question – 'When did you last have something to eat?'

Third, the source is a paper by R. E. Nisbett & D. E. Kanouse, printed in the **Journal of Personality and Social Psychology** in August 1969. It follows up a whole series of papers published in the same journal in October 1968, stemming from some research started by Stanley Schachter at Columbia, all of which went to show that obese people (defined as those who were 15% or more overweight) tended to need external cues before they felt hungry, whereas normal and underweight people tended to go by internal cues. So this is a reliable source: journals like this do not print papers unless they have passed the scrutiny of one or two referees looking for errors, vagueness, and so on. This does not mean that the papers are infallible – far from it – but it does mean that they cannot be dis-missed without some due consideration.

Fourth, the footnote says that the numbers in brackets denote *n*. This means that each dot on the graph is the result of a certain number of observations, in this case a certain number of people interviewed. We always use the letter *n* to mean the sample size in a piece of research. So the total number of overweight people inter-viewed was 149, and the total number of normal (that is, non-overweight) people was 134. This seems to be rather a high propor-tion of overweight people, but the researchers say that this would be expected from the known statistics of that particular population.

Fifth, the units used in a graph are normally two in number. There is one set of units for the vertical axis, and another for the horizontal axis. They are called axes, although on most graphs it is hard to see why; this is because most graphs only show the top right-hand corner of a space which can carry on below and to the left. The full graph would look like this:

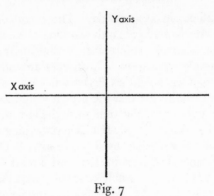

Fig. 7

It is now also clearer why the horizontal axis is usually called the X axis, and the vertical one the Y axis – we actually come to the X before the Y, if we go from left to right across the page as usual. Let us look at each axis in turn.

The X axis (also called the abscissa) usually contains the units which represent the causal element in the process under consideration. In the language of the behaviorist, it deals with the independent variable. It often represents something which is earlier in time, or more fundamental or fixed in some way. Since a base is usually flat, we can think of it as telling us about what is more basic.

The Y axis (also called the ordinate) usually contains the units which express the effect, or the dependent variable. We usually have some hypothesis in mind which tells us that we expect Y to vary in some way, as X changes. It is the X which makes the Y change, and not the other way round. This is by no means invariable, but it is customary.

So in this case the X axis tells us the number of hours since the subjects last ate. You will see that we do not have a continuous distribution, minute by minute, but that the researchers have split up the time into six sections of an hour each, with the exception of the last time span, which is open-ended. The labelling is a little curious (what happens to a person who says he last ate 2 hours and 5 minutes ago?) but we can assume that the subjects interviewed were only accurate to the nearest quarter of an hour; still, it must make some difference to the results what decision was taken about these intermediate times. We can see that those interviewed had mostly not eaten for some time; 31 less than an hour ago, 40 between one and two hours ago, 59 two to three hours before, 46 three to four hours ago, 42 four to five hours ago, and 65 more than five hours before.

The Y axis, on the other hand, deals with the variable we are looking at to see how it varies. The hypothesis we are testing says that as hours of food deprivation increase, normal people buy more food, because they are starting to feel hungry, and this sensitizes them to food cues. But obese people should not buy any more food, because they do not have these internal signals telling them that they are hungry. So the Y axis represents a variable which is directly related to the amount of food purchased – the number of dollars on the cash register when they leave the supermarket. Note that because all the amounts spent were between 11 and 18 dollars, the lower amounts of dollars are simply cut out and not shown. To indicate that this has been done, a double cut is inserted; another method is to show a zigzag line where the missing piece would be. This is an important bit of honesty; it is always more dramatic visually when only the bit is shown where something is going on, and it can be very misleading. Some good examples are given in the Moroney[12] book.

Sixth (this is equivalent to 6, 7 and 8 in the case of a table) see how the results relate to the hypothesis. Is it true that normal people spend more, if they have not had food for a longer time? The answer is yes. If they had recently eaten, they only spent about eleven dollars, on average; but if they had eaten more than five hours previously, they spent nearer seventeen dollars. This result is statistically significant – we shall say more about what this means later in this chapter.

And is it true that this does *not* hold for obese people? Yes, again. In fact – and this is surprising – the relationship goes the opposite way; we should have expected a straight line across the graph. And this may lead to further research, designed to find out why this might have happened.

Seventh, try to find anything odd about the results. We have already seen one – the downward line for the overweight shoppers. Such surprises often give the impetus to further research – often a simple replication will give the answer.

So this is how to read a graph. As with the table, it takes a long time when one first does it, but becomes simpler and simpler with practice; and as with the table, it is important to examine it critically. In fact, it is even more important than with a table, because in our daily lives we are surrounded by lying graphs, more often than lying tables.

Probability and Correlation

Having looked at graphs, let us now look at the idea of probabilities and correlations.

Percentages	1	5	25	33	50	67	75
Probabilities	·01	·05	·25	·33	·50	·67	·75

As you see, probabilities are exactly the same sort of thing as percentages, but out of 1 instead of out of 100.

Now for correlations. If we want to see whether two variables are associated, we can plot out all the observations on a scatter diagram. Let us imagine we get a hundred people, and for each one measure his or her height and weight. We might lay out height on the X axis, and weight on the Y axis, since it is usually true that the taller you grow the heavier you weigh, but not always true that the heavier you get the taller you grow. It doesn't really matter too much in this case. What we find if we then fill in a spot for each individual, showing his height and weight at the same time, is that the spots form a definite pattern:

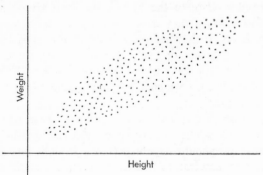

Fig. 8

And we should find a similar pattern for such things as the following, all fairly highly correlated:

INTELLIGENCE................ACHIEVEMENT
LACK OF OPEN SPACES.........ACCIDENTS TO CHILDREN
LENGTH OF SPRING............WEIGHT OF LOAD ON SPRING
SPEED OF PRODUCTION.........AMOUNT WASTED
SELF-UNDERSTANDING.........FREEDOM FROM DELINQUENCY

Usually one would not show a scatter diagram in a piece of published research, but would use it in one's preliminary work in order to see if a particular idea looked promising, before working it out properly. An unsuccessful idea would be revealed by a scatter diagram which looked rather like a plum pudding.

Now supposing our dots looked promising, and we wanted to work out the actual correlation between the two variables, as they operated in our sample. The details of exactly what to do are to be found very well and helpfully described in a book by Connolly and Sluckin,[13] and we do not intend to copy them here.

But suppose we get the result that the correlation is $r = 0.2$, or $r = 0.5$, or $r = 0.8$? Is this good, or bad, or indifferent? What does the figure mean, when we have got it? One tends at first to get the wrong end of the stick, and assume that anything above 0.5 is good. But in reality, all we have to do is to square the correlation, and regard the answer as a probability, and this also gives us the percentage of the variance which is accounted for. Look at these equivalents:

TABLE 8

Correlation Coefficient	Square to get probability	Percent variance accounted for	Angle of Cos θ
·00	·00	0	90°
·26	·07	6·7	75°
·50	·25	25·0	60°
·71	·50	50·0	45°
·87	·75	75·0	30°
·97	·93	93·3	15°

The last column represents Cos θ, and leads on to the idea of the cosine model which underlies factor analysis. Factor analysis is an important technique, entirely based upon the idea of correlations, as Diamond[14] explains very well.

Going back to our three examples in the paragraph above, a correlation of $r = 0.2$ would only account for 4% of the variation in Y which we want to explain, so that would be of little practical use. A correlation of $r = 0.5$ would account for 25% of the variance, which is a good deal better, but still leaves a great deal out of account. But a correlation of $r = 0.8$ would account for 64% of the common variance, and so would be very convincing and meaningful, unless the sample were small or biased. Nothing means very much if the sample is poor. Data can only be as good as the original observations.

The important thing is never to confuse correlation coefficients with probabilities. If you look at the first two columns above, you will see the difference very clearly.

If you are actually doing research, as opposed to merely appreciating it, it is useful to know about some very much simpler measures of association than the correlation. There are many such measures, usually called coefficients of association or similarity indices. They tell us which of several perhaps rather confusing sets of figures is the most consistent and meaningful.

Association or Similarity

In order to look at this question of association, let us take as our example a fourfold table. This will then lead naturally into a discussion of the question of significance and significance tests. A fourfold table is the basic form of contingency table, with just two rows and two columns. It is often arranged so that the two rows represent high and low, in terms of some quality, and the two columns represent high and low, in terms of some other quality – one can then see how the two qualities are associated. At other times, it may be arranged as two nominal scales, as we saw in the chapter on attitude measurement. Here is an example from an interesting series of experiments carried out by Maier & Burke[15] on the problem-solving performance of males and females. The problem was: 'A man bought a horse for £60 and sold it again for £70. Then he bought it back again for £80 and sold it for £90. How much money did he make in the horse business?' (The original problem was in dollars, of course.) Here is the table from the first experiment.

TABLE 9

	Males	Females	Total
£10 Profit or worse	42	60	102
£20 Profit or better	45	26	71
Total	87	86	173

You can see why this is called a fourfold table. There are four basic numbers in it – the others are merely marginal totals. We can put letters for each of the cells in this table, as follows, simply to give them names.

a	b	a+b
c	d	c+d
a+c	b+d	N

So the four basic numbers we have now named a, b, c and d. Now one of the simplest and best coefficients of association is called Yule's Q, which is calculated as follows:

$$Q = \frac{ad - bc}{ad + bc}$$

Why should we want to go through all this rigmarole? The answer is that we often want to compare two sets of figures, and this is very difficult to do unless we can simplify them down to one comparison. In the present case, Maier & Burke did a second experiment, where for each of the possible answers (lost £10, broke even, made £10, made £20 and made £30) a plausible set of reasons was given. This time they got this result:

TABLE 10

	Males	Females	Total
£10 Profit of worse	13	52	65
£20 Profit or better	30	31	61
Total	43	83	126

Now you may see the point. Is this a more dramatic or interesting result than the other one, or is it about the same, or how does it differ from it?

In the first experiment, 1092 − 2700 is equal to − 1608, and 1092 + 2700 is equal to +3792. If we divide the former by the latter, the result is − 0·42 rounded to the nearest hundredth. Now Yule's Q varies between zero and one, or between zero and minus one, in somewhat the same way as a correlation coefficient, so the figure of 42 is quite a substantial one; something is definitely going on here, and men are reacting differently from women to this problem. The minus sign simply means that the direction of the difference is not towards the males saying more '£10 profit or worse' but rather the other way.

If we perform the same operation on the second table, we get $403 - 1560 = -1157$ and then $403 + 1560 = +1963$, from which we obtain $-0·59$ as our final result.

What has happened, therefore, is that the second experiment has produced a more impressive result than the first. Or to put it the other way round, providing the set of reasons increased the difference between the male performance and the female performance on this particular test, if we look at the results in this particular way.

This was an interesting series of experiments, and Maier & Burke tried out various hypotheses – are women more prone to jump to conclusions, and is that why they get the right answer (£20) less often than the men? (No.) Is it because they have a strong preference for the answer 'broke even'? (Yes.) Does this preference come out in relation to other problems, too? (Yes.) Does it disappear when the problem is about a woman's problems, rather than a man's? (No.) The researchers' comments are:

> Our impression is that women are more conservative and protective. Taking chances on winning or losing are aggressive acts and these usually are associated with male personalities. Exploration of the literature supports these impressions. It has been shown that females are less aggressive, more conforming, and less willing to take extreme risks in gambling situations than males.
>
> Whether these differences in the personality traits of males and females are genetically or culturally determined remains unanswered.

(The original paper gives the appropriate references to the literature.)

So again, there is something interesting here to explore. But how do we establish what the figures are telling us? How do we decide when the pattern is so compelling that we must believe that something is genuinely going on, and when the figures look good, but could have arisen through chance variation? This is the question of significance.

Significance Testing

If an association between two variables seems to exist, we have to have some way of deciding whether it is there as a real finding of research, or whether it could have arisen just as easily by chance. Please look back at Table 9 again.

You will see that the males and females are about equal in numbers – one more male, in fact. Now if pure chance were operating, and there were no other relevant difference between men and women, the first of the marginal figures on the right-hand side of the table, that is, 102, also ought to be split more or less equally between the two; and the figure of 71 in the same way. Let us now write in the new figures we would obtain by doing this, and see what the table would look like.

Old	42	60	New	51	51
	45	26		36	35
	(Actual)			(Expected)	

We call these figures 'expected' because they represent what we would expect from the marginal totals alone, if no bias of any kind were operating. If there were no differences between men and women in the way they solved problems, then it is the second group of figures which we would expect to appear.

What many people find difficult to understand about this is why we should bring in the idea of chance at all. If there are equal numbers of men and women, *of course* we should expect all the totals in the table to divide equally, if there is no difference between men and women! That is what we *mean* by saying 'no difference between them'!

In fact, the reason why we bring in the idea of chance is because statistics has always been the province of statisticians, and the mind of a statistician seems obsessed by the tossing of coins and the throwing of dice. So when a statistician is explaining anything, he always does it by referring to fair coins and fair dice, as though we all spent our lives in the casino. And the mathematics often gets very complicated very quickly, so that the moment when the statistician really gets into his element is also the very moment when ordinary people get turned off.

Our approach here is much simpler. We simply want to point out that you must have some idea of what you would expect if there were no difference, in order to start working out how much of a difference there is.

In the kind of fourfold table we are looking at now, the difference between the actual and the expected figure is always the same for each cell in the table – in this case, 9. Can you see why it must always be the same? The reason is important, because it explains the basic idea of degrees of freedom.

The reason is that, if the marginal totals are fixed, which they are, altering any one figure makes all the other three figures change, too, if the totals are still to agree. We say, then, that a fourfold table only has one degree of freedom, because only one cell can change freely – the others are all fully determined by any such change. We shall see why we want to know this in a moment.

Now one very useful formula for testing significance is called the χ^2 (chi-squared) test. We square each of the four differences, divide each one by its own 'expected' figure, and add the results together:

$$\frac{81}{51} + \frac{81}{51} + \frac{81}{36} + \frac{81}{35} = 1\cdot59 + 1\cdot59 + 2\cdot25 + 2\cdot31 = 7\cdot74$$

This result, of 7·74, we then look up in a table of chi-square values – to be found in books of statistical tables – under the heading 'one degree of freedom', where we find that $p < \cdot01$. This means that such a result as we have found in the tables would only be likely to arise by chance less than 1% of the time, or once in a hundred times. In other words, there is a hundred-to-one probability that our results are meaningful, and point to some underlying reality. These are pretty good odds – anything better than 20-to-1 (the $p < \cdot05$ level) is considered significant – and we may then start searching for reasons, explanations, etc.

Let us try the same thing on Table 10.

Old	13	52	New	22	43
	(actual)				(expected)
	30	31		21	40

In this table the numbers of men and women are not equal, so we have to divide the marginal totals in the right proportion: there are almost twice as many women as men, so on each line there must be almost twice as many women as men. If you need a formula, in terms of our diagram on page 165, the new d (the d in the 'expected' table) is equal to:

$$\frac{c + d}{N} \times (b + d)$$

This is a very easy formula to work out on a slide rule. You only have to set it once, and just read off the answer.

So we now have our actual and expected figures for each cell, and the difference is again 9. This is just a coincidence, and no importance should be attached to it. Working out chi-squared, we now get the following:

$$\frac{81}{22} + \frac{81}{43} + \frac{81}{21} + \frac{81}{40} = 3.70 + 1.88 + 3.85 + 2.02 = 11.45$$

And if we look up this result in the tables, we find this time that $p < .001$. This means that this time there is a thousand-to-one chance that our results are not significant, or that the odds are a thousand to one in our favour, if we say that the experiment means something. This checks out with the earlier result we got with Yule's Q, which also showed that the second experiment was more dramatic than the first. We would expect any other coefficient of association or test of significance to show the same thing.

Now we went a bit fast over all that, so that the main lines would show through clearly, so now let us go back and pick up a few points.

First of all, why the chi-square test? There are two main reasons for choosing this: first, it is a very simple test to carry out, not needing long or complicated calculations, and there are good explanations of how to do it in Connolly & Sluckin[13] and in Siegel[16] and in various other texts; second, it is a non-parametric test, which means that it does not make any assumptions about the underlying distributions of the figures involved. It is therefore of more general use than a test which requires a normal distribution in order to be valid.

It is important to realize that no test can be applied purely mechanically – one still needs to apply common sense to the figures, too. If there is reason to believe that the samples (of men and women in this case) were chosen in a biased way, which would twist the evidence to suit the experimenter's purpose, no amount of statistical manipulation is going to make the figures mean anything worthwhile. It is for this reason that every decent scientific paper states very carefully how the sample was chosen. And it has been shown, as we have seen in earlier chapters, that samples can be chosen very badly.

What about the p-values? What do they mean, exactly? The p

stands for probability, and means the probability that the observed result could have arisen by chance. We have already seen the way in which probabilities and percentages can be interchanged, and the conventional level of significance is sometimes called the 'five percent level' and sometimes 'the point oh five level'; the conventional *high* level of significance is the one percent level, or the point oh one level; and the conventional *very high* level of significance is the point oh oh one level – it is very rarely called the 'point oh one percent level', probably because of the confusion which this might create!

These conventions have been challenged throughout the fifties and sixties, but they still hang on in the practice of most researchers.

What seems to have been agreed, however, is that it is better to report the actual p value than simply to say 'significant' or 'not significant'.

So this, then, is the basic idea of testing for significance. We can now go on to see how the ideas of association, correlation and significance all come together in the Pearson correlation coefficient r.

The Significance of Correlations

Having become fairly familiar with our two fourfold tables, let us now use them to go further into the idea of a correlation. One of the problems with correlations is that it is easy to assume that a high correlation means something – and this is usually correct – when actually the meaningfulness of a correlation depends very much on the size of the sample from which the figures came.

For example, Sears, Maccoby & Levin[17] report the correlation between an accepting tolerant attitude towards the child's dependent behaviour and being warm towards the child as $r = \cdot 37$: now this is not particularly high, but because it is based on a sample size of 379 (usually expressed as $n = 379$) it is statistically significant at better than the $\cdot 001$ level. But on the other hand Rokeach[18] reports the correlation between Authoritarianism and Ethnocentrism as $r = \cdot 46$: this is higher, but because it is based on a sample size of 10 ($n = 10$) it is not statistically significant even at the ten percent level.

So two morals emerge from this. One, that you need to look at the significance of a correlation before you get too impressed by it; and two, that it is dangerous to work with samples which are too low.

So let's calculate the correlation coefficients for our two tables, and see whether they are significant or not. We go in expecting that they will be significant, in both cases, and that the second table will achieve higher significance than the first one. And we know that what significance means is that women differ from men in the way in which they approach certain problems.

The product-moment correlation coefficient was invented by Karl Pearson, in order to satisfy his friend Francis Galton. For the purposes of our fourfold tables, and in the terms we have been using to name the four cells involved, the formula looks like this:

$$r = \frac{ad - bc}{\sqrt{(a+c)\,(b+d)\,(a+b)\,(c+d)}}$$

You can see that we take the products of the two diagonals, and subtract one from the other, and then divide the result by the square root of the product of all the marginal totals multiplied together.

If we do this for Table 9, we get:

$r = (42 \times 26) - (45 \times 60)$ divided by $\sqrt{87 \times 86 \times 102 \times 71}$
$= -1608$ (we worked that out before for Yule's Q, remember?)
          divided by 7378 (approximately on my slide rule)
$= - \cdot 22$

Remember that the minus sign merely means that it is a negative correlation between a man and saying '£10 profit or worse'. It is the size of the actual figure which tells us whether the correlation is significant or not. How to do this? The method is very simple for us now, after the discussion of the χ^2 test which we had earlier. The formula is:

$$\chi^2 = nr^2 \ (1 \ df)$$

So all we have to do is to multiply the correlation coefficient by itself, multiply the result by the sample size, and then look up the answer in the chi-square table under one degree of freedom. The square of $\cdot 22$ is $\cdot 05$ (actually $\cdot 0484$) and n is 173, so the product of the two is 7·97. When we look up this value in the table, we find $p < \cdot 005$, which is certainly significant.

This is a very simple method for finding out the significance of a correlation coefficient, and it takes very little time or calculation. It is not infallible, and if you go into statistics deeply you may come to be dissatisfied with it, but as a useful rule of thumb it has great value. As you can see, it does confirm what we have found previously. Let us just check Table 10 and see what we find there.

This time we find that $r = -\cdot31$, and if we apply the formula for testing significance, we find that the chi-squared value is $12\cdot11$, which at one degree of freedom is better than the $\cdot001$ level of significance. So again we have found that the second experiment produced more impressive results than the first.

You are now in a position to check any correlation you come across for yourself, if you only know the sample size.

The Importance of Statistics

In this chapter, I have tried to tell you about those things which I have found most useful myself, in reading psychological books and papers. I have not gone into the minutiae, but have stayed with the obvious and the easy. In my experience it is the obvious which is never explained properly in textbooks, and so one is always coming across things which are mystifying in some way.

Also I have tried to keep to the simple and the defensible because much of the more advanced mathematics sometimes used in psychology sometimes seems to me unnecessarily complex and indefensible. Sorokin[19] in his excellent Chapter 8 has some deep criticisms of the over-mathematical approach which can be found in sociology, psychology and worst of all in economics. He quotes Comte as saying:

> A very absurd proposition may be very precise, for example, $2 + 2 = 7$ ... and a very certain proposition may be wanting in precision in our statement of it as, for instance, when we assert that every man will die

This is an essential point, and the whole chapter is full of other points worth considering. We must never assume that statistics, or any other form of mathematics, are sufficient in themselves to guarantee that we are doing good psychology.

There is a false idea of objectivity, which says that the more remote we get from our subject-matter, and the more we remove our own subjective views from the field, the more scientific we shall be. This has been pretty thoroughly exploded in recent years, particularly by sociologists of the phenomenological school. But sometimes the criticism has gone too far, and denied the usefulness of the statistical approach at all. The best defence of statistics I know comes from Carl Rogers,[20] who can hardly be regarded as out of touch with real human beings and the way in which their actions emerge from their intentions:

> The scientist has then creatively achieved his hypothesis, his tentative faith. But does it check with reality? Experience has shown each one of us that it is very easy to deceive ourselves, to believe something which later experience shows is not so. How can I tell whether this tentative belief has some real relationship to observed facts? I can use, not one line of evidence only, but several. I can surround my observation of the facts with various precautions to make sure I am not deceiving myself. I can consult with others who have also been concerned with avoiding self-deception, and learn useful ways of catching myself in unwarranted beliefs, based on misinterpretation of observations. I can, in short, begin to use all the elaborate methodology which science has accumulated. I discover that stating my hypothesis in operational terms will avoid many blind alleys and false conclusions. I learn that control groups can help me to avoid drawing false conclusions. I learn that correlations, and t-tests and critical ratios and a whole array of statistical procedures can likewise aid me in drawing only reasonable inferences.
>
> Thus scientific methodology is seen for what it truly is – a way of preventing me from deceiving myself in regard to my creatively formed subjective hunches which have developed out of the relationship between me and my material. It is in this context, and perhaps only in this context, that the vast structure of operationism, logical positivism, research design, tests of significance, etc., have their place. They exist, not for themselves, but as servants in the attempt to check the subjective feeling or hunch or hypothesis of a person with the objective fact.

In the next chapter we shall see how we actually go about doing this when we come to looking at other people's experiments or setting up our own.

REFERENCES

1. D. Kasner & E. H. Newman, Mathematics and the imagination, Penguin 1968
2. F. Danzig. Number – The language of science, Allen & Unwin 1962
3. I. Adler. The new mathematics, Dobson 1964
4. I. D. J. Bross. Design for decision, Collier-Macmillan 1965
5. E. T. Bell. Mathematics – Queen and servant of the sciences, G. Bell 1952
6. A. N. Whitehead. Introduction to mathematics, Hutchinson University Library 1911

7. E. Schrodinger. Science and the human temperament, 1935
8. A. Einstein & K. Infeld. The evolution of physics, 1938
9. H. Zeisel. Say it with figures, Routledge 1958
10. W. A. Wallis & H. V. Roberts. Statistics: A new approach, Methuen 1967
11. R. E. Nisbett & D. A. Kanouse. Obesity, food deprivation and supermarket shopping behaviour, J. Pers. soc. Psychol. 12, 1969
12. M. J. Moroney. Facts from figures (Third edition) Penguin 1956
13. T. G. Connolly & W. Sluckin. An introduction to statistics for the social sciences (Second edition), Cleaver-Hume 1957
14. S. Diamond. Information and error, Basic Books 1959
15. N. R. F. Maier & R. J. Burke. Response availability as a factor in the problem-solving performance of males and females, J. Pers. soc. Psychol. 5, 1967
16. S. Siegel. Nonparametric statistics for the behavioral sciences, McGraw-Hill 1956
17. R. Sears, E. Maccoby & H. Levin. Patterns of child rearing, Harper & Row 1957
18. M. Rokeach. The open and closed mind, Basic Books 1970
19. P. Sorokin. Fads and foibles in modern sociology, Henry Regnery 1956
20. C. R. Rogers. On becoming a person, Constable 1961 (Chapter 10)

CHAPTER ELEVEN

Experimental Design and Social Surveys

In this book we are still interested in the science game, as we said in the first chapter. And if this is the game we are playing, we must know all the ins and outs of hypothesis-checking – because this is the name of the game.

We have already seen that one of the main tools we use in this

---

Box 1   EFFECTIVENESS OF BCG VACCINATION

Each of a group of physicians was assigned a group of children from tubercular families and told to vaccinate half of them with a vaccine called 'BCG'. The following table records the TB deaths which occurred in the subsequent six-year period, from December 1926 to December 1932.

	CASES	TB DEATHS	PER CENT
VACCINATED	445	3	0·67
CONTROLS	545	18	3·30

Analysis of these data suggests that the difference in observed death rates is more than would be expected by chance. We cannot, however, attribute the difference to the effect of BCG because the groups were not randomly formed – the doctors' choice of children to vaccinate probably tended to favour children in families where the consent of parents was easy to obtain, and these children were probably less prone than others to tuberculosis.

A second experiment was then designed in which the doctors were told to vaccinate every other child – this is not strict randomization, but an improvement over the first study. After eleven more years the following results were available:

	CASES	TB DEATHS	PER CENT
VACCINATED	556	8	1·44
CONTROLS	528	8	1·52

This difference could easily be accounted for by chance alone: hence there is no evidence that BCG did any good.

---

endeavour is the test of significance – are we kidding ourselves, or have we really got something worth pursuing? So one of the prior requirements for this is to maximize our chances of getting figures which will be significant and meaningful. We do this by using good experimental research designs.

Now what is meant by a good design? Let us get into this by looking at an example (page 175), taken from Wallis & Roberts:[1]

In this example the word 'randomization' is used, and takes up an important role in the argument. What does it mean, and why is it important?

Chance, Randomization and the Null Hypothesis

Let us make it clear what we are concerned with here. We are concerned with getting the data properly. If the data is not 'clean', we just can't tell what our results mean, because they contain so many things all going on at the same time. And randomization is a way of getting clean data.

For example, rather than allocating every other child to the experimental condition (vaccine) it would have been better to toss a coin, so that when it came up heads the child got the vaccine, and when it came up tails he or she did not. Or, what would come to the same thing, we could have looked up a table of random numbers, and allocated consecutive numbers in the table to each child, vaccinating it when the number was even, and not when the number was odd. There is something mysterious about the way in which this works. As Berelson & Steiner say:[2]

> It is sometimes hard to believe, but it is still true, that when a group has been divided at random into two groups, the groups will differ by no more than chance on *any* characteristic whatever. The proportion of blue-eyed people in the two groups, of redheads, of people under and over 5 feet 7 inches, of Catholics, of those who skipped breakfast this morning, of those opposed to capital punishment or in favour of a stronger United Nations – all will be roughly equivalent. There are statistical procedures that determine the probability of a given difference having arisen simply by such random division. Therefore, when a difference is greater than that which could reasonably be expected on the basis of random division, and the groups have in fact been randomly divided, the conclusion is not due to their division but to something that happened to them afterwards.

This is a much clearer statement than books on experimentation usually permit themselves, and it gives us the essential clue as to why randomization is found to be so important in experimentation.

There is one point which Campbell & Stanley[3] make very well, however, which is important to keep in mind. That is, that randomization only gives us the right to generalize to the universe from which the sample was taken. For example, suppose 250 students are enrolled in a particular course, and the professor wants to do an experiment needing 100 subjects. He would draw the 100 at random, and then assign them randomly to the two (or whatever) experimental conditions:

> And even if he doggedly gets all 100, from the point of view of representativeness, what he has gained is the ability to generalize with statistical confidence to the 1961 class of Educational Psychology A at State Teachers.

So with the children in the earlier experiment, we should not say that *all* children are unaffected by BCG, but that all the children in that particular catchment area are. We would now have a strong hypothesis, however, which could be tested in another area with great precision. The hypothesis we would have is that there is *no* effect of immunization; and this is a very common hypothesis to have – so common that it has received a name: the null hypothesis.

Obviously the ideas of chance, of randomness and of the null hypothesis are all closely interrelated. Let us look at an example taken from Diamond[4] where he takes even and odd numbers in a table of random numbers as equivalent to heads and tails. We know from any text on probability that if we throw coins a number of times, the pattern of heads and tails conforms to the binomial expansion: so what we are looking at is the extent to which the actual pattern we get also conforms to it.

We count the number of even digits in a series of 5 consecutive digits in the random table. This was done for 320 groups of 5 digits each, representing in all the equivalent of 1600 tosses completed without a bit of grime, with the following results:

	Number of 'heads' in each group of 5 'tosses'					
	0	1	2	3	4	5
Observed	7	47	115	95	47	9
Expected	10	50	100	100	50	10

Here the expected figures are derived from the laws of chance, in the way which Tippett[5] explains so beautifully. So the observed figures are all departures from chance. But are they systematic departures, such as might arise from a bias in the tables (or in the coin, if we were using a coin) or are they randomly distributed, in the sort of way we might expect in any sample of that size?

In order to check the null hypothesis – that there is no systematic departure from what would be expected by chance – all we need to do is to use our chi-square principle from the previous chapter. We square the difference between each pair of figures, and divide the result by the expected figure, as follows:

TABLE II

Goodness of fit in a Monte Carlo experiment, where each observation records the number of 'heads' in a group of five

'Heads'	Observed	Expected	Chi-Square value
5	9	10	·10
4	47	50	·18
3	95	100	·25
2	115	100	2·25
1	47	50	·18
0	7	10	·90
Total	320	320	3·86

So the total chi-squared value is 3·86. Now when we look this up in the table, we have to look it up under the heading of 5 degrees of freedom; we only have one marginal total, instead of the four we had before, and so only the sixth figure is totally determined – the other five are all free to move. And when we look under five degrees of freedom, we find that the result is far from being significant – it is in fact more likely than not to have arisen by chance! Which is what we had anticipated. The null hypothesis is, in fact, upheld. Even the seemingly large departure represented by getting two heads 115 times, instead of 100 times as expected, is only within the normal range of variation.

It is in this sort of way that we can start to chart the relations between randomness, chance, the null hypothesis, the significant difference, goodness of fit and so on.

Proper Designs and Valid Conclusions

All research can be looked on as a battle with the null hypothesis. In the old textbooks on experimental method, it used to be said that we do this by varying one thing at a time, and holding everything else constant. This would be a fine idea if it could be done, but it hardly ever can, and in any case we have a lot of other better ideas now. The first of these, randomization, we have already looked at. The second, the ideas of analysis of variance, we shall look at soon. But first it may be as well to eliminate two other old ideas which still hang on in practice, if not in the literature – though to be sure, they are often found in textbooks still.

The first of these two ideas we want to look at is *matching*. The concept of matching is that in order to get a good control sample, to match our experimental sample, we make sure that they do not differ on certain important characteristics. What these characteristics are, will vary from case to case. With the children in our original example, we might know, from earlier research, that living in one room was associated with tuberculosis, and we might then make sure in some way that just as many of the children who were vaccinated came from families living in one room, as those who were not vaccinated. Now if we really did know that there was such a close association, this might be a very plausible procedure.

But it would be wrong, because we would be making an implicit assumption that other characteristics of the children were not more important than the one on which we have matched them. Yet how can we know this? Campbell & Stanley have a good discussion of this whole area.

They also have much to say about the other idea we want to throw doubt on – the idea of pre and post testing. Again, this seems so obviously a good idea that it has seduced several generations of experimenters. In order to see whether an experimental intervention has the predicted effect, one tests the subjects before and after the intervention. If one is conscientious, one has a control group, and assigns subjects to the experimental and to the control group at random. Both are given the pretest, one only is given the experimental treatment, and then both are post tested. What could be better?

Simply that we don't need the pre test at all. If randomization works in the way in which we have said it does, we know already that the two groups must be comparable; so all we need to do is to give one of them the treatment, and the other not, and then test both of them afterwards.

This design was used as long ago as the 1920s, but it has not been recommended in most current textbooks. This has been due in part to a confusion of it with a non-randomized design, and in part to distrust of randomization as a way of equating two or more groups. But it is actually easier and cheaper, and just as effective for most purposes.

So these are two shibboleths we can happily abandon, and make life easier for ourselves, if we happen to be researchers. And even if we are not, it is essential in social psychology to put oneself in the position of the researcher, so as to be able to criticize him in the most productive way. And why not be a researcher, anyway? As we are finding, it is not as difficult as it has often been made to seem.

Analysis of Variance

So far, then, we have seen that we can maximize our chances of getting important results of a hypothesis-checking kind by having an appropriate experimental design, which includes randomization. But we have not so far advanced beyond the old idea of experimental design, which was to vary one thing at a time. This is called univariate analysis. There is nothing wrong with it, if it really is possible to vary one thing at a time. But this is very rarely possible in psychology, and particularly in social psychology.

If only we could include the major sources of error in the analysis of the data, and see how big an effect they made, this would actually be much more informative than merely trying to eliminate sources of error. It is a key principle in modern experimental work in social psychology that we are not interested in 'other things being equal' findings. What we want to know, about any effect which we find, is *how unequal other things can be, and the effect still hold*. This is much more practical and down to earth. And this means using multivariate analysis.

To take a simple example, look at this table:

TABLE 12

Mean time taken to arrive at orgasm.
by age and sex (fictional data).

Age group	Men	Women
Young	3 mins	14 mins
Older	14 mins	3 mins

On the basis of these results, one could not say that men reach their climax either more or less quickly than women, nor that young people reach it either more or less quickly than older people. However, the results do suggest a curious fact, that as men get older they take longer to attain satisfaction, while women undergo an opposite evolution, and take less time to reach the point of no return. Ageing is not the same thing to men and women, as regards their sex behaviour. Therefore it would be misleading to compare men and women without taking age into account, or to compare the young and older age-groups without taking sex into account. There is *interaction* between age and sex as determiners of orgasmic behaviour. And if we carefully defined several levels of age-group, it would be possible to say whether age had more effect than sex, or sex had more effect than age. For a fuller example, see Box 2.

Box 2   SEX AND CONFORMITY

Women are generally said to be more conformist than men, but Sistrunk & McDavid[6] showed that this was not the whole story. They found, when they looked at experiments on conformity, that the contents of the tests were usually male-related activities such as politics, economics, geometry and so on.

So they set up a conformity experiment where a number of statements were put before subjects, and a column was added with the heading 'Majority Response'. This said either 'Agree' or 'Disagree', and subjects were told that this represented the answers of the first 200 subjects to take the test. These agree–disagree responses were away from the truth in the factual questions, and in random alternation toward agreement and disagreement in the case of opinion statements.

There were nine classes of statements in the 45-question test:

1. Easy factual male items
2. Difficult factual male
3. Nonfactual male
4. Easy factual female
5. Difficult factual female
6. Nonfactual female
7. Easy factual sex-neutral
8. Difficult factual sex-neutral
9. Nonfactual sex-neutral

Which statements were counted as belonging to each class was established by pre-testing, using different people to those taking part in the main test. It will be seen that there are three types of statement (male, female and sex-neutral) and three levels of difficulty (easy, difficult and insoluble or opinion items).

Four experiments were carried out. In the first, it was found that overall there was no difference between men and women on how much they conformed. But there was a difference when one looked at the male and female items separately. Males yielded to the majority about the same on neutral and feminine types of items, but less on masculine items. However, females yielded less on neutral than on masculine and even less on feminine than on neutral items. The suggestion is, therefore, that women don't conform any more than men in areas where they feel they have some competence. It is just that in so many areas of knowledge and opinion men have managed to foster the impression that they are the experts, and encouraged women to take the lead from them, rather than relying on their own judgment.

The other experiments in the series confirmed these findings, and found consistently that there was an interaction between sex of the subject and sex-orientation of the items. Let us look at the analysis of variance table for the four experiments.

Summary of Analysis of Variance Effects Common to the Four Experiments

Effect	Exp. 1	Exp. 2	Exp. 3	Exp. 4
Sex (S)	ns.	ns.	ns.	ns.
Type of items (T)	ns.	ns.	ns.	ns.
Difficulty of items (D)	·001	·001	·001	·001
T × D	ns.	ns.	·005	·001
S × T	·001	·01	·001	·05
S × D	ns.	ns.	ns.	ns.
S × T × D	ns.	ns.	ns.	ns.

Often a table will give other details, such as the degrees of freedom, the mean squares and the F ratios, but these are only useful if one wants to check the calculations in detail – what we are normally looking for as consumers and critics of research is simply the significance level of the results.

From the first row of the table, we can see that sex as such was not significant on this test – the men conformed about the same as the women, overall. From the second line, we see that there was no overall difference in conformity as between male items, female items and neutral items; they all produced about equal amounts of conformity. From the third line, we see that there was a very clear effect of difficulty of items: less conformity occurred on statements concerning easily judged matters of fact than on either difficult judgments of fact or expressions of matters of opinion; and also there was more conformity on matters of opinion than on difficult matters of fact, though this information does not come direct from this table, but from another check which was carried out at the same time. From the fourth row, we find that in only two of the experiments was there a significant interaction between type of question and difficulty – but the authors feel that this has little to do with conformity, but rather with some of the actual questions used.

It is when we come to the fifth line that we strike gold. The expected interaction between sex and type of item comes out loud and clear in all four experiments. The authors' hypothesis seems to be well supported. Here, then, is a bit of evidence to show that women are not always more conformist than men.

The Sistrunk & McDavid study on conformity is a good example of the way in which a variable which has a definite effect on conformity can be put with other variables into an experimental design which sorts them out and gives an opportunity to assess the relative weight of each. In particular, it enables us to see what interactions are taking place, and what effect each one may have.

So analysis of variance gives us four advantages over straight univariate analysis: First, it enables the researcher to manipulate and control two or more variables at once. Second, it means we do not have to resort to matching. Third, it enables interactive effects to appear if they are at all important. Fourth, it is more precise and statistically superior to the univariate methods – we can have more confidence in our results.

There is just one snag. Analysis of variance does involve certain assumptions about the data, such as that the observations are drawn from normally distributed populations, all of which have the same variance. The measurement requirement of the F test is that the research must achieve at least interval measurement of the variable involved. (See Chapter 6 in Volume 1.)

However, it appears that violations of these assumptions have to be fairly large before the results are seriously affected. Boneau[7] did a large-scale study which showed this, confirming the earlier work reported by Lindquist.[8] And in any case we do not have any widely-used nonparametric tests which enable interactions to appear.

Analysis of variance is still developing, and becoming even more dominant in research practice. An interesting paper by Vaughan & Corballis[9] provides a way of estimating the strength of effects in basic one-way and three-way analysis of variance designs, and this extends it still further. Incidentally, the acronym ANOVA, if you see it quoted in the literature, stands for analysis of variance. Good explanations of the ins and outs of the analysis of variance are to be found in Kerlinger[10] and in Diamond.[11]

Sampling

In the second part of this chapter we shall be going on to the question of survey research, and the problems of sampling make a good bridge between experimental and survey research, since they are common to both.

The basic point about sampling is that somehow one has to choose people to experiment on or ask questions of, and one cannot pretend that it is irrelevant who is chosen. One must avoid bias if the results are to be replicable. And if the results are not replicable, the effect one has found is to that extent doubtful.

If one has a plate of soup, and wants to know whether it is onion or tomato (perhaps the light is too dim to see very well) one spoonful is enough to tell the difference. And if it is a one-ton vat of soup, several yards in circumference, one spoonful is still enough.

This is the principle of sampling. The size of the parent population is irrelevant to the accuracy of the conclusions which may properly be drawn. If one sip is enough from a small bowl, then one sip is enough from a huge vat, too.

But it is important that the vat should have been well stirred. Maybe some of the ingredients of the tomato soup are the same as some of the ingredients of the onion soup. If the soup is not stirred enough, it may just happen that these ingredients are not properly separated, but are concentrated here and there in the soups; in such a case we could get two spoonsful which were quite indistinguishable, just by this fault in the mixing. But if the soup is well stirred, we shall get a fair and unbiased sample, no matter where we put the spoon in. This stirring corresponds to randomization, in psychological research.

But of course this means that any sample is only a sample of the population from which it was taken. If it is a well taken sample – that is, the pot is stirred, or the selection is randomized – then it is representative.

For example, the people reported in the experiments in Box 21 were all students in Florida. In experiment 1 they were students enrolled in undergraduate psychology courses at the University of Miami (Florida); in experiment 2 students from the Dade County Junior College; in experiment 3 students from Miami area high schools; and in experiment 4 students from introductory psychology classes at the University of South Florida. So they are certainly not representative of the human race in general; nor even of America; nor even of Florida; nor even of the colleges whence they came; nor even of the classes from which they came, since we are not told anywhere that they were selected at random. So they are just some available human beings who happened to be handy.

Certainly the fact that the same result (the interaction between sex of subject and sex-orientation of the question) appeared in all four cases gives us some confidence that we are not just dealing with something weak and dubious; but we should like to see some large-scale replications to be quite sure that the phenomenon is not restricted to under-20 Americans living in the South-East, and receiving better-than-average education.

In general, it is a criticism of the vast majority of experimental social psychology that it takes no notice of the problems of sampling. There appear to be five questions which experimental psychologists ask themselves before starting a particular investigation:

1. Is it cheap? Can I do it with no materials other than duplicated score sheets – there is always plenty of paper about.
2. Is it handy? Can I do it with the people I have on hand? Can I do it without moving too far from my office?

3. Is it convenient? Can I fit it into the life of my students without disrupting their habits in any way?
4. Is it brief? Can I get the whole thing over in twenty minutes – or an hour, if I can run several people at a time?
5. Is it publishable? Will it add to my book of records, whether it reveals anything worth knowing or not? Memo: interesting statistics can help. Poor sampling will not be penalized.

One cannot help feeling that it would be better if these experimenters asked instead a different set of questions, which would be better adapted to getting something worthwhile out of their work, such as the following:

1. Is my method an adequate representation of what I am supposed to be studying? If I am studying anxiety, are my subjects really anxious?
2. Is my sample representative? If so, what is it representative of? With how much confidence can I generalize to the parent population?
3. Is my work relevant? Who suffers and who benefits from the work I am doing? If nobody suffers and nobody benefits, how do I feel about that?
4. Is my work merely descriptive, or does it lead to change of some kind? Change in what direction, and in whose interest?

In both cases, these sets of questions are of course supposed to be in addition to the normal questions of research design and accurate control within the experiment itself.

Having said that sampling is important and under-rated, there are one or two important things to be said about it. The idea of a representative sample relates to real life as part of what we mean by fairness. We come across a fruit stall, perhaps, where the stallholder puts the best apples in the display and serves his customers out of a box containing the remaining apples. If we have the courage, perhaps we point out to him that this is a very unfair practice.

Maybe he is very upset by this, and resolves to change his ways. He now gives a number to each apple, and writes the numbers on slips of paper which he mixes up in a box. He gives the slips a good shaking up in the box, and draws, let's say, a hundred slips.

He then puts into his display all those, and only those, numbers which have been drawn. It may turn out that, although ten per cent of the apples are rotten, all of the apples chosen for the display are good.

Is the sample a fair one?

The answer must be Yes. The point is that if he does the same thing each day – and assuming that he is not cheating in some ingenious way – the proportion of rotten apples on display will approximate 10% over a sufficient period of time, if that was the constant proportion in the parent population of apples. It is the *method* which is fair, not the result on any one day.

When we come to the large-scale survey, we can still apply the principle of random sampling, but we have to introduce some refinements. The main one is multi-stage sampling.

Suppose we wish to undertake a survey of the reading habits of the population of the United Kingdom. It would be unrealistic to put all the names into a hat and draw out the first 1000 names, or whatever we had decided our sample size was to be. We can do the same job both more efficiently and more conveniently by choosing a small number of administrative areas at random, and then choosing the people at random within those. Or we may have three levels – large areas, small areas and then people. If we have done it correctly, it will still be true that each person in the country had an equal chance of being picked – and this is the crucial thing.

Having picked a certain ward of a town, one gets hold of the electoral register. This contains the names and addresses of all the people over 18 in the ward. Suppose it contains 10,000 names, and we wish to choose a sample of 50 people. We would pick the first name by taking a two-digit random number and starting with the name which occupied that position on the list. And we would continue by taking every 200th name thereafter, taking the last name from the early part of the list if necessary. (If our random number was between 50 and 99, that is.)

We would then go to the addresses given, and attempt to interview the named person chosen. It would be very important to interview just that person and no other, as otherwise a person's availability could make him more likely to be chosen and thus bias the sample. So if the person is out, it is necessary to call back a couple of times to pick him up if it is humanly possible.

If we also want to interview people under 18, it is then necessary to have some special instruction which will ensure that the right proportion of non-electors is picked up. Normally this is not too difficult to arrange.

When we have used these multi-stage methods, it is usual to call it a systematic probability sample, rather than a random sample, but the same statistical laws apply to both. Such a sample is genuinely representative of the parent population.

This means that if the percentage of people with red hair is 26% in the sample, then it is approximately 26% in the parent population. There is a margin of error, which has two elements or components. One is sampling error, which is calculable, and the other is sampling bias, which is not. Sampling bias creeps in because of things which have gone wrong either in the original list of addresses, or with the interviewer's following of instructions, or with the fact that certain people are differentially available – all this kind of thing. Sampling error is in fact very easy to calculate in a crude way. In order to be certain of these percentage deviations from 50%, we need these sample sizes:

TABLE 13

% deviation	5% level sample	1% level sample
5	1400	2700
10	400	700
15	240	300
20	100	175
25	65	110
30	46	78
35	35	60
40	27	46
45	24	38

In other words, if we want our sample to be not more than $2\frac{1}{2}$% out either way (if we find 50% of the heads of household are renting their homes, and we want to be sure there are not less than $47\frac{1}{2}$% and not more than $52\frac{1}{2}$%, for example) we have to have a sample size of 1,400 at the 5% level of confidence, or 2,700 if we want to operate at the 1% level of confidence. And this is irrespective of the size of the parent population or universe. This is the point we made earlier about the soup – these figures apply whether we are sampling Hampstead, London, South-East England or the United Kingdom. People often assume that if you are sampling a smaller region, then you need a smaller sample, but this is not true.

The above figures are only approximate, and a fuller account will be found in the excellent book by Kish[12] – see also the interesting paper by Corlett.[13]

Now it sometimes happens that one cannot afford to carry out a random sample, or a systematic probability sample, which comes to the same thing. Finding electoral registers, or covering area maps, as is often done in the USA, is a time-consuming business, and the finding of selected addresses is even more time-consuming. An alternative method has been devised, which is called QUOTA SAMPLING.

Quota sampling was developed in the exciting time during the 1940s when so many of the methods of social psychology were brought into being. It is well described in Cantril's very interesting book.[14] It can be used in all those cases where we have previous knowledge of the distribution of control variables in the parent population. Thus for example, if we have previous knowledge that the main variables which have an effect on racial prejudice are age, education, sex and urban or rural residence, we can look these up in the Census or in a previous large random sample investigation, and see how they are distributed in the population we wish to study. We can then control for them directly, by telling interviewers to go out (having chosen the areas by some suitable random process) and interview so many in each age group, so many at each educational level, so many of each sex and so many in urban and rural areas, to correspond with the known levels. As Cantril points out, this often gives very accurate results, comparable to those obtained in random surveys.

Quota sampling is, however, less statistically respectable than random sampling, and is often spoken of very slightingly in books written by statisticians. One cannot apply the formula of the standard error of the normal distribution to such data, because the laws of chance do not apply; the sample has not been chosen by chance. But one can perfectly easily apply the chi-square formula to such data, and there is no real problem about tests of significance.

There are, of course, some very important practical problems with quota sampling – interviewers may go to houses which are more accessible, or pick out people who are more accessible – a lot of park-keepers get interviewed in the summer time – or pick out people who look more clean or friendly than the average; but these difficulties are more important in theory than in practice. Corlett & Rothman[15] have shown that a quota sample is about equally likely to give accurate estimates as a random sample of the same size, so far as actual sampling error is concerned. On the other kind of error – which we called sampling bias above – quota samples are more liable than random samples to show some bias, and this has to be watched and perhaps deliberately compensated for in individual instances.

This distinction between sampling error and sampling bias is in fact very important, and should always be kept in mind. Reducing sampling error is a job for the statistician, but reducing sampling bias is a job for the person in the field, or controlling what goes on in the field. And this brings us to the problem of interviewing.

Interviewing

The interviewer can bias the results of a survey, in two different ways: selecting respondents, and influencing respondents. We have already seen, in our discussion of sampling, how bias can arise in the selection of respondents; now let us look at the kinds of bias which are likely to arise during the interview itself.

It is important to realize that interviewing is a very widespread phenomenon in our society, and even more general in social psychology. Survey-type interviewing has been used in studies of consumer behaviour and family income, of fertility and family planning, of sexual behaviour, of mental health and illness, of political behaviour, of supervisor/subordinate relations and worker attitudes, of readership and media consumption, of smoking and drinking behaviour, and so on. But interviewing is also used in the social-psychological experiment, to test for anxiety or elation, increased confidence, reduced self-esteem, feelings of acceptance or rejection, and so on. The book of readings by Proshansky & Siedenberg[16] contains 61 studies, of which 37 include verbal responses in answer to some series of questions or demands by the researcher; and of the studies which do not involve interview data, all but four use written responses of subjects to questionnaire items or similar stimuli. The companion volume edited by Steiner & Fishbein[17] tells much the same story.

What are the ways, then, in which the interviewer can bias the results of such questioning? Firstly, his opinions can be a source of bias; and secondly, his appearance may be such a source. Cantril, in the book already mentioned, reports how isolationist interviewers tend to get isolationist answers to opinion questions bearing on that issue. And an experiment by Hildum & Brown[18] makes it clear how this can happen: they administered a questionnaire containing favourable and unfavourable statements on a certain issue. For some of the respondents, they said 'Good' for each response which revealed a favourable attitude; for other subjects, they said 'Good' for every response which revealed a negative attitude. The responses were significantly biased in the direction of the feedback which had been given. It seems likely, from this and other work, that not only words like 'Good', but also smiles, frowns, murmurs of agreement and gestures can have a similar or even greater effect.

Most large surveys employ trained and experienced interviewers with no particular interest in the subject under investigation – it is just another job to them. But in the social psychological experiment, the interviewer is often the researcher himself, or an assistant who may share the researcher's theoretical expectations. So the dangers of this kind of bias are often greater in the laboratory than in the field.

The second source of bias we mentioned is the appearance of the interviewer. A classic study in this field is that by Robinson & Rohde[19] on anti-Jewish feelings. A questionnaire was presented which had questions like – (1) Do you think there are too many Jews holding Government offices and jobs?; and (2) Do you think that the Jews have too much power in the United States? The interviewers were put into four groups, and the groups are shown below, together with the answers they obtained, on average, to the two questions shown.

TABLE 14

Group Interviewed by	Question 1 % Yes	Question 2 % Yes
Jewish-looking with Jewish names	11·7	5·8
Jewish-looking, no name given	15·4	15·6
Non-Jewish-looking with non-Jewish names	19·5	21·4
Non-Jewish-looking, no name given	21·2	24·3

It can be seen that the effect was a substantial one. It seems that respondents are motivated to avoid making statements which they think will be painful to the interviewer, or of which the interviewer will disapprove.

Similarly, Hyman *et al.*[20] found that black interviewers got more information than white interviewers from black respondents on the subject of resentment over racial discrimination.

Katz[21] found that interviewers from working-class backgrounds consistently obtained more radical social and political opinions from respondents than did interviewers from the middle class. The differences were marked on labour issues, particularly among respondents who were members of trade unions. For example, working-class interviewers found that 44% of their respondents favoured a law against sit-down strikes; the middle-class interviewers, supposedly with the same kind of respondents, found that 59% favoured such a law!

Ehrlich & Riesman[22] found that the age of the interviewer had an effect on information reported by adolescent girls. Older interviewers obtained fewer reports of behaviour which middle-class adults would think undesirable, and more reports of adherence to parental requirements.

The appearance of the interviewer is thus a potential source of bias, but only in fairly obvious ways, and ways which are fairly easy to take care of. Williams[23] studied black respondents, and found that racial differences became significant sources of bias only as the perceived social distance became great and the interview content threatening.

Another source of bias in interviewing is obviously the actual wording of the questions. Let us now look at this.

Questions

The form and wording of the question can affect the results considerably.

The classic work on this subject is still Payne[24] and the things he says are still very relevant. But the main change which has taken place in recent years is towards placing more emphasis on a phenomenological approach. We shall be saying more about this in the next chapter, but for the moment it is sufficient to say that we now try to get the question wording from the target population themselves. If we are surveying adolescents, we put all our questions in terms of their language and their frame of reference, and similarly with any other groups we may want to interview.

Another change which has taken place in recent years is that we now use much more sophisticated methods of attitude research. In 1948, Krech & Crutchfield were able to say – 'Because of both the need for rapport with the respondent and the need for measurement of a number of variables, then, precise scaling methods must be abandoned in public opinion research in favour of single questions designed to provide the basis for measurement.' The current routine use of such measuring instruments as the semantic differential show how far we have advanced since those days. We saw in Chapter 6 of Volume 1 how well these techniques have now been integrated into general survey methodology.

There are, however, still some controversies over question form and wording which we can look at briefly. The oldest one, open versus closed questions, now seems virtually settled. What we do nowadays is to run the survey in two waves, usually called a pilot stage and a main stage. In the pilot stage we use a number of open-ended questions, and in the main stage we close them. In other words, we make a note of the most popular answers to the question – there are usually not more than six to eleven of these, once very similar answers have been grouped together – and print them on a card, which is then shown to people in the main stage interviewing.

This is quite separate from another controversy which is sometimes confused with it. This is the question of whether you can ask people questions about something they know nothing about. In one experiment, large numbers of people expressed positive or negative attitudes towards 'The Metallic Metals Act', even though there was no such act in existence. In another, people expressed strong attitudes against the Danireans, a non-existent race of people. This again has proved to be relatively easy to deal with. The Gallup organization has developed a 'Quintamensional Plan', and other people have found the same thing under other names: all that happens is that people are first asked – 'Have you read or heard anything about . . . ' (the topic under consideration); those who say they have are then asked – 'What have you read or heard about . . . ' (the same); only if the open-ended answer reveals some real acquaintance with the topic under question are the following questions asked, about the finer details. Thus the final published percentages refer only to those people who do have some genuine acquaintance with that topic. This is also useful, in that it gives a good indication of the general level of public awareness on any given topic.

Another controversy, this time a live one, is over whether one can use indirect questions as well as direct ones. The argument for indirect questions is that the respondent does not know, or will not tell, the answer to a direct question. The argument against is that we do not know what the answers to an indirect question mean.

A good example of the use of indirect questions is to be found in the study by Lansing & Blood[25] on foreign travel. In their pilot work they found that people tend to suppress some of their fears about foreign countries, because they do not want to reveal themselves as either provincial or incompetent to the interviewer. So in addition to direct questions, two types of indirect question were used: one merely asked why the respondent thought *some people* did not want to visit foreign countries; and the other involved a series of questions about a hypothetical Mrs. Jones, who had won a free trip to Europe in a contest. Questions asked whether Mrs. Jones would or would not accept the trip as a prize, the reasons for her choice, and what some of her concerns about such travel might be. Responses to the indirect questions included more expressions of doubt, fear and hostility.

The basic form of the indirect question is the projective test. We have already looked at the basic principle of projection as one of the defences of the ego, and what we do in the projective test is to use this as a form of psychological judo, where we use the respondent's natural tendencies, instead of trying to oppose them. Survey research has used adaptations of the TAT, the Rozenweig cartoon test, the Szondi test, the Rorschach, the sentence-completion test and many others, as Newman[26] has well described.

At this point an ethical point arises, which was put very forcibly by Packard[27] in a best-selling book. What is the morality of using the most high-powered psychological techniques, often lifted from the clinician, to deceive consumers about what they are answering, particularly when the purpose behind it all may be to sell yet another new detergent?

What answers have we got to this objection? First, the purpose of the research is really irrelevant; if the technique has been developed, it can be used for great or trivial purposes, and there is no way in which it can be kept secret. And if our society runs mainly on trivial purposes, that says more about our society than it does about any special method of research.

And second, we are not really deceiving the respondent. In most cases, the respondent wants to tell us the truth. As someone once said – People do not tell lies to interviewers, but they sometimes deceive themselves. And what these methods do is to make it easier for respondents to tell us the truth.

A more cogent objection would be that by using projective questions we are manipulating the respondent, and treating him or her like a thing, rather than like a person. This is quite true, and it is also true of the more usual direct questions, so there is no difference on this score. A survey interview is basically an alienating thing, forcing people into rigid role relationships, and does just as much harm to the respondent as it does to the interviewer. We shall return to this point in the next chapter.

There is a good deal of discussion of the points we have raised about sampling and interviewing in the books by Parten,[28] Festinger & Katz,[29] Goode & Hatt,[30] Selltiz *et al.*[31] and in the chapter by Cannell & Kahn[32] in the second edition of the **Handbook**.

Survey Analysis

All the work that is done in survey research is useless unless the information obtained can be understood and used. In practice, analysis is generally of a correlative kind, but experimental designs can also be used. In every case, what we are trying to do is to check some hypothesis, or obtain facts which will lead to the setting up of some new hypothesis.

In practice, there have grown up two rather different kinds of survey. One of these is a purely descriptive survey, such as the National Expenditure Survey, which finds out family expenditure on necessities and luxuries; the Nielsen surveys of shops stocking certain goods; the British Tourist Authority surveys, and so on. These surveys simply turn out a mass of figures, on a constant basis, so that trends and changes can be seen, and general levels ascertained.

The other type of survey is the 'reason why' survey, designed to find out what influences are operating in a given area of human choice, and their relative strength. There was a lot of talk about motivational research in the 1950s which made it seem as though nobody had ever done reason-why research before then; but it is clear from books like Zeisel[33] that this is not at all the case.

We shall deal here mainly with the reason-why survey, because the points are of very general interest. Let us look first at contingency analysis, then at correlational analysis, and finally at factor analysis.

Contingency analysis for reason-why research is subject to an important logical principle, which is not immediately obvious to the naked eye. Let us look at this example, taken from an article[34] which goes into the matter in great detail.

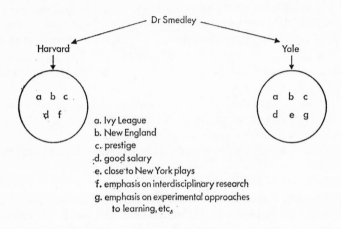

a. Ivy League
b. New England
c. prestige
d. good salary
e. close to New York plays
f. emphasis on interdisciplinary research
g. emphasis on experimental approaches to learning, etc.

Fig. 9

This shows the promising young psychologist, Dr. Smedley, trying to decide whether to accept a position at Harvard or at Yale. We have to assume, for the purposes of this example, that the factors given in the chart are the *only* influences operating.

Now if we subsequently learn that Dr. Smedley took the position at Harvard, rather than at Yale, we are in a position to answer the question Why. We know it must be something to do with e, f and g.

More important still, however, is the other side of this reasoning – a, b and c are *common* features, and therefore *cannot have been decisive in the choice*. If we asked Dr. Smedley why he chose Harvard in preference to Yale, and he replied – 'Because it is in New gland' – this would be an irrational answer. Not only would we not believe it – we would be unable even to make sense of it, because it is absurd. This is not a novel or unorthodox type of reasoning – it can be found in the Canons of John Stuart Mill in another form, and underlies a great deal of our ordinary everyday thinking.

Let us look at a numerical example, again taken from a standard work[35] on research procedures. Here are some data on baby cereals:

TABLE 15

	Among Those Women who	
	Attended welfare centres	*Did not attend*
Percentage using:	%	%
Brand A	45	43
Brands B and C	20	2
Brands D and E	10	17

From this table three things can be seen. Firstly, Brands B and C are heavily dependent upon welfare centres (they were relatively new products, for which the main promotional effort had been through these centres). Secondly, Brands D and E were bought more by those who did not attend welfare centres (they were old-fashioned products, largely disapproved of by the experts who were responsible for running the centres and the young doctors and nurses who staffed them). And thirdly, attendance at the welfare centre was irrelevant to the purchase of Brand A.

Again, it is the latter finding which concerns us most directly here. If these women had said that their main reason for purchasing Brand A was that it was recommended by the welfare centres, we would know that they were mistaken. *In fact, they did say precisely this*, and the full example in the book is very instructive in showing how useless it often is to ask people why they do things, rather than using contingency analysis.

In our discussion of projective questions, we said that one reason for using them was that people often did not know what the real reason was for their behaviour. We can now see that the projective question and the 'depth' approach is not the only way round this difficulty. In reason-why research generally, we do not *ask* people why they do things – we ask them about their behaviour, their beliefs and their values, and then we *tell* them why. In doing so, we use the principles of logical inference noted above.

The principles of contingency analysis are superbly dealt with in Zeisel's little book,[36] which also deals with the matter of the accounting scheme. He makes it clear that unless we use the principle of the accounting scheme, which takes care of all the counter possibilities, our interpretations must always be dangerous and insecure.

Similar considerations apply to correlational analysis. It is often pointed out in textbooks that correlation does not necessarily imply causation. Nevertheless, it can be very useful, particularly in suggesting patterns of relationship, and in showing the relative strengths of various relationships. Now that computers are widely available, it is simple to get out a correlation matrix – that is, a table showing the correlations between all the pairs of variables in which we are interested – and simply looking at it gives a great deal of information, as Ehrenberg has pointed out.

There is a simple paper-and-pencil way of analysing a matrix of correlations, described by McQuitty[37] who has also suggested other ideas along similar lines.[38] [39] [40] This method has been compared with factor analysis, principal components analysis and cluster analysis by Raven & Ritchie,[41] and they find that McQuitty's elementary linkage analysis is the quickest to perform, and gives substantially similar results to the other methods, on typical survey data. It therefore seems as though we have here a useful technique for trying out on data, when we are not sure whether a full factor analysis will be worth carrying out.

Let us move on to factor analysis, then. It is important to understand at least something about this, because it is used so frequently today. We have already seen that factor analysis is something to do with correlations, and this is exactly it.

Factor analysis was originally developed by psychologists, and particularly in the field of personality tests. They sought to answer whether a battery of 100 test items really measured 100 different aspects of a person's personality, or whether the data could be reduced to a smaller number of factors. If, for example, every person who comes high on 'aggressiveness' also comes high on 'assertiveness' this would indicate that these two things – which are of course logically separate – empirically hang together, and form part of a definite factor. So factor analysis has to do with patterns. Just as when we look at the sky for the first time, it seems a mass of unrelated stars; but if we keep on looking, we find that certain patterns of stars hang together in their movements – and we call these constellations. If we are measuring personality, the factor would be a personality syndrome; if we are measuring intelligence, the factor would be a basic mental ability; if we are measuring attitudes, the factor would be a fundamental outlook on the field under investigation.

There are two main forms of factor analysis, principal component analysis, and factor analysis (old style). These have been coming closer together, and old-style factor analysis is now often carried out on the basis of the principal factor solution, rendering the old distinction – still to be found in many of the older textbooks – outdated. New computer programmes are coming along all the time, however, and the maximum likelihood solution is being developed fast. All this is really to say that there are fine distinctions in this area which are not very helpful to the user. It seems best to continue to talk about factor analysis in a general sense, to include all these approaches.

For many years there has been controversy surrounding factor analysis. For an extreme example, take this quotation from Ehrenberg:[42]

> No (factor analytic) results have been reported in the literature which have turned out to be of lasting value, and protagonists seldom refer to their past work, but rather to 'promising results' of some current (but as yet incomplete) project.

Here are three counter examples to this swingeing assertion.

1. In the 1940s a number of studies were carried out on the subject of leadership at Ohio State University under the supervision of J. K. Hemphill. This led to the factor analytic work of Halpin & Winer[43] published in 1952. They identified two main factors, accounting respectively for 50% and 34% of the total variance. These were Consideration and Initiating Structure – the social-emotional and task-oriented aspects of leadership, respectively. A number of subsequent studies have confirmed that these may be regarded as the two main dimensions of leader behaviour.[44] And

they lead very naturally into such totally different work as that of Bales,[45] Fiedler[46] and Blake & Mouton,[47] all of which are very compatible with the Halpin & Winer work and reflect back on it in a constructive way – in other words, each reinforces the others. And in the 1960s this work was still being used — see for example the Fleishman & Harris paper in the Penguin book of readings on leadership[48] published in 1969. Twenty years seems to count as reasonably lasting.

2. In the 1950s a number of studies were carried out at the University of Illinois under the general supervision of Charles Osgood, leading to the publication in 1957 of *The Measurement of Meaning*.[49] This contains accounts of numerous studies using factor analysis, all of which found the same three factors, usually labelled Evaluation, Potency and Activity (though activity and potency sometimes combined to form a Dynamism factor). This work continued beyond the book, and was very widely adopted, to the point where the second edition of the Handbook[50] can say – 'Because of its vast popularity it is unnecessary to describe it here in detail.' Fifteen years ought to count as something lasting.

3. In the 1960s a number of people were inspired by the Osgood approach to attempt variants upon it, and one of the most important of these was the work of Harry Triandis, also at the University of Illinois, on the behavioral differential. This led to a great clarification of the whole notion of ethnic prejudice, and enabled prejudice to be seen as a logical part of a whole pattern of social forms of behaviour, describable in terms of five factors ranged in a two-dimensional space.[51] This work has only been going for ten years or so, but looks healthy at the present time.

So here is factor analytic work from three decades – and of course there are many more examples one could choose. All the same, there are one or two points about factor analysis which give cause for caution. The two main ones are: first, there is no mathematical way, other than an arbitrary one, of deciding *how many* factors to have – the user has to decide; and second, there is no mathematical way of *labelling* the factors – the user names them at his own risk.

The first point is not often known to the ordinary reader. One imagines – wrongly – that factor analysis is a computer thing which is completely objective from start to finish. In fact, however, what very often happens is that the user says to the computer people – 'My theory predicts that there ought to be four factors. I'd like to look at the four-factor solution – but please also let me have the two, three, five, six and seven factor solutions to see.' And it may turn out that the five-factor solution, say, makes much more sense than the four – in which case something new has been learned.

Similarly with the labelling of factors. One has the choice of leaving the factors as they are, and just calling them Factor 1, Factor 2 and so on; or of giving them some invented name – this is what Cattell does, with his Parmia, Threctia, Harria and so on; or of giving them some already known name, either derived from theory (e.g. introversion, extroversion) or immediately descriptive.

There is also a minor point which might be raised here, since it sometimes arises in the literature. Factor analytic methods put the variables in which we are interested into some specific pattern within a set of dimensions – it is these dimensions which form the factors and get the labels. But it may happen that the first print-out we get may show no pattern of alignment along the axes which we have obtained. If this happens, we can try *rotating the axes* to get a more meaningful alignment; frequently this gives us a much better because more meaningful result. There is no cheating about this – we are not moving the positions of the plotted points at all – merely lining up our explanation of their positions in a more intelligent manner. And there are two ways in which we can rotate – we can do an orthogonal rotation, which keeps the axes at right angles, and therefore retains the feature that each dimension is independent of each other dimension; or we can do an oblique rotation, which allows the axes to take up any angle to each other which makes sense of the plotted points, rather than insisting on a right angle. Where oblique rotations are carried out, it is always the case that two or more of the factors are correlated, and this correlation should always be printed out as part of the results. There is a good discussion of these points in Diamond.[52]

Factor analysis is only one of a large number of multivariate techniques, the basic principles of which are very simple, but which require a great deal of numerical computation. Until the advent of the computer, very few people wanted to do the amount of work which was involved. Now that the computer is accepted, however, even more complicated forms of analysis are possible, such as cluster analysis.

Cluster analysis is becoming much more used, because it makes a lot of sense, in such endeavours as looking for personality types, or types of television programme, or school organization, and so on. It is basically a way of finding patterns of *people* (or programmes, or schools, etc.) rather than finding patterns of *variables*, as factor analysis usually is. So it is a form of classification, and has been used in biology under the title of numerical taxonomy, to make a more objective method of distinguishing between different species, genera, etc.[53] It has also been used in market research[54] and elsewhere.[55]

Problems and Pitfalls

The further we go into modern ways of using the computer, the further we get away from the original data on which all our results are based. Will it bear all this weight of elaboration?

We saw in the discussion of the interview that it is by no means a universally safe instrument of research. There are many points at which it can become unsafe. There are also ethical problems about the interview: in training interviewers, we are training people to be apparently friendly and warm, for the purpose of lulling the suspicions of the respondent; there may be all sorts of good reasons for doing this, but it is still false, and essentially deceptive. This is, of course, no different from the ethical problem of the television interviewer or the shop assistant, the salesman or the laboratory experimenter. In all these cases one has to pretend to an interest and concern, whether one actually feels it or not.

This problem, however, bears on the psychologist more than on the salesman, because the psychologist is professionally concerned with the effect which his actions have on people. We live in a culture in which many people are severely alienated, in the sense of feeling powerless to run their own lives. As Seeman[56] says:

It would take an intolerable optimism and a blind social psychologist not to see the gravity of our problems, the public resistance to their resolution, and the massive inattention to them that a technicized social science allowed. If some current models are too one-dimensional and pessimistic by a good deal, the fact remains that there *were* concentration camps, that there *are* disreputable qualities in American life (including a widely disrespected war, at the moment), and there *will* be further urban violence born of frustrated hopes and an unrectified sense of powerlessness that many people, white and black, rightly feel.

And the psychologist cannot feel equable about contributing to this sense of alienation, this feeling of powerlessness which Seeman and others have shown to be related to ethnic prejudice and lack of political knowledge or interest. As Kelman[57] puts it:

> There is thus a danger that the widespread use of social science approaches – of psychological tests, interviews, experiments and observations – may in itself contribute to people's sense of alienation and helplessness, to the feeling that their destinies are entirely controlled by external forces; and that, furthermore, these approaches may lend themselves most readily to the purposes of those agencies who are concerned with manipulating and controlling the behaviour of individuals, with or without the consultation or the active involvement of the social scientist himself. To the extent that this danger becomes a reality, the social scientist becomes an agent and mediator of dehumanizing forces.

These are new worries, which grow out of the increasing knowledge of what leads to what in the world which the social scientist has himself created. We still know very little about what is humanizing and what is dehumanizing, except in a common-sense way, although the growing literature of humanistic psychology is now starting to change this position. Sidney Jourard is at present conducting a series of investigations which are highly relevant to this issue.

And whether for these or for other reasons, it seems to be a fact that survey research has lost some of its appeal for the social psychologist and the sociologist. All the great survey investigations took place ten or more years ago, and there have been very few recent investigations which have been either important or influential.

It seems doubtful, however, whether it is the ethical objection which is causative here, because the ethical objections actually increase when we move from the field survey to the experimental laboratory. In the laboratory, not only do we alienate the subject by subjecting him or her to techniques which diminish him or her, but we systematically deceive the subject as well. As Kelman again says:

> What concerns me most is not so much that deception is used, but precisely that it is used without question. It has now become standard operating procedure in the social psychologist's laboratory. I sometimes feel that we are training a generation of students who do not know that there is any other way of doing experiments in our field, who feel that deception is as much *de rigueur* as significance at the ·05 level. Too often

deception is used not as a last resort, but as a matter of course. Our attitude seems to be that if you can deceive, why tell the truth? It is this unquestioning attitude, this routinization of deception, that really concerns me.

His point is that by deceiving others, we are dehumanizing ourselves as psychologists. And in fact this does tie in with the common experience that psychologists are not in fact particularly warm or understanding people at all. Perhaps this links in with Jourard's[58] suggestion that the scientific ideal of prediction and control, which may make sense in the field of physics or chemistry, is very close to the adolescent dream of reading people's minds and having power over their behaviour – the kind of dream enshrined in our first ideas about hypnotism. It may also link in with another even more primitive dream, the wish to be invisible. What are our one-way observation mirrors but cloaks of invisibility? But these are unhealthy dreams, and if carried on into adult life would render us open to severe criticism and disapproval.

It seems that in psychology there is much which we need to look at afresh, with an unafraid gaze. What are we doing, to our subjects, our interviewees, and to ourselves? What underlying motivations do our actions express?

We shall return to some of these points in the following chapter; all we want to do here is to indicate that the problems of research are not only technical problems. There are human problems too, because we are dealing with human beings, and are human beings ourselves.

REFERENCES

1. W. A. Wallis & H. V. Roberts. Statistics: A new approach, Methuen 1967
2. B. Berelson & G. A. Steiner. Human behaviour, Harcourt Brace 1964
3. D. T. Campbell & J. C. Stanley. Experimental and quasi-experimental designs for research, Rand McNally 1966
4. S. Diamond. Information and error, Basic Books 1959
5. L. H. C. Tippett. Statistics, O.U.P. 1943
6. F. Sistrunk & J. W. McDavid. Sex variable in conforming behaviour, J. Pers. soc. Psychol. 17, 1971
7. C. Boneau. The effects of violations of assumptions underlying the t test, Psychol. Bull. 57, 1960
8. E. Lindquist. Design and analysis of experiments, Houghton Mifflin 1953
9. G. M. Vaughan & M. C. Corballis. Beyond tests of significance: Estimating strength of effects in selected ANOVA designs, Psychol. Bull. 72, 1969

10. F. N. Kerlinger. Foundations of behavioral research, Holt, Rinehart & Winston 1964
11. Same as ref. 4
12. L. Kish. Survey Sampling, Wiley 1965
13. T. Corlett. The standard error of the standard error, Commentary 8, 1966
14. H. Cantril. Gauging public opinion, Princeton 1944
15. Quoted in T. Corlett. Sampling errors in practice, Commentary 7, 1965
16. H. M. Proshansky & B. Seidenberg (eds) Basic studies in social psychology, Holt 1965
17. I. D. Steiner & M. Fishbein. Current studies in social psychology, Holt 1965
18. D. Hildum & R. W. Brown. Verbal reinforcement and interviewer bias, J. abnorm. Soc. Psychol. 53, 1956
19. D. Robinson & S. Rohde. Two experiments with an anti-semitism poll, J. abnorm. soc. Psychol. 41, 1946
20. H. Hyman *et al.* Interviewing in social research, Chicago 1954
21. D. Katz. Do interviewers bias poll results? Publ. Opin. Quart. 6, 1942
22. J. Ehrlich & D. Riesman. Age and authority in the interview, Publ. Opin. Quart. 25, 1961
23. J. A. Williams. Interviewer-respondent interaction: A study of bias in the information interview, Sociometry 27, 1964
24. S. L. Payne. The art of asking questions, Princeton 1951
25. J. B. Lansing & D. M. Blood. The changing travel market, Survey Research Center Monograph 38, Ann Arbor 1964
26. J. W. Newman. Motivation research and marketing management, Harvard 1957
27. V. Packard. The hidden persuaders, Penguin 1960
28. M. Parten. Surveys, polls and samples, Harper & Row 1950
29. L. Festinger & D. Katz. Research methods in the behavioral sciences, Holt, Rinehart & Winston 1953
30. W. Goode & P. Hatt. Methods in social research, McGraw-Hill 1952
31. C. Selltiz *et al.* Research methods in social relations, Holt, Rinehart & Winston 1959
32. C. F. Cannell & R. L. Kahn. Interviewing, in G. Lindzey & E. Aronson (eds) The handbook of social psychology, Addison-Wesley (Vol. 2) 1968
33. H. Zeisel. Say it with figures, Routledge 1958
34. E. C. Jones & K. E. Davis. From acts to dispositions, in L. Berkowitz (ed) Advances in experimental social psychology (Vol. 2) Academic Press 1965
35. H. Henry. Motivation research, Crosby Lockwood 1958
36. Same ref. as 33
37. L. L. McQuitty. Elementary linkage analysis, Educ. Psychol. Measmt. 17, 1957
38. L. L. McQuitty. Agreement analysis: Classifying persons by predominant patterns of responses, Br. J. Stat. Psychol. 9, 1956
39. L. L. McQuitty. Hierarchical linkage analysis for the isolation of types, Educ. Psychol. Measmt. 20, 1960
40. L. L. McQuitty. Hierarchical syndrome analysis, Educ. Psychol. Measmt. 20, 1960
41. J. Raven & J. Ritchie. A comparison of five techniques of data analysis, Government Social Survey n.d.
42. A. S. C. Ehrenberg. Multivariate analysis and marketing, Proceedings of the 15th annual conference of the Market Research Society, 1972
43. A. W. Halpin & B. J. Winer. The leadership behaviour of the airplane commander, Ohio State University Press 1952
44. E. A. Fleishman, E. F. Harris & H. E. Burtt. Leadership and supervision in industry, Ohio State University Press 1955
45. R. F. Bales. Task roles and social roles in problem-solving groups, in ref. 17
46. F. Fiedler. A theory of leadership effectiveness, McGraw-Hill 1967

47. R. Blake & J. Mouton. The managerial grid: Key orientations for achieving production for people, Gulf 1964

48. E. A. Fleishman & E. F. Harris, Patterns of leadership behaviour related to employee grievances and turnover, in C. A. Gibb (ed) Leadership, Penguin 1969

49. C. E. Osgood, G. J. Suci & P. H. Tannenbaum. The measurement of meaning, Univ. of Illinois 1957

50. R. B. Zajonc. Cognitive theories in social psychology, in G. Lindzey & E. Aronson (eds) The handbook of social psychology (Vol. 1) Addison-Wesley 1968

51. H. C. Triadis, V. Vassiliou & M. Nassiakou. The cross-cultural studies of subjective culture, J. Pers. soc. Psychol. 8, Monograph supplement 1968

52. See ref. 4

53. R. R. Sokal & P. H. A. Sneath. Principles of numerical taxonomy, W. H. Freeman 1963

54. T. Joyce & C. Channon. Classifying market survey respondents, Applied statistics 15, 1966

55. W. S. Torgerson. Theory and methods of scaling, Wiley 1958

56. M. Seeman. The urban alienation: Some dubious theses from Marx to Marcuse, J. Pers. soc. Psychol. 19, 1971

57. H. C. Kelman. A time to speak, Jossey-Bass 1968

58. S. Jourard. Self-disclosure and humanistic psychology, paper delivered at annual conference of British Psychological Society 1972

CHAPTER TWELVE

Styles in Social Research

Throughout the period of social psychology's rapid rise, it has become increasingly narrow based. The typical experiment in social psychology is carried out on a small and unrepresentative sample of students – usually second-year (sophomore) students. For example, in the *Journal of Personality and Social Psychology* for January 1972, there are about 70 people – almost always students – in each experiment; and since there are several experimental conditions in each study, actually only 10–20 subjects in each experimental condition. Sometimes the numbers are not even given, so there is no way of checking up.

And large conclusions are often drawn from such narrow bases. For example, one paper concludes that 'being crowded' is really equivalent to 'receiving excessive stimulation from social sources'. The implication of this is that in order to reduce crowding in public spaces it is not necessary to provide more space, but only to provide more partitions, fewer doorways and more elongated (rather than square) rooms. The experiments on which this conclusion is based were carried out using 10 male and 10 female undergraduates, and fibreboard models of rooms in which the subjects had to place clothespins 'with arms made of pipe cleaners' to represent people.

The answer that is sometimes offered to this criticism is that we have to be more careful in our procedures, and test each concept (e.g. crowding) in several different ways, seeing if we get similar results each time. This is the suggestion of Campbell & Fiske[1] in their classical paper.

But this seems a relatively mechanical answer, which is not fully satisfying. What really seems to be needed is a research cycle. The better and more interesting research which has been coming along in recent years has been moving more and more in this direction.

The research cycle is a concept which can be interpreted in at least two different ways. Firstly it can be seen as simply taking the old methods and using them in a more imaginative way; or alternatively, it can be seen as involving a number of new methods as well.

Research Cycle: Type One

The first type of research cycle starts with the experimenter's experience, moves straight into the laboratory, goes back to the experimenter's armchair, from there out into the field (real life situations) and from there to the final report.

A good example of this approach is to be found in the work of Stanley Schachter and his associates at Columbia on hunger in obese people. This work started in the 1960s, apparently as a result of Schachter being intrigued by an article by Bruch[2] in the *Psychiatric Quarterly*, which suggested that obese people cannot discriminate between feelings of hunger and feelings of fear, anger and anxiety, and so treat food quite differently to those of more normal weight. There was some support for this notion in an experiment carried out by Stunkard & Koch[3] which showed that if you measure the stomach contractions (normally associated with hunger feelings) of obese people, they do not correspond at all well with self-reports of hunger.

So Schachter and his co-workers[4] set up a laboratory experiment where they systematically varied the amount of food eaten, and also the amount of fear experienced. The hypotheses to be tested were that obese people should eat just as much when their stomachs are full as when they are empty, and just as much when they are frightened as when they are calm; whereas normal subjects should eat less with full stomachs, and eat more when they are calm than when frightened. All the subjects were students, and obesity was defined as being more than 15% overweight; the obese subjects actually weighed about 30 lb. more than the normals on average. And the experiment came out just as expected – all the hypotheses were upheld.

Now this was very striking, because it not only confirmed that the obese are different in not being able to tell when their stomachs are full from any internal signal, but it also threw doubt on the notion that these obese people eat more because they are more anxious. But if obese people don't get internal signals to say they are empty or full, and don't eat because of other internal signals, such as those of anxiety, fear, etc., why should they eat at all? Yet they do eat, and do report that they feel hungry at times.

Schachter suggested[5] that maybe there was something in the distinction between internal and external controls on eating. Obviously some foods 'look appetizing' while others don't, and most of us have had the experience of feeling full, but not being able to resist some extra goody, just because it looks so attractive to us. Perhaps for obese people this is the *main* determinant of eating, rather than something secondary?

After some further experiments on this theme, which again confirmed the general picture, it was decided to go out of the laboratory and test out various predictions from the theory in the field. It was found[6] that:

1. Fat Jews find it easier to fast on Yom Kippur, because they are not made hungry by the sight of food, and are able to stay in the synagogue all day.
2. Fat students are more intolerant of the food served in university dining halls, because they are more affected by its unappetizing appearance and taste.
3. Fat flyers adjust more easily to time-zone changes, because they don't feel hungry by the clock, but only when food is in front of them.
4. Fat students are far more likely to skip meals at weekends, because there is no food routine to lead them to the table at the right time, and this is irrespective of whether they are dieting or not.

From these experiments and others, it now seems clear that it is in fact true that obese people ignore any internal signals they may have of being empty or full, and go mainly by what they are seeing or tasting or smelling at the time. The field experiments, ingenious and far-reaching as they are, convince in a way that no laboratory experiment by itself could do.

The November 1968 issue of the *Journal of Personality and Social Psychology* was almost totally devoted to real-life research on important issues, and was really exciting to read. But no other issue up to the time of writing has fulfilled the promise that this was going to be the pattern for the future. This suggests that something is still wrong with this style of research.

And we do not have to look far to see what it is. Although the research is far more imaginative, and takes in far more varied situations, it all still involves an alienated relationship between the experimenter and the subject. It is still the case that the experimenter is an intelligent prober into nature, while the subject is a thing to be studied. Maybe quite an interesting thing, but still on quite a different plane from the experimenter. It is not until we challenge this, that we start to challenge what is basically wrong with social psychology today.

What we are coming to here is not an ethical issue of how the psychologist should treat the subject, but the twofold issue of what the psychologist is doing to himself *and* the subject – the relationship which the psychologist is setting up; and the image of man which is implicit in that relationship.

An increasing body of criticism is arising to say that psychology can only discover one-sided things if it insists on setting up one-sided relationships.

> You can only get answers to those questions you are asking. Questions of trust, equality and dialogue between the investigator and his subject are not being asked, since they offend against current conceptions of good methodology. But power over people in a laboratory can *only* lead (if it leads anywhere) to a technology of behaviour control. The results which flow from the unilateral inputs of the experimenter are only applicable to those exercising unilateral inputs in our culture.

This quote from Hampden-Turner[7] opens up the issue very directly, and he goes on to make a striking point:

> When we search the literature of socio-psychological experiments what do we find? We find an astonishing number of experiments on pain inflicting, prejudice, obedience, conformity, cheating, aggression, inauthenticity and scapegoating. Only rarely do we find experiments on affection or on independence and when we look more closely at these we discover that the 'affectionate monkeys' were those the experimenter left alone, and the 'independent students' were those who *resisted* the experimental pressures to conform, cheat and obey.

Perhaps this is a criticism from outside, from someone who has never had to conduct experiments himself, and who therefore does not really understand the position. So let us listen to a highly respected Professor of Psychology, Sidney Jourard:[8]

Psychologists face a choice. We may elect to treat our subjects as objects of study for the benefit of some elite; or we may choose to learn about determiners of the human condition in order to discover ways to overcome or subvert them, so as to enlarge the subjects' – that is, Everyman's – freedom. If we opt for the latter, our path is clear. Our definition of the purpose of psychology will have to change. Our ways of conducting psychological research will have to be altered. And our ways of reporting our findings, as well as the audiences to whom the reports are directed, will have to change. We shall have to state openly whether we are psychologists-for-institutions or psychologists-for-persons.

The trouble with scientific psychologists – among whom I number myself – is that we have, in a sense, been 'bought'.

Now obviously this line of thinking opens up wide vistas, affecting the whole way in which society is run and operates. It has implication both for ethics and for politics. But here we are mainly interested in its implications for research styles. What difference exactly does it make to our research if we take these points to heart?

Research Cycle: Type Two

The second type of research cycle starts with the experimenter's experience, moves to some method-oriented interaction with people, which is then revised in accordance with the actual responses obtained, a process in which the people themselves take part; this leads to further method-oriented interactions, and the process continues, resulting ultimately in a body of shared experience. Depending on the type of experience which is involved, it may or may not be appropriate to abstract the results as 'knowledge' which can be fixed in a scientific paper and used by others.

There are not very many good examples of the whole process in action – the challenge in its fully realized form is too recent for that – but there are a number of partial examples which will give something of the flavour of this research style.

Action Research is a method which came into being in the 1930s and was pursued in a number of ways in the 1940s – partly due to the inspiration of Kurt Lewin[9] who led here, as in so many other ways. One of the areas in which work was done was race prejudice. The idea was that a community which was suffering from the effects of race prejudice – anything from bad feelings and discrimination to riots – could undertake a self-survey.

A community self-survey can be described as action research in which the *members of the community themselves*, under the expert guidance of applied social psychologists, are responsible for the collection and analysis of community data. Three important objectives can be achieved by such community self-surveys: First, the facts collected will permit the realistic planning of a program of action . . . Second, the facts thus uncovered by the citizens of the community will be more readily accepted by the community than if those facts were supplied to them by an outside research agency . . . [Thirdly] quite apart from the facts collected, the intimate contact with the problems of minority-group members may have a powerful motivating effect on the surveyors.

This account of Krech & Crutchfield[10] makes the point that it is only when people actually get talking to minority group members in a face-to-face situation that they realize just how bad things are.

De Stogumber: You must see it. And then you are redeemed and saved.
Cauchon: Were not the sufferings of our Lord Christ enough for you?
De Stogumber: No. Oh no! Not at all. I have seen them in pictures, and read of them in books, and been greatly moved by them, as I thought. But it was no use: it was not our Lord that redeemed me but a young woman whom I saw actually burned to death. It was dreadful: oh, most dreadful. But it saved me. I have been a different man ever since . . .
Cauchon: Must then a Christ perish in torment in every age to save those that have no imagination?[11]

This kind of action research has been well described by Zander[12] and by Weaver.[13] It is well capable of producing both knowledge and action of a remedial kind. It may be doubted, however, whether it is very powerful in changing the basic level of prejudice. In other words, the amount and kind of discrimination in a community can be charted and changed by action research at the community level, and this is of course highly beneficial and worth doing, but a great amount of prejudice may be left intact.

It is perhaps for this kind of reason that there has been little action research reported since the end of the 1940s – but whatever the reasons, it seems a pity; there is room for much more of this kind of work.

But if we do want to get down to the deeper levels of prejudice, there is also some research in this area. Jones & Harris[14] have reported on the use of small groups to study racial attitudes. They used six to eight weekly sessions of an hour and a half, followed by a six-hour session, with groups of 10–15 people, some white and some black. One leader is always white, and one black, too. The research showed that certain phases seem to be constant – and regularly arise to be worked through as the sessions progress:

1. Introductory phase. The main theme is of white people claiming to be free from prejudice.
2. Information phase. Black members come back with details of how they have suffered. This is as far as one would normally get with the former type of action research.
3. Competitive phase. The whites come back with stories of how they, too, have experienced discrimination or persecution, because of being Jewish, Catholic, long-haired, revolutionary, etc.
4. Competitive response. The blacks then emphasize how much worse their problem is, and it becomes clearer that it is *white* society which is responsible, in their eyes.
5. Dissociation. The whites then try to dissociate themselves from white society generally, and also accuse the blacks of exaggerating. They do not accept the black statements as applying to them, one way or another.
6. Impasse. It becomes clear that the blacks and the whites are on two different wavelengths. There is a feeling of being stuck. Evasions of different kinds are tried. It seems that nothing is going to change or happen.
7. Moment of truth. Eventually one of the blacks will express unequivocal anger, strongly and honestly. The group by now knows him or her well, and cannot fail to be impressed.
8. Follow through. The other blacks in the group sooner or later support the member who has spoken out. The emotional reality of what it is like to be a black comes through clearly.
9. Realization. The whites gradually and painfully see the contrast between sympathetic understanding, warm-hearted liberalism, and the real awareness of the black experience. They see that they have been living in a different world, and systematically deceiving themselves about it.
10. Digestion. The whites start to go over their past experiences with blacks, in the light of the new consciousness they have now of what it means to be black. The blacks feel relief and surprised delight that the whites are really listening and struggling to understand.
11. Consensual validation. Both whites and blacks are able to work on their, and each other's, individual problems in an atmosphere which at last is clear.

The process is of course not automatic, and many hitches and problems may occur along the way; but already it seems clear that the kind of deep emotional readjustment which is required to do anything important about racial prejudice takes a great deal of energy and social pressure to achieve. Even in these groups, there are a few people who seem to be unreachable. But this is much more recent research, and is still going on in a number of different places.

It is important to see how this research procedure differs from participant observation. Participant observation has been an important technique in social psychology, as show the classic papers by Whyte[15] on gangs in an Italian slum, by Polsky[16] on the life of the pool hustler, by Barker & Wright[17] in their study of behaviour settings, and so on. But in participant observation, people are revealing themselves to the observer, but he is not revealing himself to them. In the Jones & Harris study just described, the researchers were themselves the group leaders, and exposed their feelings and prejudices in just the same way as other members of the group. The participant observer can often remain virtually unchanged and unchallenged by his experience, which thus becomes of one-way benefit to him and his sponsors. Indeed, the basically alienated nature of this technique is brought out in the following quote:

> Festinger, Riecken and Schachter wanted to join a secret group preparing for the end of the world ... When rebuffed in their initial effort to join, it was necessary for these investigators to have a 'psychic experience' before they were acceptable to the other members.

Karl Weick[18] gives this account without remarking on what stands out – the way in which the investigators were willing to stoop to an evil-smelling deception in order to get their data. As it happens, they were 'punished', in that their failure to confirm their original hypothesis was probably a direct effect of their deception! But investigators do not always get their come-uppance in this poetic way.

Let us look at another example of the second type of research cycle, this time in quite a different field.

How does one study the effects of a drug? The traditional experimental method is to isolate the subject, give him or her the drug under clinically controlled conditions, with a control sample given a placebo under double-blind conditions, and so on. Then an exhaustive set of tests are administered, preferably using tape-recorded instructions so as to minimize experimenter effect, and so on. This is how Timothy Leary[19] studied LSD:

1. Participants alternated roles of observer and subject, i.e., the researchers took the drug with the subjects. The humanizing effect of this procedure cannot be overestimated. Among other things the subject-object issue is clearly settled.

2. Participants were given all available information about the drug. An atmosphere of mystery and secret experimentation was avoided.

3. Participants were given control of their own dosage. A maximum dosage was determined by the research team and the maximum number of tablets was given to the subject and he was free to dose himself at the rate and amount desired.

4. A comfortable, homelike environment was employed. The sterile impersonality of the laboratory was avoided.

5. Subjects were allowed to bring a relative or friend. No subject took the drug in a group where he was a stranger.

This again shows a different way of relating to the subject, in which the experimenter actually changes places with the subject as an integral part of the experiment. None of these forms of experimentation is put forward as ideal, but simply as examples of ways in which the current orthodoxy is being challenged.

In sociology the same process can be seen at work. The vast structural-functional analyses of Talcott Parsons have given way to the much more intimate and detailed studies of Goffman[20] & Garfinkel.[21] All these movements are in the direction of greater attention being paid to qualitative research.

Qualitative Research

One of the traditional distinctions within the field of survey research has always been the distinction between qualitative and quantitative research. Qualitative research, often taking the form of group discussions or depth interviews, would be carried out first, and then hypotheses emerging from it would be carried forward into the quantitative stage. For example, in a typical large-scale exercise, J. M. Bynner[22] says:

The questionnaires used in the main investigation were designed on the basis of a series of exploratory and pilot studies. In the first of these, discussions were held with groups of boys and girls (smokers and non-smokers separately) from secondary modern schools to find out what their attitudes were towards smoking and, particularly, what they thought of the non-smokers and smokers among their peers. This study suggested a number of hypotheses about the influences prompting children to start smoking, and drawing upon the content of the children's remarks a large number of questions were designed to test and explore them further. After a pre-test these questions were modified and then tried out in a pilot survey in May 1965 of 1180 boys and girls in the first and fourth years of 20 secondary schools. (The final survey approached 60 schools and had a total sample of 5,600 boys.)

Now this is the traditional use of qualitative research – it is left behind as soon as it is decently possible to do so. Yet it is crucially important because any hypotheses which do not emerge at that stage are almost impossible to pick up later. Consequently, it is the base on which the whole later research edifice stands. And it is the only stage at which we are talking to 'real people' – at every subsequent stage we are talking to 'processed people', in the sense that they can only answer in terms of *our* questions and *our* categories. At the qualitative stage, they are using their own words and their own experience.

Now in recent years, the whole question of qualitative research has been illuminated by the intervention of phenomenological research. This approach emanates ultimately from Husserl, and states that we have observed nothing if we have not observed meanings. If we want to know what people are doing, what makes them tick, we have to ask what their actions mean to them. This actually denies the whole behaviorist theory that we can only observe behaviour from the outside, and *must not* project meaning into it.

It is the phenomenological approach which has produced the whole Goffman-Garfinkel emphasis on going into situations and teasing out the meanings which are present in them. As Harré & Secord say:[23]

The second technique, which we believe to be of very much greater scientific value, is the close study of a person who is 'passing' in a role which he or she has deliberately chosen to adopt. Garfinkel's classical analysis of the rules related to the presentation of self by adolescent girls derives from his long interrogation of a person 'Agnes', who, though originally a boy, chose to pass as a girl, and had to learn as explicit principles the conventions and rules which operate in the lives of the girls whose society he wished to join, and to follow those rules deliberately. Agnes knew, in a way which no girl could possibly know, what were the conventions of girlish life.

In this kind of work, the researcher becomes his own measuring instrument, and this opens up the whole question of how the researcher can remain objective in such circumstances. In the traditional type of research, one could simply say, that the secret of objectivity was publication and criticism and replication by the fellow scientists of the international psychology community. But we are here in an area where no replication is possible, because the researcher has changed the situation by acting within it.

The main criticism of qualitative research has always been its subjectivity – its uncheckable character. At one level this is easy to refute – perhaps one cannot repeat the investigation exactly – can one ever? – but one can certainly set up similar investigations and compare notes. But at a deeper level, it raises the whole question of what we are doing in science. As soon as one gets amongst actual psychologists, and away from the textbooks, one finds them talking like this:

– That was a brilliant paper last month by X in the journal.
– Did you think so? It may look all right, but I don't trust him. I once worked in his lab, and he is not above fiddling his results.

There is a whole lot going on in the scientific community besides science, and personal integrity is part of the story, too. Rogers[24] says about this:

Even in the realm of confirmation, the personal element enters. In a recent discussion with Lancelot Whyte, the physicist who became a historian of ideas and a philosopher of science, I was surprised to find that, for him, the truth value of a statement, even in science, could in the last analysis be evaluated by one criterion only. If I understood him correctly, that criterion is: How deeply acquainted with the phenomena, how non-defensive, how truly open to all facets of his experiencing, is the scientist who perceived the pattern and put it to the test?

If this is true even in the hard world of empirical confirmation of hypotheses by experimental test, how much more true is it likely to be in the field of qualitative research? What we are really saying is that a fully functioning person[25] in Rogers' sense is the only person who can be objective, and that this is the only kind of

The Social Individual

objectivity which really matters. It is the phenomenologists who have said this best, in their distinction between objectivity (in the sense in which we are talking about it now) and objectivism:

> Objectivity, as a human attitude, is free man's recognition of his orientation to, and being normalized by something which is not himself, insofar as this recognition finds expression, usually in an implicit fashion, in his words and deeds. It is the opposite of arbitrariness, prejudice and self-sufficient subjectivism.

On the other hand, Strasser[26] says that objectivism is a kind of reductionism of psychology to the kind of experience which can be described accurately in the language of physical science. It trusts that there is some kind of method which in and of itself guarantees scientific truth. But there is in fact no such method. Polanyi[27] gives this example:

> ...in a letter published in *Nature*. The author of this letter had observed that the average gestation period of different animals ranging from rabbits to cows was an integer multiple of the number pi (3·14159...). The evidence he produced was ample, the agreement good. Yet the acceptance of this contribution by the journal was only meant as a joke. No amount of evidence could convince a modern biologist that gestation periods are equal to integer multiples of pi. Our conception of the nature of things tells us that such a relationship is absurd.

If in the face of incontrovertible statistical evidence that there exists a significant relationship between two variables, we still prefer to trust our informed feeling that the whole thing is nonsense; that is the kind of decision which we must be making all the time, without perhaps realizing it. We cannot avoid making such decisions, so we had better become more conscious of what we are doing and how we do it, and not deceive ourselves into thinking that we are simply going by 'the facts' or by impersonal laws of proof. And it is at the level of qualitative research that our noses are rubbed most explicitly in this conclusion.

And once we do this, we find that we can use qualitative research not only at the start of a piece of quantitative research, but also during, after and instead of quantitative research.

Qualitative research DURING is the second classic use. It comes between two pieces of quantitative research, in order to answer the

WHY questions emerging from the earlier research itself. Even more commonly, it is used to improve question wording and the type of questions asked. Thus for example, Schofield[28] says:

> During this pilot research each teenager was asked to criticize the schedule of questions after the interview. Sometimes an interviewee would show quite clearly that he had not understood the questions even when he made no comment. After a series of interviews those who had volunteered were persuaded to meet together as a group with the research team. This group was then encouraged to criticize the questions on the schedule and tape-recordings of these group discussions revealed extra information on the right approach and the right wording to use.

Although the stated purpose – improving the wording – is certainly important, perhaps more important is the function of qualitative research in keeping the researchers in touch with the reality of what it is they are investigating.

In yet another way, qualitative research can be used AFTER quantitative research, in order to find out what the survey findings actually mean. Thus for example, a chain store had done a series of surveys on consumer behaviour, and found over and over again that they did badly in the area of 'quality'. Qualitative research was then used to find out what customers meant by that word, in very precise action terms. It turned out that it referred, not so much to any one characteristic of the goods, but rather to the whole image of the store, built up over a number of years.

Finally, qualitative research can be used INSTEAD OF quantitative research. The oldest example of this sort of approach is probably that of Bishop Berkeley, who put three basins of water in a row – one hot, one lukewarm, one cold. He put his left hand into the hot basin and his right hand into the cold basin, and left them there until they became accustomed to the temperature. He then put both hands into the lukewarm water, and found that his left hand experienced it as cold water, while this right hand experienced it as hot water. The same bowl of water was both hot and cold at the same time! Now it does not require large numbers of statistics to tell us this is a reliable result – once we are told what happens, we can *see* why it should be so, and we do not need any further proof.

One of the best researchers using the qualitative method is Peter Madison[29] who says:

Since 1952 I have been making detailed qualitative studies of college students, using autobiographies, repeat interviews, student journals and personality tests ... The student is studied early in his college career and followed year by year to graduation and sometimes for as long as five to ten years after ... My purposes in making such studies have been to understand my observations in terms of contemporary psychological theory and to formulate this understanding in ways that would communicate effectively to college students.

It can be seen that here, in its purest form, where it is freed from its connexion with quantitative research, qualitative research comes very close to the style we have called 'research cycle – type two'. And as Madison[30] says:

Although I have studied hundreds of students, some cases proved to be extraordinary in their power to illuminate what was going on. I have, therefore, concentrated more on these in searching for ideas ... Then, too, one can't observe a person closely over a period of time without his being influenced by the act of studying him. Any longitudinal study on such a personal level is, by definition, action research ... The student data on which this book is based, therefore, is neither objective nor unbiased. But it is highly illuminating. Once a process is revealed in a special case it becomes evident, though in a much less conspicuous form, in more everyday cases.

With the understanding of the term 'objective' which we now have, it seems that Madison is wrong in saying that his work is not objective, though it is certainly not objectivist. His understanding and care and psychological knowledge render him a first-rate observer and guide through this complex data, and his approach is thoroughly objective in the phenomenological sense. One feels all the way through that he is doing justice to the praxis of his subjects. And when he talks of the function of science as he sees it,[29] his whole approach is very much in line with this way of looking at things:

... the psychologist's role is to take ideas and observations from everyday experience and language into controlled research settings for testing. When he finds they have some merit, he can ask whether the everyday view is comprehensive enough, explore its limitations, refine and extend the idea, and explore the relation of the phenomena to events with which everyday thought would not have connected it. Once this part of his work is through, the psychologist must reintroduce the modified idea to the everyday framework of observation and language from which he borrowed it in the first place.

This is a very sophisticated view of science, which is right in line with the best thinking in sociology and in the philosophy of science at the present day. It discovers a theme and a problem in the necessarily intimate relation of the psychological observer-researcher and the observed actors in a common lived world of meanings.

The Phenomenological Approach

And this brings us into an area which we have touched on several times already. We have already seen the phenomenal self as the central concept in human motivation, and our whole discussion of perception was in terms of the different worlds of different perceivers. In earlier sections of this chapter itself, we have mentioned people like Husserl and Strasser. It seems clear that some versions of phenomenology are anti-scientific or at least incompatible with science as we have described it. But recent work in this tradition is not only compatible with a modern scientific approach, but has contributed in an important way to it.

The essential point which the phenomenologist picks on is to see that all psychological research must deal with things of which the researcher is conscious. So the researcher's consciousness is prior to any specific research interests he may have. Most research simply takes this for granted, and in physics or chemistry this may be understandable and even forgivable; but in psychology it is very dangerous to take it for granted. Psychology is a reflexive science, if it is to be at all adequate – that is, the psychologist's theory must include the activity of the psychologist himself.

Now what the phenomenologist says is that consciousness is intentional. As Gurwitsch[31] says, all consciousness is consciousness of something, or about something. And what it is conscious of is an 'intentional object'. This is necessarily a unity of meaning of some kind. As Merleau-Ponty[32] puts it, 'We are condemned to meaning.'

If the researcher is using his meanings, and the subjects are using their meanings, how is one to know that there is any real connexion between what the behaviour being studied means to the researcher and what it means to the subjects? The question has been raised most acutely over the question of deviance.

The old conception of research on deviance was that here was a problem of social control, correctly defined by lawmakers, doctors, etc. This has been called the 'correctional stance'.

This was superseded by a more scientific attitude, which welded together two separate traditions – the theory of labelling and the subculture theory. By embracing these two contrasting traditions, social psychology seemed to offer a general framework for viewing the phenomenon of deviance; the field was integrated practically by including study of rule-breaking, rule creation and rule-enforcement. This view is dominant in the field today, and we shall return to it later. But here we are concerned to point out the phenomenological criticism of this viewpoint. As Phillipson & Roche[33] say:

> ... every stage of a sociological investigation rests on the observer's commonsense understandings of the social world, of the world he takes as indubitable and known-in-common with other men ... In this sense sociology is the unclarified documentation of the researcher's commonsense and must be evaluated as such ... Phenomenological sociology, by viewing meaning as problematic in any context of description, calls into question most of what counts as evidence and theory in conventional sociology.

This dissatisfaction with conventional sociology is precisely similar to the dissatisfaction we have experienced in social psychology, and which has led to our emphasis on such things as the research cycle. And in sociology the same solutions have been found – led in the main by Garfinkel,[34] whose work he has called ethnomethodology, and who has been followed by people like McHugh,[35] Sudnow,[36] Maurer,[37] Douglas[38] and Cicourel.[39]

For an example of one such study, a paper by Alan Sutter[40] on drug use focuses on drug users' and addicts' own experiences, and on the nature of the selective processes into and out of the drug community. By doing this at the phenomenological level, he shows the inappropriateness of the retreatist or double failure hypothesis, and also questions the idea of homogeneity which is built into the concept of a subculture. He checked the authenticity of his information by submitting it to panels of drug users, and by getting them to read the research reports. Such a procedure can be used both as a validation technique and as a way of collecting more information. This is, of course, the basic advantage of the research cycle.

It is in this area that psychology and sociology come closest together – indeed at times it is hard to see the difference between social psychology and ethnomethodology. What all this work does is to show how precarious our bases are in the social sciences – all the time we are using words which may or may not do justice to the phenomena we are interpreting. And my interpretation may differ from someone else's interpretation, or more generally, one group's interpretation may differ from another group's version. But we do not need to panic. All science is like this, in one way or another. As Neurath said, in science we are all like sailors who must repair a rotting boat while it is still at sea. We depend on the relative soundness of all the other planks while we replace a particularly rotten one. Each of the planks we now depend on we will in turn have to replace. No one of them is a foundation, nor a point of certainty, no one of them is incorrigible. Popper has a similar analogy, of building on piles driven into a bottomless bog – the piles will hold our building up if there are enough of them, and if we keep on pushing more in, even though there is no rock for them to rest on. And he was talking about physics! So we can take the criticisms of the phenomenologists very seriously, without feeling that we are making psychology impossible to carry out. Campbell[41] has a very encouraging discussion along these lines.

But one of the elements in the newer sociology is worth looking at separately. It is very noticeable, when one reads any of the later work on deviance and the rest, that many of the investigations have taken a year or more to carry out. This is very different from most of the experiments we have met in this book, or in any other textbook of social psychology.

The Longitudinal Approach

It would seem on the face of it that longitudinal research – that is, research where the same subjects are observed, retested or experimented on over a long period – is more likely to reveal important patterns of meaning than 'one-off' experiments or surveys, etc.

It almost goes without saying that most participant-observer studies are longitudinal, since they almost always take a substantial period of time to complete. For example, Whyte's[42] research took $3\frac{1}{2}$ years, and Polsky's[43] took eight months.

But other types of research can go on for a long time, too. We have mentioned earlier the work of Newcomb at Bennington, covering 25 years. One very interesting project was that of Roger Barker.[44]

He and his co-workers spent a year in a town in the American mid-mid-West, identifying the 'behaviour settings' and observing people's behaviour in relation to these settings. He then spent another year doing the same thing in a Yorkshire town of similar size and type. Some very interesting things emerged from this approach; for example, when the person-hours spent in each setting were counted, it was found that English people spent 19·3% of the time out on the streets and pavements, the Americans only spent 8·3% of their time there; this was mainly because of the much higher ownership of cars in America, but also because women in England used prams and shopping expeditions as a form of sociability far more than did the American women.

A behaviour setting is simply a regular pattern of interaction – the Friday-night whist game is one, market day is another, the Express Dairy is yet another. The most striking difference between 'Midwest' (the false name for the Kansas town) and 'Yoredale' (that for the Yorkshire town) was that Midwest, with a population of 715, had 587 settings; while Yoredale, with a population of 1300, had only 494 settings. Since each setting needs one or more responsible persons to keep it going, what flows from this is that each person in Midwest has more to do. In fact, Midwest had 7·1 responsible positions per person, while Yoredale had only 2.3. And this difference, which appears at all age levels, is even higher and more exaggerated in the teenage group (actually 12 to 17 years and 11 months). This means that there is far more pressure on people in Midwest to participate, to join and to be active in regular activities than there is in Yoredale. Barker links these findings with the history of the United States, particularly the pushing back of the frontier, and the resulting need for everyone to pitch in and take part. And he wonders what will happen now that the rising population is making the reality of that situation much less pressing. Will Americans become less versatile, less willing to take on responsibility, more willing to exclude children from adult activities – in other words, more like the English?

Work like this throws up the great importance of the situation in setting up whole systems of expectations and rules, which have strong effects on people's behaviour. Many of the basic findings of this research were confirmed and amplified in other work, for example Barker & Gump[45] Barker[46] and Barker *et al.*[47] It may be worthwhile to point out that Barker was one of Lewin's pupils, and so Lewin was again the source of important work.

Some of the most important longitudinal studies have been done on questions of personality and developmental psychology. For example, in one study, nursery school children were observed by Emmerich[48] over four school terms. He found that children who were rather aggressive and outgoing at the start became socially poised and non-aggressive later, while children who began by being labelled 'co-operative' became socially insecure and awkward. The explanation of this could be that those who trusted adults may have been regarded as somewhat overassertive at first, but later their basic confidence earned them a more desirable label; while the anxious children were regarded as co-operative at first because of their obvious desire to please, but later their basic insecurity became obvious.

In a much longer study, Kagan & Moss[49] followed up a group of children who had been intensively observed, right up into their early twenties. They found that there were significant correlations for many personality variables, but the actual levels of correlation were not very high, and with a sample of only 21 males and females the precision cannot in any case be very great. The best correlation was that between school achievement at 6–10 years old, and involvement in intellectual mastery at 20+. This is of course due to basic intelligence, and is not really personality in the usual sense. The next highest correlation is for sex-typed activities, and this is of course due to social pressures just as much as to individual psychology. In fact, as Maddi[50] and Danziger[51] both suggest, most of the significant results can be reduced to sex-role conformity rather than anything else.

Although there are certain things which can only be found out by means of longitudinal studies, there are severe limitations on this type of research. In the first place, the costs are very high. And secondly, the follow-up is not always successful in locating all the members of the original sample, particularly if the time-interval between observations is several years. Even after an interval of one year, one quarter or more may be lost. This difficulty can be overcome by comparing only those subjects who were observed on both occasions. Such subjects are rarely representative of the whole group. A third point is that repeated measurements can give rise to practice effects which lead to improvements in scores. All these difficulties mean that longitudinal studies will always be the exception rather than the rule.

Cross-Cultural Studies

Another way in which we can look at our problems from another angle is to carry out similar investigations in several different cultures. We have already seen how important this is in the work of Osgood and Triandis.

There have been two main approaches to studies of other cultures, which French[52] has called the emic and the etic. The emic approach attempts to describe a phenomenon in terms of its own structure, discernible from within the culture itself. The etic approach uses some external yardstick, derived from the experimenter's theoretical position. Anthropologists have usually analysed cultures emically; through intensive analysis, they have tried to show interrelationships of various aspects of a single culture. Social psychologists, on the other hand, are usually interested in generalizations which hold good for all humans. Such generalizations require an etic approach.

Both approaches have their dangers. There is a very high risk in the emic approach that the investigator deceives himself into thinking he has got inside the culture, when in fact he has not. In particular, he is likely to exaggerate the amount of consensus he finds about cultural matters such as roles. Lewis[53] in his study of Tepoztlan concludes that:

> The picture of village life which emerges from our material is therefore quite different from the idealized, almost Rousseauan version of Tepoztlan conveyed by the earlier studies of the village by Robert Redfield and later elaborated by Stuart Chase.

Lewis interprets his data as revealing a wide disparity between actual and ideal behaviour. It seems that there is a lack of consensus on ideal patterns of the role definition of husband and wife among older and younger women and between women and men in the village, a finding not unknown in our own society.

This whole question of consensus is a very difficult one, once we get into the emic area of research, and Gross *et al.*[54] have a very sensitive discussion of the problems which arise here – problems which also arise for the qualitative and phenomenological research styles discussed earlier.

Such an orientation to the problem of role consensus suggests a series of theoretical questions that anthropologists have tended to ignore: how much consensus on what behaviours is required for a society to maintain itself? How much disagreement can a society tolerate in what areas? To what extent do different sets of role definers hold the same role definitions of key positions in society? On what aspects of role definition do members of different "subcultures" in a society agree and disagree? To what extent is deviant behaviour a function of deviant role definitions? Why do members of a society differ in their role definitions? Each of these questions suggests that systematic research on role consensus may be of importance for the development of cultural anthropology.

It will also be important for the development of social psychology, if social psychology moves in the directions we have suggested. Not that this is anything new. Already in 1951 Jacobson *et al.*[55] were investigating the different role definitions of stewards held by workers, foremen and shop stewards, and the implications of these differences for strains in occupational positions. Much more of this kind of work will be necessary in the future.

How about the etic approach? This has produced some very interesting results. For example, Sears & Wise[56] found that in Kansas City there was a positive relationship between the age of weaning and the degree to which the infant gave indications of emotional disturbance – that is, the later a child was weaned, the more disturbance he showed. But Blackwood[57] found that the Kurtatchi of the Solomon Islands do not wean their children until they are over three years old, and that Kurtatchi children show no signs of emotional disturbance. This apparent contradiction was resolved by Whiting & Child[58] by using a sample of 75 societies distributed throughout the world. Evidence was available so that judgments could be made for age of weaning and emotional disturbance for 37 societies. This showed that the level of emotional disturbance rose to a peak at the weaning age of 13–18 months, and then fell off again after that age, so that the 'over 3 years' level was comparable to the 'under 3 months' level. All the Kansas City babies were weaned at less than a year old.

This shows how useful it can be to impose our own categories on other people's behaviour. Regularities can emerge which would be quite invisible on the small scale of one society. The difficulty with the etic approach, however, is that it imposes universal categories on the data of each culture. Thus, if the categories do not fit the data, it's too bad for the data. So great caution is needed, and the research cycle, with its self-correcting character, is doubly necessary.

Unobtrusive Measures

Another style of research which has aroused a great deal of interest in recent years is that where the psychologist totally removes himself from any interaction with the subject, in order to leave the subject totally free from experimenter influence. Webb *et al.*[59] have advocated the use of such things as wear measures (how much the floor is worn in front of paintings in an art gallery, to determine the popularity of each painting); accumulation measures (number of cigarette ends in an airport lounge to determine the level of anxiety present); resting measures (frequencies at which pushbutton radios are tuned as a clue to where a car has been, or the tastes of the user); the use of archives (tombstones, *Who's Who*, *Hansard*, marriage records, voting records and volume and kind of letters sent to MPs); helicopter observation of drivers, and so on. Some of these methods get perilously close to secret spying on people, as has been pointed out by Westin.[60]

It may well be that some stages in some investigations are well served by unobtrusive measures, but they are extremely limited in what they can do. They leave out of account all the problems we have seen that psychology has to face, and encourage the investigator in the false belief that he can be totally objectivist and still do any psychology worth the name.

Even if the method worked much better than it does, it would still be ethically dubious. Is it ethically justified to get a person to reveal himself unwittingly, thereby giving information which may not help him? Are we seeking the truth about man that sets all men free? Or are the truths we discover only making some men more free and powerful, while others become more vulnerable to manipulation?

These may seem rather large questions to attach to just one method of investigation, and certainly these points are not peculiar to unobtrusive measures, but these particular methods of investigation do raise the issues in especially acute form, because of their apparent removal of the investigator from the scene, and the consequent mystification of the situation. Not only is the experimenter deceiving the subject about the observation – he is even hiding the deception. This is the double type of mystification which is most alienating, and which places the greatest difference between the experimenter and the subject.

Experimenter Effect

The reason why unobtrusive measures seemed such a good idea was, of course, the enormous storm which built up in the 1960s around the subject of experimenter effect.

Orne[61] started it all with his paper on the social psychology of the social psychology experiment – the reflexive area which we have seen continually arising in one way or another as the most problematic. He was intrigued by the way in which subjects in experiments obeyed orders in an almost hypnotic way (in fact, he had already done experiments[62] on the role-playing of hypnotic states) and did some very striking things. For example, he asked students who had come as subjects to the laboratory to tear up paper into small pieces, without giving any more reason than that. He wanted to see how long they kept on doing it before getting angry with the experimenter for wasting their time. Six hours later he wanted to go home, and had to stop the subjects, who were only too willing to carry on.

Was this because of his magnetic personality? He asked some acquaintances to do him a favour by performing five press-ups; in amazement, they asked *why*? He asked another similar group of people to take part in a short experiment involving doing five press-ups and they asked simply *where*? Orne's conclusion is that all experiments have demand characteristics, which create certain expectancies on the subject's part concerning what the experimenter wants. He quotes Pierce[63] as saying as long ago as 1908:

> It is to the highest degree probable that the subject['s] ... general attitude of mind is that of ready complacency and cheerful willingness to assist the investigator in every possible way by reporting to him those very things which he is most eager to find, and that the very questions of the experimenter ... suggest the shade of reply expected.

This general case was strongly supported by some further work of Rosenthal[64],[65] in the same area. In some of these studies, 'experimenters' were used as subjects. Different experimenters were first led to expect different outcomes in the same kind of experimental situation; then each of them worked with a different group of subjects. Despite the fact that the instructions were given to all groups in an outwardly identical way, they produced responses in accordance with the directional hypotheses previously fed to the individuals who were in charge.

It seemed clear that the experimental situation, which had been treated for all these years as a purely rational and 'clean' situation where accurate observations could be made free from bias, was actually a highly potent social field, with very strong forces operating. One practical effect of this was to force social psychologists who still worked in the laboratory to pay much more attention to post-experimental interviews, as one means of shedding light on experimenter bias and demand characteristics. They are also useful in shedding light on the internal processes relevant to the investigation.

But this is only a palliative. The basic problem remains; the university psychological laboratory is a highly authority-structured situation, in which the experimenter has very high social status. This may be the last thing the experimenter wants, but he has it, whether he wants it or not. The point is that the experimenter can vary the effect which he has, but he cannot eliminate it. For example, Hoffman et al.[66] found that people are more likely to sort photographs into emotionally positive categories with 'friendly' experimenters than they are when the same experimenters are 'neutral' in their manner. So it is not enough for the experimenter to *want* to be democratic in his approach – the situation has such strong demands that it turns him into an authority anyway, only this time it is a *nice* authority. It is almost as if the social relationship which the university has to the rest of the society (intellectual domination) were reproduced in little in the laboratory/subject situation.

So powerful are these experimenter effects that they can be communicated without words. They can even be communicated to animals, as the story of Clever Hans showed. They are thus an instance of the master-slave relationship, and should in theory be found everywhere where this relationship holds. Confirmation of this point of view is to be found in the further study which Rosenthal & Jacobson[67] carried out with schoolchildren. They carried out some intelligence tests, and then told teachers that the tests had revealed that certain children were about to bloom intellectually, giving them the names of the children to watch. These names had in fact been picked strictly at random, so these children were no different from the others (see our earlier discussion of the efficacy of randomization). Yet those children whose names had been picked and given to the teachers did in fact have much higher IQ scores when they were measured again later.

This research study was not in fact very carefully carried out or reported, and many criticisms could be made of it. But the most worrying thing about it is that the effects are biggest for the youngest children. Now if a child is labelled as bright or dull at 6 or 7 years old, it is known that this can become a self-fulfilling prophecy.[68]

So in this area of the social psychology of the social psychology experiment, it seems that we are touching some of the basic problems of social relationships in our society generally.

The Identity of the Researcher

The more we go into questions of research methodology, the more we find ourselves coming up against the problems of reflexivity – that is, the way in which the researcher is implicated in his own investigations, willy-nilly. It is not just a question of how to design better experiments – it is a question of what ground the psychologist is standing on when he conducts his experiments. As Jourard says:[69]

> Yet we must remember that a psychologist is a human being, living in a time and place, in a society with a class structure, a power structure, and he has economic interests . . . It does not seem to me far-fetched to regard the most rigorous, truth-seeking psychologist as a servant, witting or unwitting, of the agencies which pay him and his costs. The agencies which believe it worthwhile financing research into human behaviour typically believe that their interests will be furthered if man's behaviour becomes less unpredictable. They want men to be transparent to them (while they remain opaque to the others), and they want to learn how to make men's action more amenable to control . . . My hypothesis is, that unless the behaviour scientist explores the broader social, political and economic implications of his work, then he is a functionary indeed; worse, if he does not realize it, then he is being mystified by those who employ him.

It is not the intention here to go into all the details of who pays psychologists, where the money comes from, what the motives are of those who ultimately pay, and so on. All we want to do is to point out that there is a question here to be answered by anyone who wants to do good research – who is going to support him or her, and on what basis? Are social psychologists anything more than social engineers? Are they even engineers, or are they only maintenance men?

Historically, scientists have always seen themselves as being essentially more rational than other men. But the rationality they have aimed for is mainly an objectivist one – which in the case of human beings means regarding them as things to be manipulated. In so far as the irrational was studied, it was merely as a source of limitations or distortions of the rational. But the recent movements in psychology and sociology have seen man as far more than a brain on a beanstalk, even if the beanstalk had an id at the roots. They have seen man as expressing a praxis, as having projects and meanings which cannot be reduced to the old dichotomy rational/irrational. As Phillipson & Roche put it:

> It is at least a fundamental preliminary for all sociological research to make clear the types of meanings, rules and rationality employed by subjects of his study, be they primitive tribesmen, religious believers, ideology accepters, criminals, economic calculators or whatever... Phenomenology renders rationality and meaning problematic for sociology, a dimension of investigation, and not at all to be taken for granted... To render the actors' meanings and rationality problematic, and furthermore to render the sociological observer's meanings and rationality problematic is an important step to take in the development of a critical and self-aware sociology.

Both in social science and in ordinary life, it is all too easy to leave one's own meanings, one's own rationality, unexamined and taken for granted as correct. To the extent that we do this, we turn people into things, who only exist *for us*; Maslow[70] calls this rubricization, and says that healthy people resist it. He gives the example of the adolescent who is told – 'Oh, that's just a stage you're going through. You'll grow out of it eventually.' Keith Paton[71] amplifies the point:

> People like being treated as persons, and they know and hate it when they are treated as things. Wherever *praxis* is reduced to *process* we can speak of *reification*: thingification, reducing a person to the level of a dumb animal or a thing... When your parents said – 'Oh, you're just going through a phase', you probably protested and said

– 'I can decide for myself. When I need your advice I'll ask for it. For goodness sake, *stop treating me like a child.*' In our society, 'being treated like a child' *means* being reified, having our praxis denied, being explained out of existence, in short – NOT being treated like a PERSON.

Obviously this is very much the same thing as labelling – it has often been pointed out that labelling people makes it harder for them to change. Matza[72] has a very good discussion of how this works, both from the point of view of the labelling authority and from the point of view of the person labelled. So all these terms – rubricization, reification, labelling – are talking about the same thing – the process of turning a person into a thing in order to make him easier to study. But then, what is this thing we are now studying? As Laing[73] says:

Natural scientific investigations are conducted on objects, or things, or the pattern of relations between things, or on systems of 'events'. Persons are distinguished from things in that persons experience the world, whereas things behave in the world. Thing-events do not experience. Personal events are experiential. Natural scientism is the error of turning persons into things by a process of reification that is not itself part of the true natural scientific method. Results derived in this way have to be dequantified and de-reified before they can be reassimilated into the realm of human discourse.

And Laing makes the point that this also ties in with the concept of alienation. People can be alienated from other people, from their work, and from themselves, and this is all part of the same process. Social alienation, which expresses itself in feelings of powerlessness and the failure to control one's own life, is prevalent throughout our society. Laing goes on to say:

Personal action can either open out possibilities of enriched experience or it can shut off possibilities. Personal action is either predominantly validating, confirming, encouraging, supportive, enhancing, or it is invalidating, disconfirming, undermining and constricting.

Now, where does the psychologist stand in all this? Is he on the side of alienation, and helping it to be even more destructive of people and their praxis, or is he doing something more positive?

It seems clear that a great deal of psychology actually adds to the general picture of society-wide alienation. The recent work on intelligence testing shows that it has been used, quite irrespective of the wishes and intentions of its founders, as a way of keeping subordinate groups in a subordinate position, in such a way as to make it look fair, when it was far from fair. It may look at first as though the tests were all right, but the way they were used was wrong; but now that we have our present insight into the nature of what has been wrong with psychology, we can see that the tests themselves were basically reifying mechanisms, whose main function was to pin a label on a person, and thereby to reduce all other aspects of the person to insignificance. This is labelling with a vengeance! And such a procedure is inappropriate to a human psychology.

Similarly with personality tests, as used by clinical psychologists in the psychiatric framework to classify people. As Scheff[74] and Szasz[75] among others have shown, psychiatric classification is less an analogue of medical diagnosis, and more a subtle way to invalidate a human being.

And in the research laboratory? Are we engaging in a common endeavour with our subjects, or are we merely using them, and perhaps even lying to them systematically?

And in the survey field? What are the social relationships existing between researcher and interviewer? Between interviewer and respondent?

What are we doing to our subjects? What are we doing to ourselves? What is our society doing to all of us?

And when we have begun to answer all these questions, what do we actually do?

One thing which seems to be happening is that psychologists are combining work in psychotherapy or in personal growth with research. And the research tends to be in the area of finding out what enhances people and what diminishes people. For example, Jourard did research on self-disclosure[76] and at the same time allowed his psychotherapy to become more existential; the two things supported and informed each other, and began to change each other. The research increasingly came to be about shared experience, and:

> Counseling and psychotherapy, from the standpoint of humanistic psychology, become enterprises wherein patient and therapist, counselor and client share relevant experience so that the latter can become more enlightened, more liberated from influences which constrain his

growth and self-actualization. Indeed, I find myself using the word therapy less and less, seeking some metaphor more aptly descriptive of what goes on in such helping transactions. Terms like teacher, guide, guru, liberator suggest themselves, though all sound fairly pretentious. But in all these cases, one thinks not of a person manipulating another, reading his mind in order to gain power over him; rather one thinks more of a dialogue between I and You.

There is no policy which can be laid down for everybody – having once faced the issues, each psychologist has to decide for himself or herself what to do. But it should at least be clear that there are social implications in whatever action the psychologist takes. The psychologist is one of a small number of highly-educated people who have great influence in our society, mainly at the level of intellectual communication. It matters very much what image of man he holds, and what model of man he propagates.

We are entering a period of more rapid change than any we have experienced so far in human history. The human being who is going to be able to survive and contribute to this rapidly-changing society is going to be more adaptable, less rigid than any previous human being has needed to be. This means that people are going to be less predictable than before, if they are going to succeed at all. As Rogers puts it:[77]

... it is the maladjusted person whose behaviour can be specifically predicted, and some loss of predictability should be evident in every increase in openness to experience and existential living. In the maladjusted person, behaviour is predictable precisely because it is rigidly patterned ... I am suggesting that as the individual approaches the optimum of complete functioning his behaviour, though always lawful and determined, becomes more difficult to predict; and though always dependable and appropriate, more difficult to control.

It seems that it is possible for psychologists either to help in this process, by validating people, respecting their praxis, and confirming their reality as persons; or to hinder it by intentionally or unthinkingly reinforcing the rigidities which stem from the general alienation of society.

If as psychologists we opt for the former alternative, we must not be too surprised if we meet opposition. On the other hand, we should not anticipate opposition in such a way that we produce it by the sheer force of our own expectations. Social psychology is a wide field, and there is room in it for many different ways of action, many styles of being. We have to choose. We have to decide on our own projects. And we have to do all this under the pressure of a myriad forces influencing or attempting to influence us. We have to be free, while knowing that we are determined. This is the paradox of transcendence – it is at one and the same time true that we are all creatures of our age and our society, in detailed ways that we scarcely dream of; and also that we are infinite and uncontainable.[78] Psychology needs to study both; and in order to do that it must respect both. Otherwise it is not a human psychology at all.

REFERENCES

1. D. T. Campbell & D. W. Fiske. Convergent and discriminant validation by the multitrait-multimethod matrix, Psychol. Bull. 56, 1959
2. H. Bruch. Transformation of oral impulses in eating disorders; A conceptual approach, Psychiatric Quarterly 35, 1961
3. A. J. Stunkard & C. Koch. The interpretation of gastric motility: I. Apparent bias in the reports of hunger by obese persons, Archives of General Psychiatry II, 1964
4. S. Schachter et al. Effects of fear, food deprivation and obesity on eating, J. Pers. soc. Psychol. 10, 1968
5. S. Schachter. Cognitive effects on bodily functioning: Studies of obesity and eating, in D. C. Glass (ed) Neurophysiology and emotion, Rockefeller University Press 1967
6. R. Goldman et al. Yom Kippur, Air France, dormitory food and the eating behaviour of obese and normal persons, J. Pers. soc. Psychol. 10, 1968
7. C. Hampden-Turner. Radical man, Duckworth 1971
8. S. M. Jourard. Disclosing man to himself, Van Nostrand 1968
9. K. Lewin. Action research and minority problems, J. Soc. Issues 2, 1946
10. D. Krech & R. S. Crutchfield. Theory and problems of social psychology, McGraw-Hill 1948
11. B. Shaw. Saint Joan, Penguin
12. A. Zander. Centerville studies itself, University of Michigan 1941
13. R. C. Weaver. Community relations manual, Am. Council Race Rel. 1945
14. F. Jones & M. W. Harris. The development of interracial awareness in small groups, in L. Blank et al. (eds) Confrontation: Encounters in self and interpersonal awareness, Collier-Macmillan 1971
15. W. F. Whyte. Street corner society; the social structure of an Italian slum, Univ. of Chicago 1943
16. N. Polsky. Hustlers, beats and others, Anchor 1969
17. R. G. Barker & R. G. Wright. Midwest and its children: The psychological ecology of an American town, Row Peterson 1954
18. K. Weick. Systematic observational methods, in The handbook of social psychology (2nd ed) 1968 (Vol. 2)
19. T. Leary. How to change behaviour, Proceedings of the XIV international congress of applied psychology, Vol. 4

Styles in Social Research

20. E. Goffman. The presentation of self in everyday life, Penguin. See also other books by the same author
21. H. Garfinkel. Studies in ethnomethodology, Prentice-Hall 1967
22. J. M. Bynner. The young smoker, H.M.S.O. 1969
23. R. Harrè & P. F. Secord. The explanation of social behaviour, Blackwell 1972
24. C. R. Rogers. Some thoughts regarding the current presuppositions of the behavioral sciences, in W. R. Coulson & C. R. Rogers (eds) Man and the science of man, Charles Merrill 1968
25. C. R. Rogers. A therapist's view of the good life: The fully functioning person, in C. R. Rogers, On becoming a person, Constable 1961
26. S. Strasser. Phenomenology and the human sciences, Duquesne Univ. Press 1963
27. M. Polanyi. The growth of science in society, in same ref. as 24
28. M. Schofield, The sexual behaviour of young people, Penguin 1968
29. P. Madison. Complex behaviour in natural settings, in T. Mischel (ed) Human action: Conceptual and empirical issues, Academic Press 1969
30. P. Madison. Personality development in college, Addison-Wesley 1969
31. A. Gurwitsch. Studies in phenomenology and psychology, Northwestern Univ. Press 1966
32. M. Merleau-Ponty. The phenomenology of perception, Routledge 1962
33. M. Phillipson & M. Roche. Social control, deviance and dissent, British Sociological Association Conference 1971
34. Same ref. as 21
35. P. McHugh. Defining the situation, Bobbs Merrill 1968
36. D. Sudnow. Passing on, Prentice-Hall 1967
37. D. Maurer. Whiz mob, College and University Press 1964 and The big con, Signet, 1962
38. J. Douglas. The social meaning of suicide, Princeton 1967
39. A. V. Cicourel. The social organization of juvenile justice, Wiley 1968
40. A. Sutter. Worlds of drug use in the street scene, in Cressey & Ward (eds) Delinquency, crime and social process, Harper & Row 1969
41. D. T. Campbell. A phenomenology of the other one: Corrigible, hypothetical and critical, in same ref. as 29
42. Same ref. as 15
43. Same ref. as 16
44. R. G. Barker. Ecology and motivation, Nebraska symposium on motivation 1960
45. R. G. Barker & P. V. Gump. Big school, small school, Stanford 1964
46. R. G. Barker. Explorations in ecological psychology, Amer. Psychologist 20, 1965
47. R. G. Barker et al. Specimen records of American and English children, Univ. of Kansas 1961
48. W. Emmerich. Continuity and stability in early social development, Child Develop. 35, 1964
49. J. Kagan & H. A. Moss. Birth to maturity, Wiley 1962
50. S. R. Maddi. Personality theories: A comparative analysis, Dorsey 1968
51. K. Danziger. Socialization, Penguin 1971
52. D. French. The relationship of anthropology to studies in perception and cognition, in S. Koch (ed) Psychology: A study of a science (Vol. 6), McGraw-Hill 1963
53. O. Lewis. Husbands and wives in a Mexican village: A study of role conflict, Amer. Anthropol. 51, 1949
54. N. E. Gross et al. The postulate of role consensus, in P. B. Smith (ed) Group processes, Penguin 1970
55. E. Jacobson et al. The use of the role concept in the study of complex organizations, J. soc. Iss. 7, 1951
56. R. R. Sears & G. W. Wise. Relation of cup feeding in infancy to thumb-sucking and oral drive, Amer. J. Orthopsychiat. 20, 1950

57. B. Blackwood. Both sides of Buka Passage, O.U.P. 1935
58. J. W. M. Whiting & I. L. Child. Child training and personality, Yale Univ. Press 1953
59. E. J. Webb *et al.* Unobtrusive measures: A survey of non-reactive research in social science, Rand McNally 1966
60. A. F. Westin. Privacy and freedom, Atheneum 1967
61. M. T. Orne. On the social psychology of the psychological experiment, with particular reference to demand characteristics and their implications, Amer. Psychol. 17, 1962
62. M. T. Orne. The nature of hypnosis: Artefact and essence, J. abnorm. Psychol. 58, 1959
63. A. H. Pierce. The subconscious again, J. Phil. Psychol. Sci. Meth. 5, 1908
64. R. Rosenthal. On the social psychology of the psychological experiment: The experimenter's hypothesis as unintended determinant of experimental results, Amer. Sci. 51, 1963
65. R. Rosenthal. The effect of the experimenter on the results of psychological research, in B. H. Maher (ed) Experimental personality research (Vol. 1), Academic Press 1964
66. D. T. Hoffmann *et al.* 'Friendliness' of the experimenter, Psychol. Rec. 20, 1970
67. R. Rosenthal & L. Jacobson. Pygmalion in the classroom, Holt, Rinehart & Winston 1968
58. Central Advisory Council for Education (England), Children and their primary schools (Vol. 2), H.M.S.O. 1967
69. S. M. Jourard. Psychology for control, and for liberation, of humans, British Psychological Society Conference 1972
70. A. H. Maslow. Toward a psychology of being, Van Nostrand 1962
71. K. Paton. The great brain robbery, Keith Paton 1971
72. D. Matza. Becoming deviant, Prentice-Hall 1969
73. R. D. Laing. The politics of experience, Penguin 1967
74. T. Scheff. Being mentally ill, Weidenfeld & Nicolson 1966
75. T. Szasz. The myth of mental illness, Secker & Warburg 1961
76. S. M. Jourard. Self-disclosure: An experimental analysis of the transparent self, Wiley 1971
77. C. R. Rogers. Freedom to learn, Charles Merrill 1969
78. See Hegel's Philosophy of Right, para, 35 and Addition, translated by T. M. Knox, O.U.P. 1942 (1821)

SUBJECT INDEX

Abscissa 160
Acceptance 75, 114–16
Action research 211–12, 220
Activity factor 89, 200
Adolescence 47, 53–5, 93, 106–19, 121–2, 138
Alienation 36, 81, 116, 195, 202–3, 210, 229, 233–4
Anomic man 66, 77
Authenticity 116–17
Autonomy 47, 73, 76, 116

Behavioral differential 200
Behaviorist psychology 29, 35, 160, 210
Behaviour settings 224
Bias 155, 188, 190–1, 230
Biology vs. culture 121–6
Brainwashing 34–5

Career girl 129–30
Chi-squared test 168–9, 171, 178, 189
Cluster analysis 201–2
Cognitive structures 65–9, 93
Communication 100–2, 112, 235
Concrete thinking, 58 63–4, 66–8, 73–4, 77, 79
Conformity 48–9, 52–4, 73, 113
Consensus, role, 226–7
Contingency analysis 164, 196–8
Convergent thinking 94
Correlation 32, 162–4, 170–2, 198
Cos theta 163
'Cowboys' 113
Creativity 77
Cross-cultural research 31–3, 97–8, 121–4, 127, 226–8
Custodial orientation 80

Death 141, 146–7
Degrees of freedom 168, 171
Dehumanization 203–4
Desatellization 78, 108
Development of self or ego 72–3, 75, 78, 84, 109, 114–19, 133, 143–4, 234–5
Developmental tasks 107–10
Deviance 222–3
Disengagement theory 139–42
Divergent thinking 94
Drugs 109–11, 115, 118, 214–5
Dyad 99–100
Dynamism factor 200

Ecstasy 76
Ego, see Development of self or ego
Emic approach 226–7
Emotions, juke-box theory of 125–126
Enactive system 64
Encounter group 104, 114, 133, 212–14
Ethnomethodology, 222–3
Etic approach 226–8
Evaluation factor 89, 200
Experimenter effect 229–31
Eye-contact 99–100

Facial expressions 97–8
Factor analysis 163, 198–201
Family 24–5, 40–1, 78, 104, 108–9, 115–18
Fixers and wanglers 113
Formal operations 59, 64
Freak group 113–19
Freudian psychology 13, 25, 28, 35

Halo effect 95
Humanistic orientation 80, 203, 235

239

Index

NAME INDEX

Aaronson, B. 118
Abelson, R. P. 71
Adler, I. 150
Ainsworth, M. D. S. 15
Alex, C. 88
Allen, T. W. 62
Anthony, E. J. 148
Argyle, M. 99–100
Argyris, C. 116
Arnold, W. J. 41
Aronfreed, J. 33, 38–40
Aronson, E. 42, 71, 104, 105, 205–6
Atkinson, R. C. 61
Ausubel, D. P. 78–9, 106
Axline, V. 35

Bachrach, A. J. 27
Backman, C. W. 28, 34–5
Bales, R. F. 200
Bannister, D. 105
Barker, R. G. 110, 214, 224–5
Barry, H. 122
Bateson, G. 101
Beach, F. A. 136
Bell, E. T. 150
Bell, R. Q. 37, 125
Bem, D. J. 130, 132
Bem, S. L. 130, 132
Bennis, W. 40
Berelson, B. 176
Berkeley, Bishop 219
Berkowitz, L. 205
Berscheid, E. 96
Berzon, B. 136
Birch, H. G. 25
Birdwhistell, R. L. 100
Birren, J. E. 140
Blackwood, B. 227
Blake, R. 200
Blank, L. 84, 236

Blomfield, J. M. 18
Blood, D. M. 194
Boler, D. 140
Boneau, C. 184
Borrow, H. 147
Bowlby, J. 13–19, 21, 147
Brainerd, C. J. 62
Bramel, D. 95
Breznitz, S. 51
Brierley, D. W. 92
Brim, O. G. 66–7, 83
Brock, T. C. 66
Bross, I. D. J. 150
Brown, J. A. C. 145
Brown, R. 51, 84, 94, 122
Brown, R. W. 191
Bruch, H. 208
Bruner, J. S. 63–5, 67, 83
Bull, N. J. 51
Burke, R. J. 164–6
Burtt, H. E. 205
Buros, O. K. 88
Bynner, J. M. 109, 215–16

Campbell, A. 139
Campbell, D. T. 177, 179, 207, 223
Cannell, C. F. 195
Cantril, H. 189, 191
Carp, F. M. 146
Carson, R. 84–6
Casanova, Count 134
Cattell, R. B. 74, 201
Channon, C. 206
Chase, S. 226
Chess, S. 25
Chickering, A. W. 112
Child, I. L. 31, 42, 227
Chown, S. 138–9
Church, R. M. 38
Cicourel, A. V. 222